To Cliff

CREATE
WEALTH
TO BUILD
GOD'S DREAM

TOMMY REID AND *AL WARNER*
WITH AIMEE REID SYCH AND *IAIN MACDONALD*

Creating Wealth to Build God's Dream

Discovering God's Unlimited Resources

By Tommy Reid and Al Warner with Aimee Reid Sych and Iain MacDonald

Printed in the United States of America

ISBN: 978-0-9818864-2-8

Editorial Director: Dr. Larry Keefauver
Cover Design: Charity LeBlanc

KAIROS PUBLISHING®

Order from:
www.tommyreid.org

All Printing and Book Services provided by:
Heritage Publishing and Distributing
of Central Florida, Inc.
buz.swyers@heritagepd.com
www.heritagepd.com

Printed in the U.S.A.

DEDICATION

It is my great joy to dedicate this book to two families who are very personal friends and demonstrate the relationship between the sacred and the secular.

I first dedicate this book to my very close friend Darius Pridgen and his wife, Monique. Recently, they honored this Pastor by asking me to officiate at their wedding. Darius is an example of a man who has united the sacred and the secular. He serves the sacred as Pastor of one of the largest churches in Buffalo, the True Bethel Baptist Church, and at the same time serves the secular as President of the Common Council of the City of Buffalo.

Secondly, I dedicate this book to his son, Craig and his wife, Jahar. They serve the sacred as the Pastors of the Niagara Falls True Bethel congregation. They, too, serve the secular; Jahar was the Assistant District Attorney for Erie County for over ten years. She has now been elevated to serve our community as a City Court Judge. Craig and Jahar have become two highly respected leaders in our community.

My friend, Darius, has been a prominent government leader in the rebuilding of Buffalo, while at the same time serving the poor and disenfranchised.

It is my joy to humbly dedicate this book to my friends Darius and Monique Pridgen, and Craig and Jahar Pridgen.

Acknowledgements

My special thanks go to co-authors, Al Warner, Aimee Reid Sych, and Iain MacDonald. Also, thanks to my editor and friend, Dr. Larry Keefauver and to Patti Swyers, whose combined skills "put it all together." My thanks go also to Mary Collins and Kathy Black who assisted in the preparation of this manuscript.

Deep thanks go to Wanda Reid and Deb Warner who assisted their husbands and spent many weeks alone while their husbands wrote, edited, and gathered research used in this manuscript.

I also want to express my sincere appreciation to Clarence (Buz) Swyers who has assisted me in all of my publishing projects. Beyond that, he is the man God brought into my life to partner with me in birthing and growing the missions vision of The Tabernacle.

My gratitude abounds to Bishop Robert Stearns and Pastor Jim Ruddy for the support and cooperation of Eagles' Wings and The Tabernacle in this project

TABLE OF CONTENTS

Preface –   Pastor John Tonelli   vii

Why We Wrote This Book   x

Introduction - God Gives: Dreams and Resources   xiii

Section 1

We Are Born with Wealth Inside Us
Creating Wealth for the Purpose of Changing Our World

Chapter 1:   Money: What Is It?   1

Chapter 2:   Whose Money Is It?   3

Chapter 3:   Where Does Money or Wealth Come From?   11

Chapter 4:   The Master's Plan to Create Wealth   15

Chapter 5:   Managing God's Wealth through Budgeting   19

Chapter 6:   Creating Wealth through Sowing and Reaping   25

Chapter 7:   The Eternal Covenant of Blessing   31

Chapter 8:   Does Wealth Create Blessing or Condemnation?   35

              (Can You Enjoy Wealth?)

Chapter 9:   Wealth with a Reason and Purpose   41

Chapter 10:   God's Options: His Option Is to Bless You   51

Chapter 11:   Your Options: You Can Believe   55

Chapter 12:   You Will Write This Chapter on Money!   65

Section 2

This Is Our Father's World
The Worship of God Puts Money and Its Use in Perspective

Chapter 13:   Understanding Money—the Measure of Value: 81
              The Essence of Worship (Aimee Reid Sych)

Chapter 14:   True Worship Has Seen God's Worth: 87
              God Is Our Source

Chapter 15: Discovering and Aligning: Your Value System   99
            Must Be God-Centered

Chapter 16: Abundance: Changing the World is Expensive   105
            (Iain MacDonald)

Chapter 17: Partnership: Overcoming Weakness   123
            (Iain MacDonald)

Chapter 18: Increase: The Mechanism for Limitless Resources   133
            (Iain MacDonald)

Buffalo, NY: A Photo History: *Present - Past - Future*   145

Section 3

How Buffalo, New York Was Rebuilt by Dreamers
How Dreamers Found the Resources to Rebuild a City

Chapter 19: Resurrection! (Al Warner)   153

Chapter 20: Does God Hate Cities? (Al Warner)   157

Chapter 21: Buffalo: The Good, the Bad, the Ugly, the Future   161
            (Al Warner)

Chapter 22: Servant Leadership: Shepherding Stallions   165
            (Al Warner)

Chapter 23: The Son Rises over Buffalo   169
            (Al Warner)

Section 4

The Kingdoms of this World Shall Become the Kingdoms of Our God

Chapter 24: How Good and Pleasant It Is!   195

Chapter 25: Shout! For the Lord Has Given You the City   207
            (Al Warner)

Chapter 26: The New Buffalo   217

Chapter 27: Build an Upper Room and Recreate a City   223

Final Word: Delivering a Kingdom   227

Endnotes: 233

Contact Info.: Order Forms, Books, DVD's, CD's, Authors   235

PREFACE

PASTOR JOHN TONELLI
PASTOR OF RESURRECTION LIFE
CHEEKTOWAGA, NEW YORK

Tommy Reid is a true man of God, a genuine spiritual father, and a pastor of pastors. To know him is to love him, and to be his friend is to be loved by him. You can't help but tangibly feel his deep commitment to and his abiding love for our Lord Jesus Christ.

Out of Pastor Reid's unwavering relationship with Jesus, springs forth a wealth of spiritual wisdom, knowledge, and understanding of God's principles and precepts. As a seasoned minister with decades of pastoring and evangelism under his belt, he has developed a very thoughtful and well-balanced style of teaching. His gentle approach and easy delivery of the deeply spiritual topics covered in this book, give the reader a hunger for more of God, and fuel the fire for a deeper relationship with Him.

I met Pastor Reid over thirty-five years ago; I was a baby Christian. The first time I walked into his church (The Tabernacle in Orchard Park, New York) I knew I was home. I found the Spiritual Father my heart was longing for. In the years following, our relationship continued to deepen, like that of the Apostle Paul and Timothy. He taught me as a spiritual father teaches and mentors a spiritual son. He led me, as the best of fathers do, not by his teaching and preaching, but by being a living example of what God expects of His frontline leaders.

Our relationship quickly became one of the foundational relationships of my adult life. I developed an unbreakable bond and a fierce sense of covenant loyalty to my spiritual father. Not long after that, God called me to build a church and pastor a flock in a nearby suburb. Naturally, I sought out my spiritual father and to share the vision that God had given me. While speaking with Pastor Reid and relaying the call on my life and the dream that God had placed on my heart, I made a covenant promise to him. I promised that I would never do anything to jeopardize our relationship. I would protect my relationship with the Lord in the exact same way.

With that promise conveyed, he wished me well, and I am proud to say that there has not been one time in our more than thirty-five-year relationship that I have betrayed this covenant with my Pastor and spiritual Dad. I now pastor a thriving church (Resurrection Life) near Buffalo, New York. God has honored me as I have honored Him, and I have continued to honor my mentor and friend. The principle, "what you sow, is what you reap" is still just as true today as it was over 2,000 years ago, when the Apostle Paul penned it in Galatians 6:7.

As I began to establish the church that God called me to build, I encountered a problem. It is the same problem that Pastor Reid addresses in this book. I had a big God-given dream, but no money with which to make the dream a reality. That's when the Holy Spirit asked me what I was willing to give up in order to begin fulfilling the dream God had placed in my heart. I answered instantaneously, "Anything, I would give you, anything and everything!"

At that very moment God showed me an image of my brand new and almost paid for 1980 Z-28 Camaro. You need to understand some details here. That car was my baby, my dream car, my answer to prayer! I had previously earned an Automotive Degree from my first college, and that car was a huge part of my life and a great source of joy. Gloss black with three-tone red stripes and a burgundy interior. I loaded it with high performance parts and polished it within an inch of its life. Add to all that, the fact that my Savior helped me get that car and nearly pay it off.

The next instant I could hear Jesus say, "Where your treasure is there you heart will be also" (Matthew 6:21). I knew immediately that this was a test. I had been given a test similar to Abraham's, when he was asked by God to give up his son Isaac. The son he loved with all of his heart. The son he had made plans with and dreamed about. I knew what God was asking me to do, so I acted without hesitation and put the car up for sale. The phone calls started flooding in and that car sold within the very week…for a profit. The equity from the sale of that car was used to begin the spiritual journey that God had placed before me. Not once in all of these years have I regretted my decision to sell it. Why? Because the promises that God has placed in His Word are for every one of us. Verses like: "God rewards those that diligently seek Him" (Hebrews 11:6); "No good thing will He withhold from those that walk uprightly" (Psalm 84:11); "The Lord takes pleasure in the prosperity of His servants" (Psalm 35:27); and, "The Lord daily loads us with benefits" (Psalm 68:19).

My Pastor, spiritual father and covenant friend has taught me well. And the Lord has blessed me above and beyond all that I could ask or think. You simply can't out give God! You just need to obey His voice and step out in faith and trust Him in the area of finances. He will teach you how to flourish and prosper. He will, "GIVE YOU THE POWER TO CREATE WEALTH!"

So now, I encourage you to pull up a comfortable chair, turn on a reading lamp, and get ready to enjoy a book that will ignite your dreams and inspire your heart. Jesus has so many wonderful plans for your life and important assignments for you to fulfill. Resist the urge to pull back. Don't be afraid. Just trust Him. He will strengthen you for the tasks at hand and will anoint all that you do for Him and His Kingdom. I wish you Godspeed as you embark on the journey that our Father God has placed before you.

WHY WE WROTE THIS BOOK:
CHASING PLASTIC RABBITS

Before you read the pages of this book, I want you to know why we wrote it and what I mean by the phrase, "chasing plastic rabbits". This is a serious book about purpose and destiny and the creation of wealth to fund the dreams of destiny that are inside every person. The problem with our lives is that we tend to chase the unimportant things as if they had great value.

The story is told of a racing greyhound at the dog track. The greyhounds were motivated by a large, plastic, mechanical rabbit that "ran" ahead of them. One day, a dog by the name of Aladdin who had been running at the track for many years caught the mechanical plastic rabbit. He bit down, lost three of his teeth on the plastic surface, and suddenly discovered that for years he had been chasing something he could not use and did not want.

It is said that Aladdin never ran again. He now knew that the rabbit was plastic, and there was nothing in it that he wanted or needed. From that day and for the rest of his life, he never graced another track or ran another race.

Many people in our world chase after something they do not need. Many, like Aladdin, once they catch what they've been chasing, don't want what they've finally caught.

This is especially true of money. All over the world, you'll find people chasing after money. When they finally acquire a large sum, they find it fulfills nothing. Common thinking is that "if I could just get more money, I'd be satisfied," but satisfaction never comes. I know billionaires; yet, I have never met one who has found satisfaction in the acquisition of money.

Money itself is the plastic mechanical rabbit that doesn't have the ability to satisfy us.

However, if we can discover the true purpose of money, that purpose can, and will bring us great satisfaction.

So, what is money for? I believe the purpose of money is to fund the dream and purpose God He has implanted within you. Do you have a seeming lack of money? When you discover that God gives you power to create wealth for the purpose of building God's dream, you will walk into a world where money is without limits.

The old Chinese proverb says, "He who chases two rabbits catches neither." But when you discover the God-given purpose of money along with the truth that it is God who gives you power to create the wealth to build His dream on the earth, you will discover that He is the Source of limitless resources.

Take a look at a dollar bill. Our forefathers understood the purpose and limitations of money. After they designed the currency, they placed a statement in the center of our money that said simply, "In God We Trust." In their own dramatic and non-compromising way, they told us that no matter what the amount written on that currency, it literally had no value. The value of our currency is God. He is our Source and our Supply. Their statement not only said that we must trust in God, but more forcibly that, we must not trust in money!

Chasing money is like chasing plastic rabbits which is exactly what so many do in our materialistic culture. I hope you'll quickly learn several indelible lessons and etch them in your mind and heart. It's essential you know and live out these keys to creating unlimited wealth:

You cannot trust in money.

You must never chase after money; it is only a "mechanical plastic rabbit" that has no value.

Never pursue money to get rich. Riches are never an end but only a means to fund God's dream.

When you have a dream from God, the resources for that dream are inside you, and creating them is a journey of faith that is easier than I can describe.

MY PURPOSE IN WRITING THIS BOOK IS TO HELP YOU DISCOVER THAT WHEN YOU CREATE WEALTH TO FUND GOD'S DREAM, YOU WILL DISCOVER A WORLD WHERE MONEY IS WITHOUT LIMIT.

In the following pages, we will answer some major questions including the discovery of who owns all the riches of the world. We will also discover that Jesus taught us that we are mandated to take God's money, invest it, and grow it. Then, we will uncover the purpose of money -- to fund the dream that God has for the earth.

Part of this book will tell the story of a prophetic word God gave this author over forty years ago to speak to the dry bones of his dying city to rise and walk again. Through a series of what we call spiritual renewals, God raised up a Nehemiah team of believers who have literally catapulted our city into a period of growth and the rebuilding of the walls and superstructure of a great city.

At the time of this writing, a city that was given up to die a generation ago now has billions of dollars of construction either in process or in the "pipeline." A city has come alive! We tell the story of men and women who have created wealth through their faith in God. And, all of them knew the purpose of their wealth creation was to re-create their city.

I hope you will never chase the plastic rabbit of money again. I hope you will seek God with all of your heart, discover God's dream for your life, and embrace the wonder of God, enabling you to create wealth to fund that dream.

So forget chasing the plastic rabbit of money and as Tommy Tenney said, "Chase God." God will give you a destiny, a cause, a purpose, and the creativity to create the wealth to fund God's dream for our world.

- Pastor Tommy Reid
- Buffalo 2015

Introduction

God Gives—Both Dreams and Resources

As I look back at over sixty years of what people have called a successful ministry, I become more and more aware of the leading of a Sovereign God in each of our lives. After pastoring a church for over fifty years, I now feel called of God to go across the world and teach people how to find the destiny that God has written for them.

Many years ago, when Who's Who asked me to write a concise statement concerning my purpose for life, I wrote these words: "I believe that EVERY PERSON HAS SIGNIFICANCE, PURPOSE, and DESTINY, and it is my calling to teach people how to find their destiny." That, in essence, is who I am, and the purpose of this book is to assist you in finding your destiny and in discovering and creating the resources to fund your destiny.

Let me say something briefly about the word, "destiny." I recognize that its etymology is not rooted in a single, biblical word. If you did a concordance search, you would not find a corresponding Hebrew or Greek word for "destiny." Its origins are French and its denotation is much more secular than the way I use it. So, permit me to take some editorial license and baptize this word for our use in this book.

I see destiny as a combination of biblical words like purpose, plans, future, dreams, desires, and hope. God actually puts His desires, purposes, and plans in our hearts and minds to fulfill His dream for us, for our families, our cities, our culture, and our world. God inspires us with His dreams and provides us with creativity and power to create the resources and money to bring His kingdom in heaven to earth. As you walk through this book, you will discover many facets and connotations to this word, destiny. And you will be inspired to add to its meanings some of your own.

While I clarify how I use words, let me mention the word, dream, as well. Sometimes in the book I may capitalize or bold the word, dream. In context, I generally mean the big Dream that God has for your life, which includes all of the smaller dreams He has for you. For example, God's big Dream for you is to create wealth to resource all the other dreams. I believe He deposits dreams into us to build His Kingdom in our world.

In our recent book, *How To Live Out of a Dream*, I wrote that before the foundation of the world, God wrote our names or our destiny in His Book. For instance, Henry Ford was created by God to put America on wheels and change how we do life. Henry Kaiser was born and created not only to build dams and roads, but when there would come world crisis, Henry Kaiser was born to find an answer to a major problem.

Now, we come to the primary question of this book: If God has a plan, dream, and destiny for our lives, where do we get the resources to build the dream that is inside of us? It is obvious that God has created tremendous resources on this planet. Those resources of gold, silver, precious metals, and iron to make cars, airplanes, ships, buildings, and many other resources are beyond our ability to calculate. In this book, we will not focus on those material resources, but rather the phenomenal resources within us that enable us to harvest and reinvest those resources thereby changing the world around us.

The resources I am writing about are resources that are within you. They involve your destiny—your dreams for your future, your creative and witty mind, your ability to imagine and dream, and your ability to discipline and focus yourself on the achievement of goals.

I would also like for you to look inside of not only your mind and your natural talents, but at an amazing resource that goes beyond your natural man and your natural abilities and connects with the abilities of God and the mind of Christ. I would like to suggest to you that perhaps your greatest asset and your greatest resource is a hearing, spiritual ear where you can hear the voice of God. Almost all of Jesus' accomplishments when He lived on this planet came from His spiritual ear that had the ability to hear the voice of His Father. The Scriptures reveal that He limited His human behavior to those things He saw the Father do and heard the Father say.

I cannot write this without constantly reminding you that the ability to create wealth according to the Scripture comes from within you. Solomon did not have millions of dollars dropped off in his "mailbox," but found within himself, the ability to create wealth.

The wonder of being able to accomplish and fulfill the dream inside you will come from those resources God has placed inside your heart. Moses had an innate ability to lead and a natural sensitivity to hear the voice of God. Joshua led the people of God not just to a natural victory in Jericho, but to a miracle victory that came from the deep resources of His spirit, and His spirit connected with God's spirit.

We will all look inside ourselves to discover the source of the resources that will finance the dream that God has given you. If it is a God-dream, it will be bigger than you. If it is a God-dream, it will cost more than you have in your hand right now. God looks at you and says, "What is in your hand?" I assure you that the rod in your hand and in your heart has the potential of changing the world.

Let's look for a moment at some of the people that I have observed in my life who have changed our world.

- Henry Kaiser: When America and our allies were facing annihilation from the Nazi powers, President Roosevelt called Henry Kaiser into his office and said, "Henry, we are going to lose this war because we do not have the ships to take our troops and their weapons to the battlefields in Europe and Asia." Kaiser asked the president why he would call him about this matter. The president told him that every ship builder had said it was impossible to build the hundreds of ships we needed. Kaiser rose to his feet and said, "If it can't be done, then I will do it."

  We won that war because of the creativity of Henry Kaiser who built a 450-foot ship in four days, when previously, the shortest time for the building of a ship that size had taken over one year and four months. Henry Kaiser was the creative genius who contributed immeasurably to our victory in World War II.

  That was the purpose for which Henry Kaiser had been chosen. In other words, that was his ultimate destiny. It was not to make millions, though he did make millions, but to be the creative genius with the ability to build ships on an assembly line as we had made automobiles. God wrote that purpose for Henry Kaiser before He made the universe. And every one of us has a destiny: a destiny that was written by God in His book.

- Paul Crouch: I grew up with Paul Crouch. Day after day, a ten-year-old boy told me about his dreams for the future. Paul and his wife, Jan, launched the largest Christian television network in the world. Trinity Broadcasting Network (TBN) was a dream, a vision, and a plan birthed in the heart of God.

- Dr. David (Paul) Cho: I lived and traveled with Dr. Cho as he told me about the church he was called to build. I sat with Dr. Cho as my own father prophesied to him that he would build the largest church in human history.

But now I raise another question in this book: *If God wrote your destiny and my destiny, then how can we fund that destiny?"* To create a destiny takes time, talent, and the wisdom of God. Creating a great destiny may also cost millions or even billions of dollars. Where does that resource come from? How do we discover the funds that we need to do something God destined for us to do?

I have thought a lot about that question. My life has been one miracle after another. God has provided millions of dollars to fund ministries in Buffalo and around the world.

A Parable Filled with Clues for Creating Unlimited Wealth

We begin with the "Parable of the Talents." To me that parable is the description of the funding of every vision. In this parable, Jesus indicates that we have the responsibility to increase the wealth that He has entrusted to our stewardship. God also gives us the power to create wealth, and the creation of wealth is how God will finance the vision that He has placed in our hearts.

I was born at the height of the Depression. Like most everyone else, my family was poor. However, it was not always that way. Both my mother and father were born into affluent homes. My mother's family owned the largest business in their town and employed a large percentage of the population. But life changed.

The family fortune and business were left to the eldest son who was expected to divide it with his siblings. That did not happen. The elder brother disposed of the family business, took all of the assets, and moved to another part of the country leaving my grandfather and his family with barely enough to put food on the table. Shortly after losing a fortune, my grandfather was injured and became crippled.

I remember visiting a cousin of mine many years later. When she opened the door and realized who I was, she looked at me and said, "Oh, Tommy, you are from the 'poor' side of the family." I gazed into her eyes and thought, "Well, we would not be the poor side of the family if your father had not stolen our part of the family fortune!" We learned that riches can vanish in a moment of time and my mother was like many others—one moment rich, and the next moment poor.

My Dad's side of the family had experienced a similar sequence of events. Two circumstances changed the economy of a city and nation that caused the little rich boy, who became my father, to be exposed to a life of near poverty.

His father was a very successful restaurant owner on Exchange Street in Buffalo, New York as well as a prominent political figure of that city. He had built one of the largest restaurants in the city. My father and his brother lived in a home that enjoyed all of the trappings of success and prosperity.

Then came 1929 and two unbelievable events turned this successful family into one that found it almost a miracle to come up with enough money to put food on the table. First of all, Buffalo revolved around the railroad, and Exchange Street where the Reid restaurant was located faced the train depot. The Reid business was in the center of the traffic in the hotel and restaurant corridor. Then one day, the train depot was moved to another location, and Exchange Street became deserted. Within months the crash of 1929 hit America, and my entrepreneurial grandfather lost all of his business investments and the family was thrust into poverty. Perhaps that story is where I should begin, because I came from wealth that was lost – families who were rich and became poor in a very short period of time.

My two grandfathers responded differently to the loss of their family fortunes. Both of them died in 1936, within four years of the loss of the family money. I was brought up knowing both sides of the economic tapestry of America. My parents knew what it was like to be rich and what it was like to be poor.

Nevertheless, I watched as my parents accepted the challenge of believing that God had a covenant promise to bless them. I watched as they both lived, not in a state of despair for what could have been, but in faith for what was going to be.

My mother had watched as her father became angry and lost his desire to live. I lived with Fenton Rice and remember his bitterness for his loss. The one thing I remember about "Papa" was his delight in tripping me with his cane and watching me fall. It is a sad memory.

Thompson Reid (after whom I was named) never expressed bitterness or anger, but lived a life, from what I remember, of despair. The only one of his properties he was able to save was a small farm in East Aurora, New York.

He loved the city. He loved crowds and the excitement and the wonder of being in the center where thousands of people passed by his door every day. But now, his days were spent looking at and milking the few cows on his farm to earn a living. The "city boy" hated this life and within four years, in great discouragement, Thompson Reid didn't wake up one day – he simply could not accept poverty.

I watched my parents, as young Christians, take on a whole different attitude. Within a few years they were in ministry. We had a brand new, luxury automobile. I had toys. We stayed at the finest hotels and ate at the best restaurants.

My parents were not rich, but they were rich toward God. They gave liberally. They had famous and wealthy friends, and no one would believe that they had been poor. And, to make it even more miraculous, this was still in the waning years of the Depression.

They both believed that God could do anything and that He had a covenant with them to prosper them. When Albert Edward Reid was about to die, he called me to his bedside and reminded me of the fact that God had provided for me a great life of abundance. I remembered the beautiful new cars, the boats, the beautiful hotels where we stayed, the trips we made when few people traveled. In spite of the fact that we lived a very rich existence, we were never rich in terms of large amounts of money. It was because of my father's faith that we always lived a life of abundance.

Within hours of his "home-going" he looked into my eyes and said, "Tommy, you know I have given everything away: our home, our cars, our money...all of it has been invested in the Kingdom. I have less than $500.00 in the bank. I only leave an insurance policy with enough to bury me and a few thousand dollars. Your stepmother has taken care of me for almost twenty-five years, and I must leave everything I have to her. Because I have given everything to God, I know that God will take care of her. Watch the miracles that God will perform for her.

"For you, my will gives you a total of $500.00. Take care of Wanda with that. But I have one more thing to leave you with – My Faith. That faith has provided the cars, the boats, the hotels, fine restaurants, all the blessings we have enjoyed. God has always provided everything. So, I leave you my faith; a faith that will provide for you all of your life."

That was forty years ago, and I can say today, that the greatest inheritance a father could leave to a son, was the faith for God's prosperity that Albert Reid left his son. I had a vision or destiny that needed funding. My Dad did not have the resources I needed, but He did leave me the faith to create those resources.

And…how it has worked! I have lived a miracle life; a life very few rich people ever enjoy. I have lived as if Albert Reid had been a multi-millionaire. My father left me His Faith.

This book is the story of how God sees money and how He provides money.

Here is what Albert Reid taught me:

God has planned and predestined for his children to prosper!

Prosperity is not an option in the Kingdom of God; it is A Mandate! If you understand the spiritual context of this parable, you will have to come to the conclusion that prosperity is mandated for the people of the Kingdom.

We will deal with the principles of this parable throughout this book. However, take a moment to remember what Jesus said in this amazing story. Each parable has an amazing amount of heavenly truth. They must be the central and the most important things God actually said when Jesus was present among us.

This individual parable has one central truth. Man was designed to be the steward of God's wealth. As a steward of that wealth, the faithful steward will take God's wealth and increase, grow it, or multiply it.

The consequences for not making profit or increasing the wealth of God which we are to steward are severe. First of all, if we take good care of them and protect them, but do not make a profit and increase them, they will be taken away and given to one who has faithfully made profit with what was given to him.

At the end of the parable, the whole story takes on a supernatural and heavenly context. The punishment for the steward's failure to increase God's wealth is directly linked to a heavenly or eternal consequence. The unfaithful steward is cast out of his eternal relationship and sent to a place that appears to be the place of eternal punishment.

I will not attempt to exegete that passage except to say that the consequences of a steward's failure to make profit or to prosper in the area of things over which God has made him a steward is linked to the eternal kingdom. It is obvious that increasing God's resources has been a mandate ever since the Garden of Eden when man was ordered to sow seed and multiply God's resources. Man was also commanded to subdue the earth, or extend the wonder of the garden to all of the earth.

We Are Born with Wealth Inside Us!

All of us begin our lives with a deposit of talents or wealth inside us. Wealth does not begin by someone dropping an unexpected check in our "mailbox." Let's take a look at what each of us has within us when we begin our lives:

Asset #1: Our God-Written Destiny

First of all, the greatest asset inside us is our God-written purpose or destiny. Scripture says that it was penned by God before the foundation of the world. It is undoubtedly the most powerful asset in our life. Because it was written by God, before matter itself was created, it is more powerful than nature itself. The destiny of Moses was greater than the Red Sea. Therefore, since the destiny of Moses was greater and more powerful than the sea, that body of water was forced to bow to the superior ranking of the destiny inside of Moses. The same was true with Joshua and the sun. The sun had to bow to the greater ranking of the destiny inside of Joshua. I submit to you that the greatest wealth inside of you is your God-predestined destiny.

Asset #2: The Person of the Holy Spirit Dwelling Inside Us

Nothing can be more powerful than the wealth of knowing that God, through the Holy Spirit, lives inside of us. Scripture says that Christ is in us and is the Hope of Glory! Did you know that your greatest asset is certainly that you have the mind of Christ? He knows how to build the church or the business you dream of building.

Asset #3: Our Natural Talent or Ability

Every one of us has God-given abilities. You may not have discovered them yet, or you may not have developed them yet, but they are a wealth inside of you.

Asset #4: Our Spiritual Inner Ear

You have an "inner ear" that can hear the voice of the Holy Spirit. It may not yet be something that is highly developed within you. But as you spend time in prayer and meditation on the Word of God and carefully listen to the voice of God, you will be able to hear what God is speaking to you about your future and your destiny. The inner spiritual ear that can hear the voice of God is your greatest asset. Moses heard that voice at the burning bush. Joshua received God's instructions on how to conquer Jericho as he listened with his inner spiritual ear and heard the voice of God.

So, take a journey inside yourself and discover not only the purposes of God for your life, but the power to become the man or woman that God dreams you to be and fulfill the purposes that He dreams of you creating.

Let us never forget that God made us for success and destiny. He placed great resources and wealth inside of us. Perhaps we need to realize that success, destiny, and purpose are not gifts that come from outside of us, but rather gifts that are already inside us. We begin life with great wealth inside of us.

This book is a sequel to our book, "How To Live Out Of A Dream." In that book, I shared about God's dream for your life or discovering your own destiny. This book is about how to discover and create the resources you will need to fund that vision and create your destiny. Yes, it is the story of money, the money you need to create your destiny. But it is your story. It begins with the greatness that God has placed within you. It begins with the fact that the power to create the wealth you need to fulfill God's dream is really inside of you.

Let's make the great discovery together as we find the hidden treasure of the provision you need to fulfill God's dream for your life.

THE PARABLE OF THE TALENTS
(MATTHEW 25:14-29)

For the Kingdom of Heaven is like a man traveling to a far country, who called his own servants and delivered his goods to them. And to one he gave five talents, to another two, and to another one, to each according to his own ability and immediately he went on a journey.

Then he who had received five talents went and traded with them, and made another five talents. And likewise he who had received two gained two more also. But he who had received one went and dug in the ground, and hid his lord's money. After a long time The Lord of those servants came and settled accounts with them.

And he who had received five talents came and brought five other talents, saying, "Lord you delivered to me five talents, look I have gained five more talents. His lord said to him, "Well done good and faithful servant, you were faithful over a few things, I will make you ruler over many things. Enter into the joy of your Lord."

He also who had received two talents came and said, "Look, I have gained two more talents besides them". His lord said to him, "Well done good and faithful servant, you have been faithful over a few things, I will make you ruler over many things. Enter into the joy of your Lord."

Then he who had received the one talent came and said, "Lord I knew you to be a hard man, reaping where you have not sown, and gathering where you have not scattered seed. And I was afraid, and went and hid your talent in the ground. Look, there you have what is yours."

But his Lord answered and said to him, "You wicked and lazy servant, you knew that I reap where I have not sown, and gather where I have not scattered seed. So you ought to have deposited my money with the bankers, and at my coming I would have received back my own with interest. Therefore, take that talent and give it to him who has ten talents."

For to everyone who has, more will be given, and he will have abundance; but from him who does not have, even what he has will be taken away. And cast the unprofitable servant into outer darkness. There will be weeping and gnashing of teeth.

Section 1

WE ARE BORN WITH WEALTH INSIDE US

CREATING WEALTH FOR THE PURPOSE OF CHANGING OUR WORLD

"My destiny will cause mountains to move,
seas to roll back,
and the sun to stand still.
I believe in the power inherent in the destiny inside of me. "
(From Tommy Reid's Destiny Quote of the day)

"Asking who ought to be the boss is like asking
who ought to be the tenor in the quartet.
Obviously the man who can sing tenor."
(Henry Ford, 1863-1947)

"Whatever you birth by the flesh
you have to sustain with the flesh.
Whatever you birth by the spirit
is sustained by the spirit."
(Larry Szrama)

Chapter 1

MONEY: WHAT IS IT?

Money. What is it? Or perhaps a better question would be, "Whose is it?" Is it evil, or is it good? It is obviously important to all of us because it feeds us, houses us, clothes us, provides medicine and medical care when we are sick, provides transportation, and educates our children.

So, I guess you could say it is important. As Christians we generally are confused about money. We argue about the doctrine of prosperity, and yet we would all like to prosper. We know we should properly budget our money, but most of us live a life of instant gratification, which causes us to be a servant to our debts. We work hard for money, and yet something inside of us really believes that it probably is evil.

Therefore, I want to share with you what I believe is the biblical view of money. The Bible talks more about money than it does about faith or eternity including both heaven and hell.

I do believe in prosperity. I must believe in prosperity because the Bible teaches us that God wants us to prosper or increase the talents or wealth He has entrusted to us.

Don't put this book down yet because you think you might disagree with my deductions. You might want to put it down because you think I may put you under condemnation for not budgeting your money properly or that I am against that new car you want to buy on the installment plan. I think you will like what I am going to say about getting excited about budgeting your money and systematically increasing your wealth. Remember, it is the Lord who gives you the power to create wealth.

Perhaps you think I am going to talk to you about sowing seed and reaping a harvest. I will, because I have lived all of my life sowing seed and reaping harvests. I also have more good news for you, and that news is that I know that God wants you released from the condemnation of thinking you are giving to get. I have an idea that will change your life.

And what about wealth? I will be honest with you: I am going to talk to you about building or creating wealth. That, I believe is a biblical mandate. Abraham was not the only person in the nation of Israel who was wealthy. He was wealthy, but so were many of his people. Wealth is good! Greed is bad – very bad! Therefore, let me talk to you about the biblical logistics of building a portfolio of wealth.

My purpose is to bless you, not with pie-in–the-sky theology, or the overly simplistic formula to put your money in the offering, sow a seed into the good ground of a specific ministry, and you will reap a harvest. You properly will if you do that, but perhaps we should sit back for a moment and examine the full implications of a lifestyle of giving.

Now I want to get down to the nitty-gritty of the money world.

- We will dream together.
- We will plan together.
- We will build a structure of building wealth in our lives that will not, nor can it fail.
- We will talk about the covenant God made with us to prosper.
- We will prosper. You and I both will prosper because it is the covenant that our Covenant God made with us.

Let's get started with our first question: Wealth, to whom does it belong or whose money is it, anyway?

Chapter 2

WHOSE MONEY IS IT?

I have to begin with a question. It is the primary question of wealth and the first question we must answer in order to understand God's philosophy of blessing and wealth. Let's begin with the primary truth of this book, the answer to our question. Who is the owner of true wealth?

EVERYTHING BELONGS TO GOD!
Yes, I said, EVERYTHING!

The richest man in the world owns nothing. Donald Trump owns nothing! The queen of England with all her silver and gold and her real estate owns nothing. They are both penny-less! Not a penny, or a nickel, or a dime belongs to them. God teaches us this truth in the book of Genesis. Without understanding that, we will never understand money or finances.

In Genesis we read that God makes a garden of wealth and places his man and woman in that garden. They are not to own it, and they are not to claim any kind of ownership – it is God's garden!

God instructs them to "tend the garden" and "subdue the rest of the earth." That is their job description. That is how they will build, manage, and increase the wealth that belongs to God. In order for Adam and Eve to understand His ownership of everything completely, God places a tree in the center of that garden. That tree had one major purpose: to let Adam and Eve declare daily to whom the garden belongs.

Day after day they walked by that tree and never ate of its fruit because they knew it was God's tree. Their obedience in abstaining from the fruit of that tree acknowledged the ownership of God over every tree and over the total garden.

That tree was God's way of beginning to teach man about the law of first fruits or the law of the tithe. As the tree demonstrated to man that the first fruit of the garden expressed the ownership of God over all the rest of the garden, so the tithe, or the first fruit, also acknowledged to God that He owned everything.

As we examine this truth, let's look at another biblical story beginning in Joshua 6:16. God had promised that He would give a very special land to His people. It was a covenantal promise. In fact God had sworn by himself that Abraham and his family would inherit the land. Abraham asked God, "How shall I know that you will give me this land?" God then gave Abraham an amazing vision. Through this vision God said to Abraham that although He was making a covenant between Himself and Abraham, in reality He was making a covenant with Himself so that it could never be broken. Abraham saw the pillar of fire (representing God the Son) and the smoking furnace (representing God the Father) walking between the sacrifices making covenant with each other. God was saying that nothing could destroy this covenant.

It now comes time for the family of Abraham to enter in and inherit God's promise. However, before they could enter the Promised Land, God told them that they would be required to recognize His ownership by giving Him the first city, Jericho. In fact, this is the way that God said it, "Now the first city shall be doomed by the lord for destruction." Then in verse 19 He further tells Abraham, "Now all the silver and gold and vessels of bronze and iron are consecrated to the Lord...they shall come into the treasury of the Lord."

Adam and Eve learned that the first tree in the garden was the covenantal tithe portion, or the first fruit. They were told to abstain from its fruit thereby, acknowledging God's ownership. Then, notice how that truth is expressed in this story of Joshua and the destiny of the first city of the Promised Land. In the story of Joshua and the city of Jericho, it becomes obvious that Jehovah is requiring this the same principle of abstinence be expressed by their first act of giving the first city in the land of promise to God. They must signify the ownership of God of the entire land by giving the first-fruit city to God.

The Lord has given the city to you.

Remember, God has said that you are to, "Shout for the Lord has given you the city!" (Joshua 6:16). Jericho is the first city that is a part of this covenantal promise. In the next verse, God says, "Now **the first city** shall be doomed (accursed) and you must abstain from the accursed thing" (emphasis added).

The first city must be brought back to God.

Every time I read this story, I am brought back to my strong faith in the tithe or first fruit. **It must be brought back to God!** However, there is another truth in this story that amazes me. The first city is called by God the "accursed or doomed" portion. It tells us that this city is "doomed for destruction" and all of its silver and gold are to be brought to God's house.

The first city is the "accursed city."

Isn't it interesting that the Bible says, "Jesus became a curse for us that we might inherit the promises God made to Abraham." Here is the way I believe it works. When we bring the first fruits or the first portion to God, we acknowledge His ownership also over the other 90 percent. God calls this first portion "accursed." Therefore, when we bring the accursed portion to God, the entire curse that was brought upon the earth in the book of Genesis is placed on the accursed portion (the tithe or first fruits) as the curse was placed upon Jesus.

When the "curse" is placed on the first city, the curse will then be removed from the other nine cities.

If the curse is taken by the first fruit and brought to God, then the curse is removed from the other 90 percent so that everything can be brought under the blessing. Listen to Paul as he states, "Jesus became a curse for us so that we might inherit the blessing of Abraham."

It works like this: we take the first 10% of our income to the house of God. As Jesus, the holy and totally righteous one became the one who took our curse, so the accursed portion that now becomes God's portion, assumes the entire curse and all of our finances. The curse that has been upon our increase is now released.

Carefully note Romans 11:16, **"For if the first fruit is holy, the lump is also holy, and if the root is holy, so are the branches"** (emphasis added).

We are commanded not to touch the first city.

Now, Israel is about to enter the land of covenantal promise. So that divine order can be followed, God orders them to take the first city and bring all of the silver, gold, and precious things to His house.

Joshua follows the command of God, except that one man, by the name of Achan, takes some of that sacred portion for himself and buries it in his tent. When he is discovered he says, "When I saw among the spoils a beautiful Babylon garment, two hundred shekels of silver, a wedge of gold weighing fifty shekels, I coveted them and took them!" In Joshua 7:7, God says, "You have transgressed my covenant, you have taken accursed things and you have stolen and deceived." In verse 13, God further says, "Achan, you cannot stand before your enemies until you take away the accursed thing from among you." Achan pays for the trespass with his own life.

The first truth of this book is simply this:

GOD OWNS EVERYTHING;
WE OWN NOTHING.

The way we express the ownership of God is to bring the first fruit of our lives to the altar of God to express to Him our faith in His ownership.

I understood this as a child. It was in the middle of the Depression and my parents could not afford to buy a house so they rented. The cost to purchase a new house was $2,200.00. The cost to rent was $20.00 per month.

Since it was the Depression era, my parents had no way to find $2,200 to buy a house, so they rented at the rate of $240.00 for an entire year, or $20.00 per month.

To teach his son stewardship, every month, my father took me as we went with that $20.00 bill to Mr. Smith's house. Before my eyes, he paid the rent so we could live in Mr. Smith's property. We had the responsibility of being a steward over that house. Dad was attempting to teach me about what Adam did every day when God told him not to take anything from that single tree that represented God's ownership of the garden.

Daily, as Adam passed by that tree, he said to himself and to God, "That is Your tree, the symbolism of Your ownership of this garden." When I put aside the first fruits of this garden, I recognized that You own everything.

It was just like that $20.00 bill. That bill was the symbol that Mr. Smith owned the house and that our family was "stewarding" the house for him. Since we were the stewards over his property, we could enjoy the full benefits of life in that house.

As I grew older, my Dad and mother provided me with twenty-five cents a week allowance. They told me that all of that twenty-five cents belonged to God, and I was to declare his ownership and my stewardship by giving God at least 10 percent as recognition of His ownership of everything. I would carefully lay aside at least three cents (usually five), acknowledging that God owned everything.

Later, I went into fulltime ministry with my father. It was then that he taught me an even greater lesson about God's ownership.

While I grew up during the Depression, my Dad work for educational institutions. We always lived in housing provided for us by the schools or colleges where Dad worked. Over the years, Dad and Mom began to put money aside in the bank to buy their first house.

There are times when God asks some of us to acknowledge His ownership by giving everything back to God. My father and mother taught me the tithe to honor His ownership of everything. And they demonstrated obedience in those times when we had to give everything we had back to a Sovereign God. To properly understand my concept of money and the ownership of God, I need to tell you how my parents demonstrated to me a biblical philosophy of money and wealth.

Because of the Depression and our lack of family resources, my parents were never able to purchase a home. But, they saved what they could, and when I became a teenager and was attending Bible School, they finally had enough money to build their first home on North Woods Drive in Springfield, Missouri.

How exciting to see the first home we had ever owned under construction! I remember helping them choose knotty pine paneling in the living and dining rooms in that beautiful new country home. I remember them buying matching furniture. I remember the day Mom, Dad, and I moved into our first home. Wow! That is all I can say. It was ours...or, was it really? I knew in my heart it belonged to God.

Three years passed, and we were in full-time ministry traveling from city to city, state to state, living in our dream house and planning that when God blessed our finances enough to buy tickets overseas, we would go to Asia.

One day, Dad came into the living room overlooking the woods. It was a holy moment. Dad was about to give it all to God. Within weeks the house would be gone. As he began to explain to us, he told us of our need for a tent, chairs, sound system, and other things we needed to preach the Gospel.

I knew at that moment, the house was gone because my Dad had given it to God in his heart. So, my parents sold the house, and with the profit we bought the tent, the semi-truck and tractor to move the tent from city to city. We purchased hundreds of chairs, and designed and purchased a sound system all from the proceeds of that house.

I remember climbing behind the wheel of that old 1951 Ford F7 truck hooked to the thirty-two foot trailer that would haul God's tent cathedral seating 1,300 people. I can still see that old truck with this unseasoned truck driver at the wheel as I pulled away from our dream house and watched another family move into the beautiful house Dad had designed and built for our family.

We would never see that house again, for Dad's entire life savings were now invested in that Ford truck, Fruehauf trailer, tent, hundreds of chairs, and other related equipment. Dad looked at me and his tear-filled eyes said it all, "Tommy, that house was never ours. It was always God's house. He owns everything we have."

In order to understand money, we have to begin with my first premise. It is the most important thing you will ever understand about money:

EVERYTHING ON THIS PLANET BELONGS TO GOD.

We are only stewards of God's wealth. So, my first statement to you is that you will never own anything. It all belongs to God.

God is the best investment genius in the universe. Prosperity is inevitable if your belief is right, because we are all responsible for properly investing and managing God's portfolio of riches. We are responsible to make it grow!

That is why Jesus talked about this in parables. As he prospered Abraham and gave him power to create wealth, this powerful man of faith increased the wealth God had entrusted to him. In the parables, Jesus teaches us that the steward of God's possessions is responsible to take everything entrusted to him and make increase of what God has put into his hands.

The parable of the talents says it best. Jesus talks about different kinds of stewards. The first steward takes the one talent, buries it and protects it from being lost. Jesus tells us that he is an unfaithful servant because God expects us to take what He puts in our hands and cause it to grow and increase. Two talents are to become four, and five are to become ten. According to Jesus, we are responsible to grow God's wealth because:

GOD GIVES US POWER TO GET WEALTH!

Jesus infers that every one of us has been made responsible to grow what He has given us to steward for Him. Know this: **Prosperity is not an option!** Prosperity is a responsibility of our stewardship of the abundance that God has given us and expects us to increase. Creating wealth is a mandate from God. Our responsibility is to increase, not our wealth, but God's wealth. Prosperity is not only a covenant promise of God; **it is a mandate.**

Chapter 3

WHERE DOES MONEY OR WEALTH COME FROM?

I know what you think I am going to say. I understand that that raw wealth comes from the riches of the earth such as silver, gold, diamonds, or other precious things buried in the soil. Or, you may think that money comes from the wicked, who will surrender it to the man or woman of faith. In other words, you think that money comes from somewhere besides where you are standing right now. You believe when God blesses you, resources will come to you.

However, in reality, money or the blessing of God comes to you from the wealth of God inside you, not from somewhere outside of you. The provision of God is within you because Jesus and all of His wisdom to create wealth is within you.

THE PROVISION OF GOD IS ACTUALLY INSIDE OF YOU!

When God made a covenant with our faith-father Abraham, God said to him, "I will bless you; I will make you a great nation." Essentially, what God was saying was that God inside of Abraham would produce the blessing. Blessing would not come to him; it would come from him.

I submit to you that no one came to Henry Ford and gave him millions of dollars. The money that Henry Ford made from the sale of millions of automobiles came from the genius, wisdom, and creativity inside him. What was inside of Henry Ford, created wealth. Listen to the words of Scripture: (Emphasis added throughout.)

- "Honor the Lord with your possessions and with the first fruits of all your increase. So your barns will be filled with plenty, and your vats will overflow with new wine." (Proverbs 3:9-10)

- "Riches and honor are with me, **Enduring riches** and righteousness. My fruit is better than gold, yes than fine gold." (Proverbs 8:18)
- "The hand of the diligent makes rich. Blessings are on the head of the righteous." (Proverbs 10:4, 22)
- "The fruit of the righteous is a tree of life." (Proverbs 11:30)
- "By humility and the fear of the Lord are riches and honor and life." (Proverbs 22:4)
- "Through wisdom is a house built. And by understanding it is established; By knowledge the rooms are filled with all precious and pleasant **riches!**" (Proverbs 24:3, 4)
- "As for every man to whom God has given riches and wealth, and **given him power to eat of it, to receive his heritage and rejoice in his labor**…this is the gift of God." (Ecclesiastes 5:19)

Note the amazing words of the writer of Ecclesiastes when he talks about the one who has been given riches and wealth and the power to eat of those riches. It talks about **God's power** to earn **riches** and **wealth and God's power** to receive His heritage. The emphasis is on the fact that it is the power within him that is the source of riches and wealth.

The blessing of God that made Abram the richest man in the entire world came from **God Who** made him into the man that produced those riches. Abram's riches came from the wisdom, power, creativity, and strength that God put within him.

Solomon became the richest man who has ever lived. Today, Solomon would be at the top of the list of Billionaires in the world. How did he become so rich? True, he inherited wealth from his father David, but he far surpassed the riches of his father. He not only had the power to create wealth, but he also had the power to enjoy or eat of his wealth. He himself, states that both the power he had to create wealth and to enjoy wealth came as a gift of God.

But this amazing gift that came from God was placed within Solomon. His riches and his wealth came from something deep inside him. In his writings, he refers to it as wisdom. Remember that he said, "Riches and honor are within me."

Let me share with you how powerful that force to create wealth is even over the power of nature itself. Remember the power of your destiny.

Your destiny was written by God before the foundation of the world. Revelation 17:8 states that your name (or your destiny) was written in the Book of Life before the foundation of the world. Hebrews 4:3 states that your works (or what you will create) were finished before the foundation of the world. Ephesians 1:4 states that He chose us in Him before the foundation of the world.

That power is within you. Deep in the recesses of your heart is a vision of your destiny. Deep in the recesses of your heart is the power to create the wealth that will fund your destiny.

We keep looking for letters from heaven to fund our destiny. We dream about winning the lottery or having a rich uncle die and leave us a fortune. I have even had people share that God was interested in giving them special wisdom in the buying of stock or futures so they would be blessed. Forget it! Riches do not come from outside of you; they come from within you.

Abraham gave Lot the better piece of ground. Abraham knew that the productivity of a piece of land did not come from the seeming fruitfulness of the land but rather from the faith and belief inside of the man who owned and tilled it.

Go to the source of your wealth and your riches. They are inside you. Remember Scripture states, "Christ in us, the hope of glory." (Colossians 1:27) Look within you. There you will find the Source of blessing and the Source of riches.

Not a single wealthy man in the world believes that his wealth came from outside of himself. He was the one who had power to create wealth. I cannot even imagine what would happen in our world if people, who are born again by the Holy Spirit and have Christ dwelling within them, would realize the power of Who lives inside them. God, Himself, lives inside of you. You have the mind of Christ. It is that same Christ who spoke the universe into existence, and His very power and wisdom lives inside of you.

YOU HAVE POWER TO CREATE WEALTH!

Chapter 4

THE MASTER'S PLAN TO CREATE WEALTH

Now that we have discovered that all wealth belongs to God, we are ready to get down to business of increasing God's wealth. If the wealth that we sometimes think is ours really belongs to God, then God demands that we make His portfolio grow. Increase is a mandate from God! If it is the mandate of God to grow God's resources, then let's get really practical in this chapter. How do we do that?

I would suggest first of all that we are to believe! Believe that we are responsible to create wealth and increase the wealth that He has entrusted us to steward. Then we are to believe that we have the power to create wealth. Ultimately, we are to believe that it is a spiritual thing and a divine mandate to prosper.

PROSPERITY IS NOT AN OPTION.
IT IS A DUTY.

The first question I ask is: "Who has greater wealth, the child with a million dollar inheritance or the child with an idea?" I believe the greatest wealth is in ideas, not in money in a bank. One idea can create a billion dollars. Just ask Henry Ford! So, let's begin with faith.

I believe that inside you and inside me are unlimited resources. God has placed those ideas inside of us to create wealth. But, just how do we begin?

We begin with a plan. Even as a teenager, you can develop a plan to reach specific goals and create wealth within certain periods of time. It's also never too late, to begin setting goals. Do so in five-year increments so you can see progress. You must set wealth goals.

Measure your "wealth quotient."
(What are you worth?)

What is your worth? Perhaps you do not know. You might even have a negative net worth and owe more than you own. So let's be very practical:

MEASURE YOUR WEALTH QUOTIENT.

At the end of this chapter is a chart I want you to fill in. Here is what needs to be in that chart:

Assets	Value of Assets
Cash in Bank, Bonds, Securities, etc.	(?)
Equity value in Real Estate	(?)
Value of Furniture, etc.	(?)
Equity Value in Automobiles, Boats, RV's and other valuable items	(?)
Value of Post-Secondary Education (Remember: this is an asset.)	(?)
All other items of value	(?)
TOTAL WEALTH	**(?)**

As you look at this chart, you will develop a way to measure your wealth quotient. Examine your life and your resources. How much do you presently have in the bank? What is the value of the property or properties that you own, less the amount you owe on those properties? What is the equity you have in your car? You might be surprised to find out what you are worth.

Then, set your goals. If you have $15,000.00 in the bank, and you have equity of $22,000.00 in your home and your car has a value of $10,000 less than what you owe on it, add them together to place a value on your worth.

For example:

My home equity value:	$20,000.00
Equity in a car = Value less amount owed:	$3,000.00
My clothes:	$5,000.00
Value of Insurance Policies:	$10,000.00
Money in Savings and Checking:	$12,000.00
Boat or sports equipment:	$10,000.00
My Value:	$60,000.00

Set Goals for Creating God's Wealth

Next, set goals for where you want to be by five or ten years from now. For example, if you presently do not own a house, then you need to increase cash in the bank so you will have adequate funds for a 20% down payment.

Then, set goals for every ten years. Where do you want to be when you are thirty, forty, fifty, sixty, or seventy years of age?

You may want to add other goals, which may or may not include starting a business, owning your own insurance or sales agency, but always set some goals.

You see: it is God's will that you prosper. It is God's desire to prosper you so you can reach God's goals for your life. This is why that story of the talents is so important. Increasing wealth is a mandate of the Kingdom.

Look at the next few pages and begin to set goals for your life.

Ask yourself...

1. Why are we mandated in Scripture to create wealth?
2. Am I creating wealth now?
3. Do I have goals for wealth creation?
4. Prepare a chart of your present wealth using the following categories
5. Set specific goals for creating wealth for your future. Measure your worth. Then set goals on an incremental basis and a final goal for your life. Following is a chart to measure your wealth quotient:

LISTING OF MY ASSETS	VALUE OF ASSET
Cash in Bank, Bonds, Stock, Securities	
Value of Real Estate	
Value of Autos, Boats, RV's, Other Real Estate in addition to home, etc.	
Value of Post-Secondary or Special Education	
All other items of Value	
Less mortgages, loans on listed assets including mortgage on my home	
TOTAL WORTH	

MY AGE	PRESENT WORTH and/or MY GOAL
MY PRESENT AGE	
10 YEARS FROM NOW	
MY AGE _____	
THE YEAR_____	
20 YEARS FROM NOW	
MY AGE _____	
THE YEAR_____	
30 YEARS FROM NOW	
MY AGE _____	
THE YEAR _____	
40 YEARS FROM NOW	
MY AGE _____	
THE YEAR_____	
50 YEARS FROM NOW	
MY AGE _____	
THE YEAR _____	
MY GOAL IS TO BE WORTH THE AMOUNT OF _____	
AT 70 YEARS OF AGE	

Chapter 5

Managing God's Wealth through Budgeting

L et's return to our premise. First, whatever wealth God has already entrusted you with really belongs to God. Secondly, every Kingdom citizen has a responsibility to grow the resources that God has placed in their hands. However, before we can successfully create wealth we have to properly manage the talents or wealth that God has placed in our hands.

It is not enough just to believe for wealth or to expect that the wealth of the wicked is laid up for the righteous. True, the wealth of the unrighteous is laid up for the righteous, but how does that happen? We are responsible to create wealth and to see it grow. So, let's get down to the nitty-gritty of wealth management and wealth creation. The plan of God is to increase what God has given us and turn what may be a small amount of "talents" into the abundance of God.

One of the mistakes we make in management, especially in the western world, is to think that we create wealth by buying things that make us feel as if we are blessed even though we're buying them with borrowed money. That approach actually depletes God's resources.

Take a moment and "measure" your assets and your debts. Because your wealth is only the equity you have in a car, a house, a business, or whatever you think is wealth. If you are upside down in your equity, then you have a liability instead of an asset.

How do you manage God's money? First of all, you must manage God's money through budgeting. How can you balance your budget? I've prepared some charts to help you create a budget for your life. You will never create the wealth you dream of creating without a budget and without living by that budget.

You may be thinking: How do I pay off my credit cards when I simply do not have enough money? One of the things that I want you to do in this chapter is to think about how you can use budgeting to pay off your debt.

Let's examine the wonder of the budget process. You need to think about a budget as one of the most exciting things in your life, because it will assist you in reaching your goals. Take a moment to look at all of your credit card balances. They have bothered you and discouraged you, and you really think they will "always be with you." Not so, IF you begin to utilize the excitement of a goal-setting budget.

Remember, the budget is not your goal. It is only a means to an end. The goal is creating wealth that is measurable. The budget is only a way to assist you to reach that goal. So get your mindset on the goal and take it off the alleged pain of the process. We are going somewhere.

One of your first goals must be to eliminate debt by paying off all of your credit cards! That begins with a promise to you and to God. Remember every debt you eliminate adds to your actual wealth quotient. We can do all things through Christ who enables or strengthens us!

After perhaps fasting and praying for one or two days, get on your knees and make a promise to God that:

YOU WILL ELIMINATE
ALL OF YOUR CREDIT CARD DEBT.

If you are going to eliminate all of your debt, my suggestion is that you take those credit cards out of your purse or your wallet. Get rid of them!

Where do you get the money you need to pay off your credit cards?

Set up a "resource pool" that you can use to eliminate all credit card debt. Let me list a few simple sources of a fund you can build:

- Example: Starbucks coffee purchases – Do you frequent Starbucks? How many Starbucks coffees do you buy a month? One every day, two a week, four a week or may be one every day of the week? Eliminate those expenses totally, or at least reduce them to a very small number. Let's say you usually buy four cups of coffee a week. Say that a cup of Starbucks regular is $3.00. Multiply the number of cups times the $3.00 average cost. In this case, 4/week X 4 weeks is 16 cups/month X $3.00 each. The total cost of sixteen cups is $48.00/month. If you reduce the number to one/week for a total of $12.00/month, that gives you a savings of $36.00 each month to be applied to your credit cards. This is one example. Most everyone has a regular habit of buying something that isn't essential for life and wellbeing. You can save money by breaking that habit.

- Example: How many times a month does your family eat out? Twice a week? In today's culture, it's often more than that. Let's say that the cost of dinner for a family of four is $50.00. If you cut back to eat out only once a week, your savings would be $50/week and $200/month! More dollars to apply to those credit cards.

- More examples: How much do you spend a month on non-essential items? Or what about changing your vacation plans? Instead of flying to California, vacation near home. (When Aimee was growing up, we eliminated all of our travel vacations for over ten years. Instead, we planned and budgeted savings so we could take that money and purchase a beautiful 28" cabin cruiser. That boat became part of how our daughter grew up and how we enjoyed ourselves as a family. And it wasn't an added expense but was derived from our budgeted savings.)

Just think about your spending habits. Begin by destroying the cards. Find the funds to pay them off in your budget, and set goals to pay them off in specific periods of time. Begin with the smallest balance. This is important because you will immediately see yourself reaching a goal. Goals are important in this process.

In the next few pages, you will find two charts. The first chart is a goal-setting promise to God to eliminate your debt. The second contains your sources of funding to eliminate your debt.

Dig in and begin the process! First, prepare a budget. I've included an example for you to consider. Then, propose a way to pay off all of your credit cards.

You may have other ideas that will work. Get ready to start a program to save enough from your present income to totally eliminate all of your credit card debt.

AN EXAMPLE FOR YOU TO CONSIDER

CREDIT CARD (Listed in order of balances owed with smallest first)	BALANCE OF CARD DEBT	GOAL DATE FOR ELIMINATION
Sears Card	$140.00	First Month
Department Store Card	$ 280.00	First Month
Master Card	$845.00	Third Month
Visa Card	$1,845.00	Sixth Month
Amex Card	$ 2,180.00 (vacation to Bahamas charged to this account)	Tenth (or twelfth) Month
2nd Master Card	$ 4,000.00 (used for purchasing refrigerator and other improvements for kitchen)	Eighteen Months

You can see that I have paid off the smallest card balance first. Some people pay off the card with the highest interest rate first. However, it's important that we set goals we can reach and goals we can visualize. When you get three or four cards paid off and destroyed, you'll feel very fulfilled.

You may be able to accomplish this even faster than I have suggested. When you get started with your budget you will find further savings each month because you will be reaching goals.

Stop now and take a look at your credit cards. Immediately determine that you will totally eliminate any new credit card debt, and begin today to find the resources for total elimination of all credit card debt.

Remember, goal setting is important. Reaching goals motivates us and causes us to get excited about the process. Too often our goal is a bigger house or a nicer car. The first goal of God is to take our two talents and make them into four. Building wealth is a reachable and spiritual goal. Let's do it.

Action Steps…

List all of your credit cards and the total balance on each. Make a promise to God that you will pay off all of this indebtedness in a specific time frame. Use the following chart to list all of this debt.

I MAKE AN ABSOLUTE PROMISE TO GOD THAT I WILL PAY OFF ALL MY CREDIT CARD DEBT IN _____ MONTHS.

Use the following chart to put your promise in writing:

CREDIT CARD	BALANCE OWED	GOAL DATE FOR ELIMINATION

Where will I get the money to eliminate credit card debt? Here are some ideas.

SOURCE OF FUNDING FOR CREDIT CARD DEBT ELIMINATION	ESTIMATED MONTHLY CASH SAVINGS
Elimination of Coffee and Restaurant Purchases	Starbucks etc. $_____ monthly Other Restaurants $_____ monthly
Elimination or Postponement of Major Purchases	$ _____ monthly
Eliminate Purchase of Auto and Continue Driving Present Vehicle	$_____ monthly
Change Plans for Vacation from Distant Trip to Local	$ _____ monthly
Other Ideas	

Chapter 6

CREATING WEALTH THROUGH SOWING AND REAPING

As soon as we open our Bibles to the book of Genesis, we are immediately confronted with God's major truth concerning growth, seedtime, and harvest. Increase is harvest, and the sowing of seed is what God designed to give increase and growth to anything on this planet. Whether it a tree, an animal, a human being, or an entire forest, everything on this planet grows through a system of sowing seed and reaping a harvest. That is the way God's world works.

This is not the invention of Oral Roberts who taught seed faith or a television evangelist raising funds for his ministry. This is a basic truth and is the source of *every miracle of increase!* The beautiful garden in my back yard, planted by a faithful son in the Kingdom, is not just a dream. It is the work of a man who labored to plant a seed so we could all reap a harvest.

Everything in your budget is a seed that is sown. You may sow it in a bank account or you may sow it into a mission project, but everything is a seed that is sown from which you will reap a harvest if it is sown in good ground.

The first seed you sow is *always your tithe!* Secondly, you sow into missions or other projects that God lays on your heart. You may sow into your education or the education of your children.

But never forget that when you sow, you must sow in faith and in expectancy. It is faith in God and His economy that ignites a fire inside of you to give beyond your means to send a missionary, sponsor a television ministry, or build a church. Sow in faith – in faith and expectancy that *you will reap a harvest!*

IF YOU ARE TO REACH YOUR GOALS, SOW SEEDS INTO YOUR FUTURE.

I have lived a life of sowing seeds, seeds that were really beyond my natural ability, but were sown in faith. Everything I have accumulated in life is a result of the sowing seed.

Every true servant of God can share with you a multitude of experiences concerning the miracles of provision they have received from the sowing of seed and the increase that God gives of 10-fold, 100-fold, or even 1,000-fold. I have seen it time and time again.

Allow me to tell the story of how God has asked me to sow seed beyond my natural ability in the thousands of dollars. Remember, I am retired largely living on Social Security.

Recently, I sat on a platform with a spiritual son, Pastor Benny Hinn. I am always amazed at how God has anointed this man who was a very young evangelist of just past twenty years of age when I first met him and invited him to the United States and then assisted him in scheduling meetings throughout the country. I admire him both for his anointing and integrity.

As I sat on the platform, God began to speak to me about sowing a seed into his ministry. I had already purchased very expensive air tickets for Wanda and myself to travel to that meeting, and I began to argue with God that He was asking too much of me. But, I knew that God wanted me to sow a significant seed into Pastor Benny's ministry.

A week or so later, I was at a meeting of another spiritual son, and again, God spoke to my heart about another large seed that I must sow into that ministry!

So, I reminded God that when we were finishing our last building program ran short on funds to purchase chairs, and sound and video equipment for the new building. We needed thousands of dollars. Because someone on our board felt we should not purchase the equipment until we had paid off every bit of the bridge construction loan from the bank, we wouldn't be able to use our new facility. I knew I could not face the congregation with a building that did not have chairs, sound, and video equipment. So I went to my retirement fund and borrowed about $40,000.00 to finish the project without telling anyone what I had done. It was the last building I would every build as a pastor, and at nearly eighty years of age, I wanted to see that building completed. I explained to the Lord that I had sown adequate seed already.

Then God began to deal with me about another seed I was to sow into the church. I have been a collector of antique and special interest automobiles for over forty years. A man came to me and offered a beautiful Ford Thunderbird with only 39,000 actual miles. God spoke into my spirit that I was to accept the gift, completely restore the automobile, and give it as the first gift toward a Capital Fund Campaign at The Tabernacle. I reminded Him that I am no longer the pastor of this church, and that the restoration of a high quality automobile is very expensive. But God has always been persistent with me and said, "I am asking you to sow that as seed into your future ministry."

Again I added the numbers and reminded God of how generous I had been and that I'm now retired, living mostly on Social Security. But the Holy Spirit persisted. So, I obeyed and restored the car and gave it as seed to the Lord.

I remembered sitting at those two meetings with my spiritual sons and arguing with God at how much seed I had just sown. I told Him that He should not be expecting me to sow more. But the Holy Spirit didn't let up on me. He reminded me of how He was dealing with me about **obedience!** He reminded me that it was not man, but He Who had asked me to sow these seeds. And although I thought they were beyond my ability, He reminded me again that He was dealing with me about **obedience!**

Then God spoke another "word" into my spirit. That "word" was **expectancy!** The Holy Spirit reminded me that I must sow these seeds expecting a harvest!

I began to look at the harvest I was already reaping. At nearly eighty-two years of age, I was finding myself in an unbelievably busy speaking schedule at major venues and churches. My last book was selling amazingly well, and the blessing of God was being poured out on me both financially and in my health. So, I sowed new seeds with **obedience** and **expectancy!**

I close this chapter with a story from back in 1959. We were planning a missions trip to Asia, and one day I realized that if we were going to make the trip on schedule, I would have to sow a very sacrificial seed into that trip. I looked outside at the beautiful baby blue Cadillac Eldorado convertible I used in my travels around the country as an evangelist. I was going to put it in storage so that in a few months, when we returned to America, I would still have that beautiful car to travel in from church to church and city to city.

As our departure time neared, I realized we didn't have the funds to buy tickets. So, we called the Cadillac dealer, sold that beautiful car, and bought our tickets. I will never forget the emotion that I felt as I watched that dealer drive out of our driveway in "my" baby. It was gone.

So, I said to God, "Lord, I gave you my Cadillac. I'll need a car when we return, and You know the one car I dream of." As a friend talks to a friend, I looked into the face of Jesus and said, "Jesus, I have sown the seed of my Cadillac into good ground. I'm trusting that You'll give me a harvest of a very special car." I had one in mind and knew that only 465 of those cars were made. I had actually never seen one except in a picture. It was almost an impossibility to find one to buy, let alone be able to afford this rare collector car.

We spent two years in Asia in very successful ministry. When we arrived in Manila, we were asked to assume the pastorate of the largest church in the Assemblies of God in Manila. It was a wonderful time of exciting ministry. But then, we came home and my beloved Cadillac was gone.

I reminded God about my request. "I have sown my seed and given You my Cadillac, but I'm expecting a 'miracle of miracles' to replace my Cadillac."

A few weeks later, we were driving down the White Horse Pike near Atlantic City, New Jersey where we were preaching a meeting. We passed many auto dealers, and as we rounded a bend, there sat my miracle!

I had never seen a Kaiser Darren sports car in person, but there it was waiting for me. Just to see it was amazing! Within hours it was mine, and I drove it for over ten years. When I sold it, it won first place in a national automobile show. (I guess I sold it too soon because recently one went over the auction block for $180,000.00.) Well, I never saw those kinds of dollars, but I did get to drive it for ten years—it was my miracle of seed faith.

"SOWING AND REAPING" IS GOD'S METHOD OF CREATING WEALTH!

Ask Yourself…

- *Have I sown a significant seed recently? Did I reap a harvest from that seed?*
- *Did I believe and expect a harvest? In what way did I exercise my faith and reap a harvest?*
- *What have I learned about sowing and reaping as a means of creating wealth in the economy of God?*
- *Write your most significant testimony of sowing a seed and reaping a harvest.*

Chapter 7

THE ETERNAL COVENANT OF BLESSING

This is a chapter I could not wait to write. It is the very core of my belief system. I believe that God has **a covenant promise of blessing for my life!** The blessing of God is inevitable in your life and my life IF we believe.

You can't get a dime out of your bank unless you have enough faith to write a check on the money you own in your checking account or use your bankcard. Writing a check on your assets is still a matter of faith, faith that you have money in the bank. When you make a determination to create wealth, you enter into the covenant that our God made with all of His covenant children to bless us. Go back with me to one of the most amazing stories of covenant blessing in all of Scripture.

God came to His servant, Abraham, and made covenant with him. He covenanted with Abraham to give him a son. He said He would bless Abraham and his family and make them into a nation that would bless all the nations of the earth.

To make that covenant of blessing very specific, God promised to bless Abraham with a specific piece of land we know as the Holy Land. God described that land including its borders and its wealth. Abraham questioned the God of covenant, "How do I know that you will give me this land?" God answered this question with a most dramatic visitation and covenant Truth in Scripture.

God spoke to Abraham, probably in a dream or vision, "Abraham, take three animals, slay them and make a sacrifice to God with them by dividing them into halves and place each half on either side of the path. Then, take birds and lay them as a sacrifice on either side of the path. The makers of covenant will walk between the blood sacrifices and cut an unbreakable covenant so you will know that I will covenant with you to give you that land."

Then, something very interesting happens. Instead of God and Abraham walking between the sacrifices to "cut" covenant, Abraham watched an amazing thing took place. A smoking furnace (representing God the Father) and a flaming torch (representing God the Son) stood at either end of the sacrifices.

At that moment, God the Father and God the Son faced each other and walked between the sacrifices and made covenant between the Godhead. It was God making covenant with God. It is an unbreakable covenant.

God is saying to Abraham, "You will live in this land because I can never break this covenant!" That is how specific the God of covenant is about the blessing He has covenanted to provide to us. God has sworn by God, and therefore, this covenant of the promise of blessing must be fulfilled!

If God covenanted in that dimension to provide a land for the family of Abraham, I believe our covenant for blessing is an unbreakable covenant. God has made an unbreakable covenant with every believer to bless us, or more specifically, to bless and covenant with Himself. For we are in Christ and everything we have belongs to Christ, so the covenant of blessing is between God and God.

GOD HAS MADE AN UNBREAKABLE COVENANT WITH YOU, OR MORE SPECIFICALLY, TO BLESS AND COVENANT WITH HIMSELF.

But remember, all of the wealth that others think you have is God's wealth. When He blesses you, He blesses Himself and multiplies His wealth. When I get up in the morning, I lay my hand on God's billfold, and look inside and remind God that everything I have is not mine, but His. I remind Him that He has made covenant with Himself to bless His possessions, because everything that I have belongs to Him.

Remember, God made a covenant of blessing with our faith father, Abraham. In the middle of a world that was under the curse, God covenants with one man and his family to bless them, give them a land, and prosper the work of their hands.

The problem is that as a people and as a family, they consistently failed to keep their end of the covenant. Sometimes they were carried away into captivity, and sometimes they lost the land that God had covenanted to give them. In Deuteronomy, we read that God had told them that they could walk under the curse or under the blessing. Often they chose a life that put them under the curse. But in the book of Galatians, Paul the Apostle tells us something amazing. He says that **Jesus became a curse for us, that we might inherit the blessings of Abraham!**

I understand the blessings and curses of Deuteronomy 28. I realize that both Israel and the church have violated the blessing covenant. But Jesus... when I fail, has become the curse, and that releases the blessing of Abraham upon me.

I have been "grafted into" the covenant God made with Abraham. I live in covenant! I walk in covenant! When I fail to live in the full dimension of covenant, I throw myself onto His grace and declare again, "Jesus, you became the curse for me **so that I might inherit the blessing of covenant You gave to Abraham!**"

One of the very few times that our God swore by Himself was when He made a prosperity covenant with our faith father, Abraham. When Jesus told the parable of "The Lost Coin," He attributed eternal consequences to not being the kind of steward of God's wealth that would give increase to the Lord's riches.

I believe this infers that God will not entrust us with spiritual blessing until we are faithful with our stewardship of His earthly riches.

YOU MUST REALIZE THAT COVENANT BLESSING IS NOT AN OPTION – IT IS A MANDATE!

So, set your goals! What are you worth now, and what do you want to be worth when you are forty, fifty, sixty or seventy years of age. God loves people who permit Him to set their goals. Now, I want you to...

BELIEVE THAT BLESSING AND INCREASE ARE
A COVENANT PROMISE FROM GOD!

Ask Yourself…

When God made a covenant with Abraham and his family, how did God answer Abraham's question, "How shall I know that we shall inherit the land?"

- Did God ask Abraham to make covenant with Him or did God swear by Himself?
- Write the vision that God gave Abraham of God swearing by Himself concerning this covenant.

Is this covenant ever revocable? What if Abraham's family failed to keep their end of the covenant? Would that negate it, or would God, swearing by Himself, guarantee the covenant?

What has God covenanted with you? If Abraham's goal was to take his family to the Promised Land, describe your goals for the fulfillment of your covenant.

Chapter 8

Does Wealth Create Blessing or Condemnation?

(Can You Enjoy Wealth?)

It was one of those amazing summer seasons. We were enjoying where we lived in the Midwest, the warm and beautiful weather, and the blessing of God upon our lives. I was a young emerging evangelist and things were going well. We were preaching in some of the largest churches, and renting large auditoriums to conduct "city-wide" crusades. We were also part of a group of evangelists who published a well-known magazine, The Voice of Healing. It was truly a wonderful time in my life. But, I had a desire in my heart.

I had always dreamed of traveling in a Cadillac and will never forget the day when our car dealer, Ben Hopkins, placed the keys of that beautiful baby blue Cadillac Eldorado convertible in my hands and said, "Enjoy your travels." I thought to myself, "How can you help but enjoy your travels when you sit behind the wheel of this amazing convertible and point that beautiful chrome hood ornament toward the destination of your next meeting!"

That special day, I drove the Cadillac home, parked it in the garage, and cleaned myself up for dinner. Later, walking toward the kitchen across the black floors that gleamed with the sunshine, I looked ahead and there were my car keys on the countertop. The keys to that beautiful Cadillac stood out like the Empire State Building rising above every surrounding structure. They magnetized me, and I said to myself, "How can I possibly enjoy this gift from God?"

I smiled and picked up the keys. I had dreamed for years of owning this car, and now it was mine. Those keys burned into the skin of my hands. What an amazing moment! My dream was reality. As I walked out the back door and put the keys in the ignition, everything around me took on a different feeling.

The huge V8 engine came to life. I put it in reverse, backed out of the driveway, and went on to my appointment. I thought, "Life can't be better than this. A new Cadillac and it is mine…wow…I cannot believe this!"

I had always loved cars, and this was my dream car. So I wanted to enjoy it, and enjoy it I did, for over three years, until that day when God walked into my room and said, "Is that Cadillac yours or Mine?" I had to admit who owned it, and realized that I had no choice. Though I had enjoyed it for three years, it was really God's Cadillac.

One of our first trips in that car took us to Dallas, Texas to be with the man who was probably the leading healing evangelist in the world, outside of Oral Roberts. He was also part of the Voice of Healing family. As we turned the nose of the beautiful Cadillac into the dusty parking lot where his tent was pitched, I looked out of the corner of my eye and noticed this famous evangelist headed directly toward my car. As I rolled down the window, he reached in, patted my shoulder, and said, "So you joined our club! You're driving a Cadillac."

My mind went into a tailspin as I thought about his words, even though he said them in jest. I questioned where we had come as this group of evangelists. Did we think that we deserved beautiful automobiles, or that it was some kind of a badge of success? I felt confused.

As he walked back into his tent, I determined to examine myself as to what that Cadillac meant to me. I now had the same questions as those I had asked the day I drove it home, "Did I have the right to enjoy it or not? Should I be driving such an opulent car? Was I part of a 'private blessing club' with a few evangelists, or was it okay to own this car? And now, how can I drive it without finding myself with feelings of guilt?"

My mind raced back through my life, where I had been and where I wanted to go. I thought of my mother and father, amazing Christians! Maybe in their story I could find what all this is about?

Mom and Dad had married at the beginning of the Depression, and life was difficult to say the least. They met when the man who would become my father managed a hotel dining room. That summer, he hired a schoolteacher (who would become my mother) who was looking for employment while she waited to return to the little schoolhouse where she taught in Eldred, Pennsylvania. She had worked hard to obtain her college education in the 1920s to fulfill her dream to be a teacher. For Helen Rice, child of a wealthy father who had lost a fortune during the Depression, that job was the best she could do to put food on the table.

Albert Reid was also the son of relatively wealthy parents. His family had lost everything in 1929 as the Depression wiped out their restaurant business. But he did have this amazing skill he had learned in the family business: he could cook and manage a successful restaurant.

As Helen and Albert worked together, they fell in love, married, and had one son. They both had an interesting philosophy of money. Children of parents who had lost everything, they found themselves still happy in life. Both were skilled in their professions. Perhaps, they desired to have wealth again, but they both knew that wealth was not the secret of happiness.

Their philosophy of money was a healthy one. Wealth was not a route to happiness or success, but their experience of failed wealth had also taught them that wealth was a good thing and that money could be enjoyed. They believed that it was good to be successful and that wealth never should make you to feel condemned.

So, life treated them well in the middle of the Depression. Since Dad was in the restaurant business, we always ate very well. Since food was our business, there was always sufficiency and abundance, and it was part of the way Dad was paid. That left money left over to purchase things other people didn't have during those years. They could afford to buy toys for me that other boys did not have. We traveled when others could not. Life was good for us even though we were poor by today's standards of measurement. But we enjoyed what we had.

I watched as Mom could only afford one good dress each year, and Dad budgeted to buy one suit each year. Then one year, our pastor was to be ordained. Mom and Dad knew that our pastor did not have the money to buy a suit for his ordination, nor did his wife have the money to buy a new dress. So my parents made a decision. This year's suit and dress would be eliminated and that money would buy Pastor Granter and his wife a suit and dress for the ordination.

That's the way I learned that it was good to have things and enjoy things, but they must always be under the authority of God. When God asks for them or someone needs them, everything must belong to God. They taught me that it was the will of God to bless us. And, God did bless us, to the extent that in the middle of the Depression, my parents could bless others. They lived a life of generosity and giving that still challenges me today. Always, I saw it rewarded. They sowed seeds of generosity, and God gave them an abundant harvest.

I remembered all of the lessons Mom and Dad taught me about wealth and the blessings of God. They lived on the miraculous blessing of God and enjoyed His blessing and never felt condemned for what God had given them. They knew that God is a good God Who loves to bless His people.

Life was amazing. This family, from the Depression now owned our first home, and today I owned this amazing baby blue Cadillac Eldorado convertible. Life was good, but was it okay for it to be this good?

A Cadillac Convertible Teaches Me Lessons about Wealth

My memory went back to that day I walked across the floor of that room and saw the keys to the Cadillac on the kitchen counter. I was overwhelmed with God's amazing provision for his son and thinking, "God, I still can't believe you are so good to me, but thank you. I will enjoy driving your car."

I HAVE A RIGHT TO ENJOY THE COVENANT BLESSINGS OF GOD.

That Cadillac taught me several lessons about wealth. God's abundant gifts are, first of all, the result of His blessing, and they are to be enjoyed. God showers the blessings of covenant upon His children. And, wow, did I enjoy that blue convertible! At the same time, I understood, **This car belongs to God not to me.**

I also remembered the another lesson; I was only to own it for a little less than three years because it would be the car I sold to buy our tickets to go to the Philippines as missionaries. God would use it to show me His blessings and then use it to be the means of sending us to the mission field.

Yes, God's blessings are to be enjoyed and celebrated. But they also always belong to Him. He is the owner, and the only way I can prove He is the owner is to obey His voice when He tells me that He wants me to give it back.

I still celebrate the blessings of God to this day. I love the house that God has abundantly provided. I love the Toyota convertible that still graces my driveway. I loved my Cadillac convertible and the beautiful 28' Chris Craft cabin cruiser we had when our daughter was growing up. Today, I love our forty-acre farm with all of its animals. Life has been very good to us, and I am so grateful for the God who gave me His blessings. I have enjoyed without condemnation but with much thanksgiving.

So celebrate with me the blessings of our covenant God. The Queen of Sheba watched King Solomon celebrate the massive riches that God had given him and said, "The half has never been told."

Prepare for blessing, prepare for covenant fulfillment, and…

CELEBRATE! CELEBRATE! CELEBRATE!

It is perfectly acceptable to God for you to enjoy His blessings. But, always remember every one of those blessings belongs to Him. God is the owner. And, when God calls one of those blessings back to Himself, He requires immediate obedience.

Ask yourself…
- *Do I feel condemned or unworthy when God blesses me? Describe your feelings and why you feel that way.*
- *Can I enjoy and celebrate the blessings of God without condemnation? If you have enjoyed and celebrated those blessings, describe your feelings.*
- *Who is the owner of the blessing God shared with me? Why?*
- *If God came to you tomorrow and asked for the blessing that He had given you, would you be willing, without hesitation or reluctance, to give it back to the Owner? Would you have joy in doing so?*

Chapter 9

WEALTH WITH A REASON AND PURPOSE

"The wonder of fulfillment overwhelms me when I discover not only who I am and what God has destined for me to do, but when I also discover the wonder and adequacy of the resources that He has placed within me to build the dream that He has destined me to create!"

(Destiny Quote of the Day by Tommy Reid)

Say out loud with faith, emphasis, and impact, "I have the power to create wealth." Yes. You have power to create wealth, but for what purpose? Why does God give you that power? Is it so you can have a better home or a more expensive car, or to travel all over the world first class? Is there a reason for God to grant you this power? It is certainly not for you to hoard it or, as the man in the parable, to bury it.

What is the reason for the wealth you create?

There is a reason. You are the reason. Long before the foundation of the world, God wrote your name. But that is far more than the name your parents gave you. It is the name that God gave you. That name was your "destiny" or your "purpose" for being. It was the life and the very essence of "why" you were born. As you grew, God began to speak into your spirit. You may or may not have understood His voice. Those dreams of destiny were the very purposes that God wrote in His book before the foundation of the world.

The Cost of God's Dreams

God's dreams are very costly. It took a great deal of money to build the wonderful churches that men have dreamed of building. It took a great deal of money to build corporations, but someone had to create the wealth that would be invested to make Henry Ford's dream or Walter Chrysler's dream come true.

So, let's talk about the purpose of the wealth that God has destined you to create. Let me go back in my story when I was entrusted with a small amount of wealth created by a very faithful family of church people in Buffalo, New York.

It was September 1963, and for the first time I was to stand in the pulpit of the South Buffalo Tabernacle. Up until this time, life had been good. At twenty-six, I was pastor of Bethel Temple in Manila, Philippines, the largest church in the Assemblies of God. At thirty, I worked with Dr. Paul Cho in the first year of what was to become the largest church in the world. In the ten previous years I had preached in our own 1,300 seat tent, conducting city-wide crusades in the northeastern United States. Yes, life had been good. But it was to get better…but not right away. Now would come a time of struggle, a time without success, and a time of seeing my dreams come to a complete standstill.

I didn't realize the time of struggle that was about to come. Walking with great enthusiasm to a pulpit I would fill for over fifty years, I thought that life could not be more exciting than this. I was where God wanted me to be, and it was the time I knew that God wanted me to be there.

I looked around me. I had just become steward of what those pastors who preceded me had left to my stewardship. The people, the buildings, the parsonage, everything was all now my responsibility to manage. But, I also knew something else deep inside me. It was now my responsibility to take the "talents" that my predecessors had left to me and make them grow. I did know that this was the church God had shown me in my dreams at the altar of the little Assemblies of God church when I was a boy of eight. At that time, I thought that my church would explode in growth immediately, but I had to handle the philosophical issue of God's ownership and my responsibility to grow God's wealth before He could bless this church.

What are the assets you have been asked to steward?

God had now made me steward over the assets that a faithful group of sacrificial church members had created. I began to count. The church had paid $50,000.00 for the beautiful old brick Lutheran church. The church had also purchased a lovely city home for a purchase price in the late 1950s for $10,000.00. And, of course, there were church furnishings and other assets, but for our purpose, let us assume that the total assets were about $75,000.00.

I asked myself, "According to my understanding of the parables, what is my responsibility?" I knew that Jesus mandated me to grow what He had placed in my hands. And, I knew I must become a faithful steward and grow God's wealth.

Over the last fifty years, we have. Today, our main campus is valued at over fifteen million dollars. The branch campuses have been valued at over ten million dollars, or a total value of over twenty-five million dollars. There are also other assets around the world. It all began with God asking me to steward $75,000.00 in assets.

As I stood in God's presence recently, I looked into the face of Jesus and said, "Lord, I pray you have considered me faithful." Our ministry has led thousands to Christ all over this city. We have built a very successful church, a television ministry, a Bible School, mission churches around the world. The $75,000.00 equity left to me by the pastors who preceded me has been multiplied to over twenty-five million dollars ($25,000,000) of real estate including our main campus and all of the satellite churches. I have always attempted to see the Parable of the Talents and the responsibility that it gave me as a guiding force in my life.

That story illustrates exactly what I am trying to say in this manuscript: God has given us assets, personal talents, and abilities. He mandates that we grow, increase, and multiply them to fulfill the dream He has put in our heart.

That is the true purpose of wealth and God's mandate to us to create wealth for the dream in our heart. Wealth has a reason and purpose! And because of the importance of that purpose and reason, it is mandated by God that we increase it in order to fulfill His dream for our lives.

In my life, we not only increased the physical value of the wealth created by that small congregation, but we also used those assets to change the world. Thousands came to Christ over the next few years, over ten branch churches were established, our Bible School produced hundreds of ministers who went all over the world, we built churches in other countries, and produced thousands of television programs aired around the world. All of this cost millions of dollars.

It all began with the seed of a small group of people who sacrificially gave to God in the 1950s and through the early 1960s. They passed on to the new leadership assets of a little over seventy-five thousand dollars. And, over the next fifty years, the people of God invested that seventy five thousand dollars, multiplied it, and touched the world.

Enjoying Wealth

Of course, I have enjoyed wealth. I have loved my cars, my boats, my vacations, my travel, my motor home, and the beautiful property and house where I now live. God's abundance has provided much happiness and fulfillment for me and for my family. But enjoyment and happiness are only byproducts of productivity. Everything that God has entrusted to me, and everything that God has created under my stewardship of His wealth has a purpose.

Before the foundation of the world, God had a dream for you. He said in His Word that, "He wrote your name (your life's purpose) in His book before the foundation of the world" (Revelation 13:8 paraphrased). He said that He wrote your "works" in His book before the foundation of the world.

BEFORE THE FOUNDATION OF THE WORLD, GOD HAD A DREAM FOR YOU!

The dream that God placed in your heart may well cost millions of dollars to fulfill. But, God has placed a seed in your hand. It is a small seed.

God had placed about 120 people and $75,000.00 worth of real estate in my hands. He mandated that I grow it, reproduce it, and reach a city for God.

The dream inside you is an amazing one. Of course, it is beyond your ability to fulfill. But God has placed a small seed in your hand. For me it was that small congregation and their real estate, but God has used that small beginning to touch a city, a nation, and the world.

Take a moment. Look in your hand.

As the prophet asked the widow, "What is in your house?" At first she said nothing. Then she admitted, "a cruise of oil and a little bread." To paraphrase, he said, "Take what you have, lady, pour it out, and it will feed thousands." So, look in your hand.

Of course, what you see in your hand is never sufficient to do what God has commanded you to do. But, take what is there. Pour it out to God. It will increase and will be more than enough to fulfill the dream in your heart.

You see, the blessing of God, the increase of God, the multiplication of God was never meant to simply bless you. All blessing is for a purpose, and the increase that God gives you will touch a city, touch a nation, and oh, yes...touch the world.

The Miracle of Buffalo

Let me illustrate this with a story of my friend, Byron Brown, Mayor of Buffalo, New York. Buffalo has had amazing renewal during his tenure. Billions of dollars are being invested in the city. This includes the huge new HarborCenter, the Canalside Waterfront Development, the new Buffalo-

Niagara Medical Campus, and Larkinville. The new Buffalo-Niagara Medical Campus alone is projected to grow to 20,000 jobs by 2020. This is roughly the equivalent of the number of jobs lost when Bethlehem Steel left the city.

These billions of dollars have created new construction and the development of the new waterfront. Additionally, the building of a hockey center is expected to attract 500,000 visitors to our city annually. Buffalo has not seen a building boom like this since the 1950s. The city pulses with new construction.

About three years ago, we sat across the table from my friend, Mayor Byron Brown. We talked Buffalo, what was happening, and how both of us were dreaming of the future of this great city.

I mentioned to him what I believe was his greatest asset: thousands of acres of vacant land where houses had been torn down as almost 200,000 people had left the city. This acreage had full infrastructure with water, sewers, and electrical service. That vacant land could be used to build housing developments for middle and upper income families who would be employed in the medical corridor and other new companies coming to our city.

We talked about gated communities for professionals who were moving to our city and would like to live close to their employment. I said, "Mayor, you are the steward of a very valuable resource and God has made you responsible to steward it properly. It is in your hands to use for good and to do what Jesus told us all to do in the parable of the talents. This is one of the 'talents' that Jesus has given you and you can use it for increase and growth. We can either view this vacant land as a liability or an asset."

The Silent Walk to the Elevator

At the end of a rather spirited and certainly entrepreneurial discussion about the future, instead of leaving the conference room and returning to his office, he stood to his feet and said, "Can I walk you to the elevator?"

This handsome and stately African-American man, who had dreamed of being mayor and changing a city, walked by my side. It was a mostly silent walk with few words. But as the elevator doors opened, I prayed silently that

God would show him the resource that was in his hands to rebuild our city. I knew he had already seen his asset, and it was about to come alive under his administration. And it has!

Activating Dreams Is a Costly Investment

As I walked into that elevator and said farewell to my friend, the door closed and the face of Mayor Brown disappeared. I thought about the cost of dreams. To fulfill his dream of changing a city would be costly. Billions of dollars would have to be invested. But other costs would be involved.

Every great leader has to endure the cost of criticism. Just ask the great dreamers of the world. Jesus had a dream, and He paid for it with his life. Mother Theresa had a dream, and she paid for it by living a life in the worst ghetto in the world. As I climbed into the elevator and the Mayor said, "See you soon," I thought about the cost of dreams.

They are costly. The will cost you your life. Sometimes they will take millions of dollars to create. That is the very reason Jesus told the story of the Talents. You see dreams are the language of heaven that God uses to talk to us about His destiny for our lives.

Though the cost of a dream is expensive, the "expense" of the dream has a source. That source is within you and includes the talents or abilities that God places in your hand. Not only does God give a dream to you, but God also places resources in your hands to create His dream. Those talents or resources may come in several forms.

Think of those God-given talents: money, education, ideas, friends, and a thousand other things that are in your hand. The cost of success in creating God's dreams for His world **though** your life, demands everything that He has placed in your hands. You have within you the talent of creativity and God ideas. Remember: you will be tempted with many "good ideas" in life. Good ideas may meet your needs or even the needs of others. But, God ideas accomplish His desires for you and others.

So, why settle for good ideas when you can receive the unlimited wealth God has dreamed for you and others to accomplish His desires for the world? Everything must be invested in the dream. For what you have is not to provide toys for you to enjoy but rather to create wonders that will change the world.

GOOD IDEAS MAY MEET YOUR NEEDS OR EVEN THE NEEDS OF OTHERS

BUT, GOD IDEAS ACCOMPLISH HIS DESIRES FOR YOU AND OTHERS.

You are wealthy! You have the ability to create wealth. Wealth can be enjoyed and create an abundant life for you. But all wealth—including yours, must belong to God. It is never yours or mine. It is His!

The Cost of My Dream for Asia

I dreamed of going to Asia, but little did I know the cost of that dream. It cost five years of my life. But I also remember the day when Jesus walked into my room and asked for the Cadillac He had given me. I gave it to God and bought a ticket to Korea.

I did not know whom I would meet in Korea or how significant my time in that nation would be. When I got there, I met my interpreter, a young man by the name of Paul (David) Cho. For an entire year I would live with him, travel with him, preach the first revival in his new church, and be asked to spend the rest of my life in Korea. I never dreamed that the church he would create that year would become the largest church in the history of the world. But it did!

As we saw the work begin to grow exponentially, I boarded a train with him for the southern tip of the country. As the train wound its way through the hills, Brother Cho and I sat in a small private compartment. He turned to me and asked if I would give him the rest of my life to be the co-pastor of the church.

At that moment of intense conversation, I looked at him and said, "Brother Cho, I would love to stay with you here in Korea, but God's dream for me is the city of Buffalo. Seoul is your dream. You do not need me, and my dream is Buffalo. That is where I am called. I love you and I love what God is doing in this nation, but I must pursue my dream. I must invest my love for Korea, my success in Korea, yes even my close friendship with you, Brother Cho, in the dream that God has given me for Buffalo."

I returned to Buffalo and pursued the dream that God had placed inside my spirit, and my friend pursued the dream inside of him. Twenty years later, when the church had grown to hundreds of thousands of people, he asked me to come back to Korea and bring my family to celebrate the twentieth Anniversary of the church. His congregation had grown to nearly 500,000!

As I walked to the platform, looked at over 50,000 people in that single service. That day, I preached four times to a total of 200,000. I saw his dream. Tears began to stream down my face.

I remembered the year I had ministered with him and the Cadillac I had invested into that church. I felt the bricks. I touched the pulpit. I stood before the microphone. I saw the crowds. I felt the spirit. I heard the prayers, and God said, "Was this worth the investment of your Cadillac?"

Of course it was! That day, I realized the purpose of wealth. I remembered the day when that beautiful baby blue convertible was sold and invested in the trip to Korea, and I also remembered the day I left Korea and invested my love for that nation in the dream God had for me in Buffalo.

One day, like that day in my life, when you have created wealth and invested it in the dream of God for your life and into His Kingdom, you will touch the bricks of what you have built and say, "Wow! This is the power of wealth and the creative ability of sowing it into the Kingdom of God!"

As I write this story, let me tell you that my decision was to take every risk God asked me to take. I would invest those assets into His Kingdom and what He was doing on the earth. I would sometimes take great risks, but I determined to make them grow. Fifty years later, we have seen the results.

We continue to build, to dream, and to invest our resources in the dreams God has given for our future. Today, we are building a ranch for trafficked children in the Philippines, we plan for new construction at our home campus, and we are building facilities around the world.

Remember, everything God has given you belongs to God. It is all at His disposal. I never dreamed when I gave God that beautiful Cadillac convertible that it would be invested in creating the largest church in the world. God's dream is at your fingertips, but it requires an investment, the investment of everything you have! So…

GET READY! GET READY TO GIVE IT ALL!

Ask yourself…
- *Describe what you believe is the PURPOSE or DESTINY of your life?*
- *Estimate the cost of creating the dream that God has given you.*
- *List your present assets:*
  - *Physical assets including money, real estate, etc.*
  - *Value of Education*
  - *Value of my Vision*
  - *Friends who will partner with me*
  - *Other assets*
- *Estimate the cost of creating the dream God has given you.*
- *What do you feel is the relationship between your present wealth and the dream God has given you?*
- *Are you willing to invest **everything** in your dream?*

Chapter 10

God's Options: His Option Is to Bless You

God has many options. He can sovereignly bring blessing or even cursing into your life. However, it is His will and His purpose to bless you! So, let's talk about God's option to bless you.

The Sovereign Blessing of God upon Our Earth (Amazing Grace)

Of course, I have to admit that I believe strongly in the Sovereignty of a loving and benevolent God. Look at the magnificent universe that He has given us to enjoy! There is no doubt that He has sovereignly chosen to bless this planet and His people who live in this blessed place. We can call His blessing by the appropriate word: Grace. The best of God's abundant grace is everywhere visible. He has blessed this planet with abundance of wealth and resources which are the product of His grace.

We sing the song, "Amazing Grace" referring to our salvation, but that grace is more than salvation. Salvation is the product of God's amazing grace. The rain, sun, air, gold and silver, food--everything is the expression of God's grace. He is the author of and the creator of what we call grace.

However, there is another dimension to His grace. That is the blessing of "Sovereign Grace." He wants to reveal and show His grace to a hurting and damaged world, so He chooses a man through whom He will reveal and show His grace.

God Chooses Individuals to Reveal His Sovereign Grace

I believe that God chose Winston Churchill to show the British Empire and the world the grace of God. It was the sovereign will of God to save England and ultimately the world during World War II.

I also believe that God chose Henry Ford, who not only put America on wheels but changed how business was done in America and created a middle class of people. Men like Churchill and Ford, who changed the world, are a gift of the "Grace" of a sovereign God.

GOD'S GIFT OF GRACE IN YOUR LIFE: THE TALENTS OR RESOURCES IN YOUR LIFE DEMONSTRATE HIS GRACE.

There is a grace upon your life. It is the "grace of choice," a God who sovereignly chose you. It is the grace of resources, time, talent, education, influence. Everything you have is a gift of grace.

I hear preachers go to the pulpit and say things like, "I do not believe in the prosperity Gospel." I do not understand that statement. Prosperity is the "Good News" or the "Gospel." We are not just saved to go to heaven. We have been given responsibilities. One of those responsibilities is to take what God has given us and multiply it. One of the ways this happens is through God's supernatural blessing on our lives.

That is why I believe that the blessing of prosperity is not an option. It is a mandate or a responsibility. Your talents and your resources are a gift of the Grace of God. We are responsible to grow in grace or literally grow the grace of God in our lives so that we may impact our planet with the Good News of the Gospel.

That is the way God grows His Kingdom. The parable of the talents clearly shows that the alleged option of blessing is not really an option at all, but rather a mandate. You must increase what God has given you or it will be taken away. But in the parable, the consequences of failure to increase God's wealth will also result in eternal consequences. Could this parable demanding increase of resources allude to the fires of eternal punishment?

Jesus may have been using a Jewish form of exaggeration to present a truth, but the failure of a disciple to use the resources that God gives him and to increase them will result in eternal consequences.

The Option of God: To Bless or Not Bless Us

Our problem is not blessing. It is that lack of faith that will withhold the blessing from us. God has an option of whether to bless us or not. And His blessing is contingent upon our faith and expectancy. First of all, acknowledge the blessing or grace of God in your life by discovering and measuring the resources that God has placed in your life: your talents or abilities, your vision and your dreams, your faith, your education and, of course, the resource of physical assets.

Secondly, this book attempts to help you measure those assets, grow them, and use those assets to build the dream that is inside you. I urge you to think about and discover what is in your hand. Remember when God asked Moses, "What is in your hand?" Moses looked and saw only an ugly rod of wood with which he herded sheep. The widow woman had only a small cruse of oil. What God can do with what is in your hand is beyond your wildest imagination.

So, plant the seed. Believe for the harvest. You have power to create wealth. Believe that. Imagine the world we could recreate if we truly believed that God, who took a simple rod in Moses' hand and used it to lead a nation through the Red Sea, had an awesome plan to use what He has placed in our hands.

And remember, when you plant a seed into the Kingdom of God, have faith and expect. God does have options, and He can make a decision whether or not to bless you. Granted, it is His decision, but it is based on your faith.

BELIEVE AND EXPECT!
IF YOU DO THAT, THEN GOD HAS ONLY ONE OPTION— HE HAS TO BLESS HIS CHILDREN— THAT INCLUDES YOU, WHO EXPECT A HARVEST!

Ask yourself...

- *What thoughts, feelings, and actions are part of my daily life that demonstrate to me and to others that I believe and expect?*
- *If those thoughts, feelings, and actions don't exist in me, when will I start thinking, feeling, and acting in such a way that it's evident that I believe and expect?*

Chapter 11

YOUR OPTIONS: YOU CAN BELIEVE

God came and made a covenant with Abram to bless him. God's covenant blessings included a son, a family, a land, and the blessing of great resources. God was so definitive about this covenant that he literally swore by Himself so that Abram would know that God really was serious about this covenant blessing.

Abram responded to God by believing. The scripture says that "By faith, Abraham believed God and it was accounted to him as righteousness." It seems obvious to us that we have the final determination as to whether we are blessed or not. God made a covenant with Abraham to bless him, but that covenant was contingent upon Abraham believing God.

I have come to believe that the difference between blessed people and people who seem to live without blessing is faith. Everyone has a measure of faith according to scripture and that measure is sufficient to receive all of God's blessings. However, the option is whether we believe or not. Abraham believed, and God tells us that this was accounted to him as righteousness.

God has options of whether or not to bless you! But His options are based on our options. I learned this from my parents who taught me how to live by faith.

ENTREPRENEURIAL PARENTS TEACH THEIR CHILDREN THAT THE RESOURCES FOR ANY DREAM ARE INSIDE THEM.

The resources for any dream are always found within the individual. My father taught me that when I was a child. Let me tell you the story of one of his dreams. It was a dream to feed a student body of 500 Bible College students nutritious food in proper balance that included good meat, vegetables, and other items essential to a healthy diet. This is a story of how a man who had almost no money for the task believed that the resources to meet his need were inside him.

On one of those beautiful warm spring evenings in the city of Springfield, Missouri, our family was taking one of our frequent evening drives. We turned toward Booneville Avenue for our usual warm weather evening snack at the A & W Root Beer drive-in.

We would pull in with our blue '37 Ford, attach a tray to the window, and order a hot dog and a frosted glass of root beer. Something about these typical evenings made the three of us a warm family unit. Before I relate the story though, I must tell you about my Dad.

The son of a very successful businessman, he had inherited his father's entrepreneurial talents. He was a dreamer. He was full of ideas and always fulfilled his employment duties by changing things with his dreams. This is the story of how he dreamed the answer to his problems.

When we arrived in Springfield, Missouri for Dad to assume the responsibilities of cafeteria manager for the Central Bible Institute, he went to W. I. Evans, the head of the school and his immediate superior. He asked "Brother Evans" what his per capita budget was for food. The aging spiritual head of the school looked over his horn-rimmed glasses and said, "You have a budget of no more than fifteen cents a day to feed our students."

Dad, having left the employment of a school that served the wealthiest families in America was shocked. He looked at the Dean and said, "Brother Evans, the only thing we could feed them for dinner would be macaroni and cheese or Spanish rice." That famed dean looked back at my Dad and said, "Brother Reid, that is all we can afford." Dad thought about that problem as our car rolled toward the A&W Root Beer drive-in.

As we made our way to the A&W, suddenly sirens began to fill the air. Fire engines flew past us. Now, you have to understand my dreamer father. He loved excitement. Wherever there was excitement, Dad wanted to go. Fire engines were no exception; he loved to follow them.

He put that old 1937 Ford into second gear and began to press the accelerator following the fire engines. That was his usual response to excitement. And soon we arrived at the scene. It was a clothing factory and flames ascended into the sky. It was obvious that everything would be lost.

As we got out of the car to join scores of people who lined the streets, Dad spotted the owner of the factory, Mr. Lurie, and Dad said, "Mr. Lurie, I am so sorry." The elderly man looked at him and exchanged a few words.

I knew intuitively what was going to happen next. I could see the wheels turning in my Dad's head, and I knew what his next question would be. Dad saw an opportunity to make some money. I remember thinking, "what in the world can Dad find in that mess to make some money?" Then a second thought passed through my thirteen-year-old brain: "My father is thinking about money to buy food to feed the students." I was right.

I lived with a father who always dreamed an answer to every question. Nothing ever was too big, too complex, or too impossible. Inside of the man who was my Dad, was an idea, a solution, or the resources to fund any dream or any problem.

Mr. Lurie looked at Dad and said, "Sure, I'll sell you the wool, but sir, it's singed and burned. What are you going to do with it?" Dad turned and said, "Mr. Lurie, I'll find a way to salvage that material."

It was near the end of World War II, and you could not purchase quality material, especially the quality of wool used for the clothing made in this factory. That moment, Dad and Mr. Lurie struck a deal. This teenage boy looked at his Dad and said, "Daddy, what in the world are you going to do with all that material?"

I soon found out. Several trucks were filled with the hundreds of bolts of costly wool that were singed on both ends by the flames. Every bolt of material smelled of smoke. But, Dad looked beyond the smell and the fire singed ends and saw the resources to feed a student body for a year.

He got back to the school and hired about twenty-five students for a month. They took the bolts of wool and lay them out on several acres of vacant land. He did it immediately so that the students who were getting out of school for the summer could find a month's employment to pay their next year's tuition. I will never forget the sight of scores of acres of wool material with singed ends lying on that vacant land.

Dad realized there was a market for that wool material. It didn't matter if it was singed. In the middle of a war, you couldn't buy wool, and he knew that. News got out to the missionaries who were leaving Springfield for their assignments around the world. Preachers in need of new suits came. Housewives came. Within a week, every yard of that material was sold, and Dad had raised enough money to feed the students of the Bible School for a year!

My handsome Dad, a former professional athlete, looked at his amazed son and said, "Tommy, always remember that the resources for any dream or any need are always inside of you. I was told I had only fifteen cents a day to feed these students, but now I can give them steak!" I learned that day that no matter how big the dream or the problem, the resources to fund the dream or solve the problem are within your heart. Dig deep enough inside, and you will find a gold mine.

1700 Pairs of Ice Skates

Nothing ever discouraged my Dad. He believed that within his heart was the world of conquering the impossible. Let me share another story of how Dad thought and how he taught me to think and believe.

At forty-five, the man I called Daddy was always finding something to buy that he could sell and make a profit. One day, he found 1,700 pairs of ice skates in a government surplus sale. They were available to him at a very low cost. He immediately jumped at the opportunity to make a profit. I remember when the truck arrived with all 1,700 pairs of aluminum ice skates. I was a teenager, but I thought at the moment that Dad had gotten a real bargain and, as usual, he was going to fund one of his dreams with this purchase.

Upon their delivery, Dad began to search for ideas on where he could sell them. He had an amazing idea and went to the owner of a chain of shoe stores. Dad suggested that they run a major shoe sale and give a pair of ice skates to every person who bought shoes in the 100-degree summer heat.

This, he thought, would gain the attention of the entire city. The chain of shoe stores would break all of their sales records, and the whole city would think about buying their shoes from this "crazy" shoe store operator."

But when they unloaded the ice skates to arrange for the sale, much to his dismay, Dad discovered that the 3,400 ice skates were all for the left foot! Nobody knew why. Nobody understood where all the right foot skates went, but the shoe sale idea evaporated with that discovery.

However for Dad, there was never a problem that did not have an entrepreneurial solution. I remember: night after night, Dad's eyes showed the signs of him thinking about a solution to that ice skate problem.

In a few days, Dad walked into our living room and said, "We are going to Jefferson City, the capital city of Missouri." I said, "Dad, why are we going to there?" Dad answered, "We are going to meet with the head of the State Department of Education." I responded with, "Why the Department of Education?" He said, "You'll see." Then I began to argue with Dad and reminded him that he had bought those ice skates from the Department of Education, and why would you go back to the man you bought them from a few weeks ago?

The drive seemed so long and to me, so unreasonable. I knew it was about ice skates because I saw a box of those ice skates in the trunk of our Frazer. I was embarrassed for my Dad as I thought how foolish it was for him to go back to the man from whom he had purchased the ice skates.

Little did I know the simple but creative idea inside my Dad. I did not go with him into the capitol building. Mom and I stayed outside. It seemed so unreasonable. It seemed so impossible. Actually, it seemed so foolish. Why go to the head of the Department of Education? I thought, "Dad, he will think you are crazy."

As Dad returned to the car, he was smiling. He said, "I sold all of the ice skates." I thought, "Surely not at the Department of Education?" But he was right; the department bought all of the ice skates! I asked, "Dad, why did you go there?" He said, "I had an idea. Every school system has a shop and needs metal. There is a lot of metal in those ice skates that can be melted down.

They may all be left-footed skates, but that doesn't matter if you're going to melt them down."

Dad said that the head of the department never thought of that. Obviously, the dreamer was right. No matter what the obstacle, no matter what the impossibility, there is always an idea inside you for every problem you face. When I heard of the profit he had made, I was amazed.

My Dad looked at me with eyes of wisdom and said, "Tommy I bought those ice skates to show you that nothing can keep you from being successful even when you buy 3400 ice skates and they are all for the left foot. You just have to find a customer who can use 3400 left-footed ice skates!" My special Daddy taught me that nothing was impossible. All you need is an idea that is already inside of you.

My Father's Faith for the Blessing of God

When my father sold our first home, gave everything to God, and invested it all into His Kingdom, that was my Dad's faith. But my father not only had faith to sacrifice and give everything he had to God, there was another kind of faith he would have to exercise. It was not enough for Dad just to give in faith or sacrifice in faith, he must have faith to believe that God would bless him and take his seed and turn it into a harvest.

Dad sold our home and gave everything to the Kingdom of God. With that money, we purchased our large revival tent, semi-truck, chairs, public address system, and other related equipment. About two years later, we sold my Cadillac and with that money, purchased one-way tickets to the Philippines on a Norwegian freighter. Now everything was gone: our home, our new car. We had nothing except our one-way tickets.

We stored the truck, tent, and chairs in a barn near Williamsport, Pennsylvania and sailed for the Philippines. Dad and I looked to God and said, "We have invested our home, our car, and our lives into this venture. God, bless it and increase it!"

After three weeks at sea, the 450-foot Fernsea, tied up to the dock in Manila. We had an expectant passion to touch a whole nation for God. Our lives were invested in this, everything. There was nothing left. We knew this was God's call upon our lives, and we had to invest everything we had and everything we were into this vision and call.

Our close missionary friends, Alfred and Lillian Cawston met us and welcomed us to the Philippines. We saw them waiting as the ship slowly came to dock. It was a thrill to be in a nation on the other side the world and see their familiar smiling faces.

However, the news they brought us was not good. They were returning to America and with their departure, there was no missionary home where we could live. We immediately questioned where we would get the funds to pay hotel bills.

And, there was more bad news. Many evangelists had converged on the Philippines to invade the nation with the good news of the Gospel. Because we were one evangelistic party among many famous evangelists, most all of our meetings were cancelled. That meant we had no place to preach.

We stood on that dock stunned at the news. The Cawston's assured us they believed God had sent us to the nation and that everything would work out. They said they had made us reservations at one of the large hotels in the city.

As we checked in, we wondered how we would ever pay the bill. To make matters worse, we had come (some say foolishly) on one-way tickets with no money to return home. If we had the money, we would have left. Instead, we had to believe.

Added to that, Dad became very ill with a tropical disease. He was on the brink of death. But we had an option – an option to believe or not believe!

GOD ALWAYS GIVES YOU OPTIONS— TO BELIEVE OR NOT TO BELIEVE.

But some things were very exciting. Our friend and fellow Voice of Healing Evangelist, Morris Cerullo, was conducting a huge miracle crusade in Manila. I played the Hammond organ for the crusade and assisted him. Things were so busy that, for a few days, I tried to forget our dilemma and poured myself into the crusade ministry.

But when I came back to the hotel room where Dad lay ill, I tried to pray for his healing, but he wouldn't let me. I attempted to pray for money, but again he said, everything was all right. He said that God had already provided because of the promise that God had made to him. I tried to pray for open doors to preach, but again he said that God had already scheduled places where we would minister. Every time I tried to pray for something, my father stopped me. He said we were not to pray; we were to believe! What an option!

Do not pray limited prayers for healing or money. Instead, believe for destiny.

Two weeks later I stood at his bedside and asked again, "Daddy, let me pray for your healing and that God will provide money to get us home." Dad said, "No, we cannot pray for our will to be done. We must believe for God's will. We are on an assignment. We are not going home, and we do not need money for a ticket…God is in this!"

Then, he looked into my eyes and said, "Tommy, in a few minutes that phone will ring, and a voice will say, 'You are the new pastors of Bethel Temple.' And we will stand in the pulpit Lester Sumrall built. That is why we are here." I wanted to argue with my father, but I knew I must honor him. The best I could do at that moment was to humor him because I knew the desperation of our circumstance. He kept saying, "You are not to pray for healing, for money, or for places to preach. You are to pray for our destiny, our purpose for being here."

I knew how absurd his words were. I was in my early twenties. Dad had never pastored a church. He was a converted restaurant man who had been saved and had spent most of his ministry managing food facilities for corporations and the church. I was young and had just graduated from Bible School. Never would they ask the two of us who were untrained and not ready to pastor a church to become the pastors of the largest church in their denomination! That, I thought to myself, was absurd. It would never happen.

Thirty minutes later, the phone rang. It was the Missions Department of the Assemblies of God and a voice said, "You and Tommy have been selected as the new pastors of Bethel Temple." That one phone call changed everything! We were now in the prestigious position of pastors of this church of thousands. We knew that would open the door to solve every one of our financial problems. It would give us a place to live, and we would have the funds to travel back and forth across Asia to minister and even back and forth to America.

That day, my father, Albert Reid had an option. He believed that when we sowed the seeds of our home and a Cadillac, yes when we sowed the seeds of our lives, that we would reap a harvest. And, what a harvest! We were on our way to one of the most exciting missionary journeys any two men have ever taken.

Like Albert and Tommy Reid, you have an option. That option is to believe. God's option of blessing is contingent on your option to believe. Provision is always attached to faith. For over sixty years, I have seen the amazing provision of God. I could never write this book about money without this chapter on faith.

EXERCISE THE RIGHT OPTION:
BELIEVE!

Ask yourself…
- What keeps you or hinders you from believing God?
- If you are in a "not to believe" mindset, what will you do to repent, change, and begin exercising your option to believe?

Chapter 12

You Will Write This Chapter on Money

"There is a light that God put inside of me that is greater than the darkness around me! That light was formed by God to light the world of darkness that surrounds me. I WILL CHANGE THE WORLD WITH THE LIGHT INSIDE OF ME!"
(Destiny Quote of the Day by Tommy Reid)

"I am a man of faith writing my story of a fulfilled life. A man or a woman of faith experiences mountaintops and valleys. I love the euphoria and exuberance of the mountaintop, but I also have learned to love the solitude and intimacy with God that the valley provides for me. Both are part of my life and I have decided to rejoice when I am in the valley or on the mountain top."
(Destiny Quote of the Day by Tommy Reid)

Here is where this book is different than probably any book you have ever read. I wrote the other chapters…**YOU WILL WRITE THIS CHAPTER!** But, before you begin, let me go back in my life to a turning point that set me on a course to reach my destiny.

It was a beautiful day in Korea. Spring had come, the sun was shining brightly, and the temperature was in the seventies. Korea is a beautiful nation, with amazing mountains, beautiful rivers, and lush gardens. The old American train with its puffing steam engine ran quite fast through the beautiful countryside. The evangelist in me thought that I had reached the pinnacle of ministry.

From Seoul we went to several cities and in each one, the crowds were amazing, the miracles attested to the Lordship of Jesus Christ, and the altars were filled every night with hundreds finding Christ. This was what I was born to do, and I felt fulfilled. In fact, I felt jubilant about where I was and what I was doing. These thoughts were surging through my mind as that old steam engine pulled the train through the mountains of Korea.

I thought about the success of the crusades. I thought about how I had conducted the first revival crusade in the church in Seoul that would become the largest church in the world. As he stood by my side in Seoul and all over Korea, I developed an amazingly close friendship with this young man who was almost my age. We had become like inseparable brothers. The church in Seoul was exploding in growth, and I knew the question that would come when we would sit down in our compartment on that train.

Before I took my seat beside him, I had to wrestle with myself. What would I say when he asked the question I knew he was going to ask. As I walked through the train, peering out the windows at the beautiful Korean landscape, I knew I would have to give him an answer. The train lurched and climbed up the next mountain. I knew what God wanted me to say and do. It would be hard to say "no." I would have to say no, no matter how attractive his offer would be. I knew that decision day had come, and I would have to make and declare my decision.

I entered the door of the private compartment and took my seat across from my friend then known as Paul Cho. As I took my seat the expected happened. He looked at me and said, "Tommy, I want you to give me the rest of your life and be my co-pastor in Seoul." I didn't know then that this church would become the largest church in Christian history.

Full Gospel Church was already exploding in growth and was becoming a church of thousands. As soon as he opened his mouth, Brother Cho said to me, "You are probably the only man in the world that has pastored a church in Asia with thousands in attendance. You know how to pastor a large Asian church. Please, Tommy, take the role of co-pastor of the church that I believe will become the largest church in the world."

I knew the answer I had to give. I loved Asia. I loved Korea. I loved working with my friend. But, I knew this was not the calling of God for me. I had to go back to Buffalo, New York and fulfill the dream that God had given me when I was eight years old.

With tears and great emotion, I took the hand of the man in the seat across from me and said, "Brother Cho, no one has ever placed this kind of trust in me. I love Korea. I love you. But, I have to say no to you today because my call is not to Korea or the Philippines, it is to Buffalo. I have a church inside of me, a dream in my heart that God put there when I was eight years old at an altar of my church in East Aurora, New York. I must go back and leave all of this success. I have nothing. I do not have a single member. I do not have a building, but I have a call! I knew you were going to ask me, and I knew it was my moment of decision. This moment will be the pivotal point of my future and my life. I have to obey God and say 'no.'"

My young brother, Paul David Cho squeezed my hand and said, "I understand. Go to your calling."

That day I made my decision for destiny, my course had been set. Yes, the Philippines, where I had pastored the largest church in the Assemblies of God was an exciting season, but it was not my destiny. Yes, working side by side with the man who was destined to build the largest church in the world was exciting, but it was not my destiny. I had to make my decision, and I did. I knew my destiny was Buffalo, New York.

So, today, I want you to follow my example. I want you to make a decision. This book requires a decision. We have presented these decisions in chapter after chapter, but now it's time for you to write the rest of this chapter.

I pray this book will cause you to make a decision like I made my decision that day. Please make your decision, and say yes to God. Without hesitation, I can tell you this will change your life as mine was changed that day as the train climbed through the hills of Korea.

COVENANTS WITH GOD

Here are the questions, and you must write the answers as your manuscript. Let's take them one at a time. Before you write your specific declarations, make these COVENANTS WITH GOD!

1. I COVENANT WITH GOD TO DEFINE MY DESTINY AND COVENANT WITH GOD TO CREATE WEALTH TO FULFILL MY DESTINY.
2. I COVENANT WITH GOD TO TITHE AND BRING MY FIRST FRUITS TO GOD'S HOUSE TO DEFINE WHO OWNS EVERYTHING.
3. I COVENANT WITH GOD TO SET SPECIFIC GOALS FOR THE CREATION OF HIS WEALTH.
4. I COVENANT WITH GOD TO PROPERLY MANAGE GOD'S MONEY.
5. I COVENANT WITH GOD TO GROW GOD'S MONEY AND TO INCREASE HIS WEALTH.
6. I COVENANT TO LIBERALLY SOW SEED.
7. I COVENANT WITH GOD TO BELIEVE FOR THE INCREASE OF GOD'S WEALTH.

Now, it's time for you to write your portion of this book. As I made a decision to come back to Buffalo and to reject what looked like instant success, this book requires a decision. Here is the place for you to declare your future and write your story:

1. I will declare and demonstrate from this moment on that God is the owner of everything, and I am simply a steward of His riches.

_____

_____

_____

_____

_____

_____

_____

2. This day I will declare to tithe and bring my first fruits to God every week before I spend one cent of the money I earn.

a. Where will you bring your tithes that will express the ownership of God?

_____

_____

_____

_____

_____

_____

_____

_____

_____

_____

b. If the City of Jericho was the first city and God called it the "cursed city" and its total riches were to be brought to the house of worship, I will spend my life by bringing my "first fruits" to God. In doing so, I declare that the other 90 percent (or other 9 cities) are removed from the curse and will be blessed for the rest of my life.

MY DECLARATION

_____

_____

_____

_____

_____

_____

_____

_____

_____

c. I will believe and express the Lordship and ownership of Jesus Christ over everything that I have. My faith confession is that from this day forward, God will bless what He owns.

_____

_____

_____

_____

_____

_____

_____

_____

_____

d. I will confess today that when I sow a seed, I will believe that God's plan is to always give me a harvest.

MY DECLARATION

_____

_____

_____

_____

_____

_____

_____

_____

_____

_____

_____

_____

e. I will this day examine all of my resources and my wealth, and I will put a value on everything that God has given me to steward for Him.

Take this space to examine everything that God has entrusted you with and put a dollar value on everything.

AN INVENTORY OF THE WEALTH THAT GOD HAS ENTRUSTED TO ME

_____

_____

_____

_____

_____

_____

_____

_____

_____

Place a dollar value on your total worth, or more specifically God's worth that He has given you to steward. Set incremental goals for every ten-year-period of your life until you are at least 70 years of age:

TODAY, MY WORTH IS $_____

10 YEARS FROM NOW I WILL BE WORTH $_____

20 YEARS FROM NOW I WILL BE WORTH $_____

30 YEARS FROM NOW I WILL BE WORTH $_____

40 YEARS FROM NOW I WILL BE WORTH $_____

50 YEARS FROM NOW I WILL BE WORTH $_____

In order to reach these goals, I must pay off all of my credit card debt and any other debt that does not build equity in God's estate. Set goals for the payment of all these debts.

_____

_____

_____

_____

_____

_____
_____
_____
_____
_____

List your credit cards. Devise a plan and get busy today to totally eliminate debt that cannot increase the value of your worth. Remember, it is God Who gives you power to create wealth!

MY DECLARATION CONCERNING MY CREDIT CARDS

_____
_____
_____
_____
_____
_____
_____
_____
_____
_____
_____
_____

You have now written your future. May this be an important and transformational moment of your life! May your future be greater than your past and may every financial goal you have set come to pass.

CONGRATULATIONS!

THE WONDER AND FULFILLMENT OF BEING BLESSED: REMOVING WHAT KEEPS US FROM SEEING OUR DESTINY.

I drove along the Niagara Parkway with the top down on my Toyota convertible, my hair blowing in the breeze and I thought, "My life is so perfect, and believe that I enjoy a total fulfillment of what life is about." I looked ahead over the hood of the beautiful red Toyota convertible and remembered that it was really a gift from my friend, Rodney Howard Browne. The gift was so meaningful that I have kept it as my personal vehicle for over fourteen years. With the memories of my friend, I turned the car into Riverside Park. Parking it beside our motorhome, I began to look heavenward in worship as I thanked my Lord for His faithfulness in giving me such a fulfilling life.

Then I asked myself: "What is fulfillment? What is sustaining joy? Is it health? Is it wealth, is it stuff? Is it the things we enjoy? Is it a good marriage? Is it a beautiful family? Is it living in just the right place? Is it being ready to go to heaven?"

No! All of those things are fulfilling but real fulfillment is inside us. It is who we are. It is a peace that as the Scripture says passes even our understanding. It is Abraham walking beside the water, counting the sand and the stars and dreaming of a family that was impossible in the natural. He was totally fulfilled at that moment. He worshiped under the stars as he counted his future. It is Jesus as He prays John 17 and says, "Father, I thank you for all those you will give me." Fulfillment is faith. Fulfillment is when our faith is in the process of producing something.

Life was designed to be enjoyed, and this book is about that kind of fulfillment. In this book, I am attempting to give you a road map to fulfillment. Abraham was as fulfilled when he dreamed about a family and children and when the day finally came that Isaac was born.

Over thirty years ago, Wanda and I went to Maui to spend several days with our close friends, Robert and Arvella Schuller. During that week together, Bob and I were walking on the Baldwin Estate. We both commented about the beauty of the island and especially the beauty of the Baldwin estate. We stopped for a moment and looked across the beautiful Pacific to a neighboring island. Bob, in his typical demeanor, raised his long arms and pointed to Molokai. He said, 'Tommy, do you know what happened on that island?" Since I knew I said, "Yes, but you tell me the story again."

He shared how Molokai was originally a Leper Colony and everyone who lived there was a leper, banned from society. One day a Catholic missionary, Father Damien, went to the island to bring the Gospel. After several years of ministry, not one leper had come to Christ. But one day Father Damien looked at his hand and realized that he, too, was now one of them. He was a leper. One of the lepers noticed and news spread. The next Sunday, every single leper on that island came to church and many became Christians. I thought to myself, "that is fulfillment." For this missionary, fulfillment happened when he became a leper.

Let me give you my definition of fulfillment. I believe that fulfillment in destiny pales negative circumstances.

Fulfillment is the joy that comes when we experience destiny.

A few minutes later, Bob Schuller said something I will always remember. As he gazed again toward that beautiful island, we both noticed the huge electric lines that blocked some of the beauty of the view between the islands. I had been with Bob Schuller so many times I knew how he disliked power lines and the distraction they caused. Bob looked at me and said, "I would love to have the money to remove those power lines and place them underground so the view of that beautiful island will not be obscured." He then immediately launched into a discussion of how could fund that vision.

At that moment, I thought to myself, "what is it that blocks our view of total fulfillment? What keeps us from a full view of our own destiny? What stands between every one of us and the full purposes of God?"

May I suggest that this book is about the ugly "power lines" that block the view of the fulfillment of your destiny or purpose? How different would your life be if you could remove those distractions so that you could see the perfect fulfillment of your life?

Perhaps the distracting power line is lack of faith. You just can't see fulfillment because you can't believe you can reach it. I want to encourage you to remember that your destiny was written before the foundation of the earth. If you can believe that it is God's will and plan for you to find the fulfillment of His destiny for you, then it will be possible to have a beautiful and amazing view of your destiny. You can believe…just believe what God has written for you.

Or, perhaps your lack of finances or resources is like those power lines, and they obscure your view of the fulfillment of your destiny. Make a decision today to remove that obstruction from your life.

The first decision you must make, before God can bless you to the extent of His will, is to recognize that God is the owner of everything. This requires that you become a systematic tither, for your tithes are an expression of your faith that God is the owner of everything and that you are a steward of God's riches. It is only when you systematically tithe that you are given the power by God to increase His finances. It is from this very decision that God gives you the power to increase God's wealth as the steward of His wealth.

Remove the "power line" of doubt from your life. Confess that God has placed faith and creativity inside of you to create the wealth you need to fulfill your destiny. Then begin the plan to measure your wealth. Set goals for the creation of wealth over a specific time frame.

Remove the "power line" of forgotten dreams. Know that your dreams have been given to you by God and were written in His book before the foundation of the world.

If the "power lines" that stands between you and your fulfillment happen to be the way you fail to control your budget, change what you do! If the "power line" that stand between you and reaching your destiny is your failure to create the wealth to fulfill your dream, make your plans now to tear it down.

When you get to the end of your life, will Jesus say to you, "Well done you good and faithful servant, you have fulfilled your destiny!"

The Michael Cardone Story—Dusting Off an Old Dream

My phone rang and on the other end of the line I heard the voice of my friend, Michael Cardone, owner of the largest company in the world dedicated to the rebuilding of automobile parts. I have had the privilege of seeing many people who have accomplished great things and have changed the world. Perhaps one of the most successful was Michael Cardone.

Michael said, "Tommy, I want you to come down to my place in Florida for a week or so, and let's talk." Then he said, "I want to give you a choice on where to stay. I have a beautiful guesthouse on the waterfront here in Ft. Lauderdale, and you're welcome to stay there. Or, I will provide a room at the most beautiful luxury hotel in Ft. Lauderdale. Or, last of all, you can use my 68' Hataras yacht, and I'll give you a captain to take you any place you want to go." Of course, being a boater, I chose the yacht. We went to Florida and did I ever enjoy sleeping in the owner's suite on that two million dollar yacht.

Michael Cardone built a huge manufacturing company that employed thousands of people in several countries. From a poor family employed in the coal mines in Pennsylvania, Michael had dreams that made him one of the most successful men on this planet.

I have had the privilege of enjoying the use of one of his Rolls Royce automobiles, living aboard yacht, and eating with him at some of the most expensive restaurants in the world. I remember how he rebuilt a windshield wiper motor in his basement, and God gave him the idea to rebuild windshield wipers, generators, and carburetors. The Cardone Company became the leading re-manufacturer of automobile parts in the world. But Michael Cardone had a dream that had never reached fulfillment. Let me share that with you. Maybe you, too, have a dream that needs to be dusted off and brought to fulfillment.

An Unfulfilled Dream

Michael Cardone had accomplished so much, but there was one thing that he seemingly could not accomplish. He felt that God had called him to create a large church in northern part of the city of Philadelphia. He built factories all over the world, but the dream of this church was unfulfilled. I sat with his son, Michael Jr., one day at the Oral Roberts University Board of Regents, and he shared with me how frustrated his father was that this dream of building a large church in Philadelphia was not happening. He had sent a large amount of money to a denomination to fund the vision, but no one was doing anything about his dream. How could such an amazing dreamer have an unfulfilled dream? I looked at Michael and said, "If you can't find anyone to help your Dad build that church, that is what I do. I build churches, and

I will build another with your Dad in Philadelphia." We began the process. I suggested, "Let's dust off your Dad's dream and get busy helping him do it."

It was an amazing experience. One of the most fulfilling parts of my ministry was to commute between Buffalo and Philadelphia as we conducted the planning meetings, worked with about six or seven leadership families, brought the first pastor on staff, and launched the church.

Within a few years, the church grew to over 2,000 members with a complex of buildings valued over $25,000,000. When his dream became reality, Michael Cardone went to be with the Lord. Dusting off his dream and helping him in its fulfillment, was what God wanted me to do.

When Michael went to be with the Lord, I was unable to attend the funeral because of a scheduling conflict. I called his son Michael and apologized for my inability to attend. I will never forget his words to me. He said, "Tommy, don't worry about attending the funeral. You gave my Dad the best gift any man could have given him. You helped him build the church of his dreams." To Michael Cardone, that church was his fulfillment. We simply helped him dust it off and helped him make it become reality.

Dust off your dream! If you will believe, perhaps like Michael Cardone, someone will be sent to you to help you build it. You can reach your dream. You can do it. You must begin by believing that your dream is from God and that every resource you need is within you.

This book is about the question of where you find the resources for the dream or the destiny in your heart. My answer is that the resources for your dream are inside you.

God owns everything, and I mean everything! He has made you a steward of limited resources. Those resources are not sufficient to build your dream, but God has given us the ability to create wealth, not for ourselves, not for our own ego, but to fulfill the God-given dream that is inside you.

WALK THROUGH THE DOOR OF DESTINY!
CREATE WEALTH AND FINANCE THE DREAM!

MAKING A COVENANT WITH GOD

MY COVENANT

I desire to make a COVENANT BEFORE GOD concerning my faith in the provision of God and my personal faith declaration concerning my individual finances. Today, I will make a covenant with God.

_____ I believe that God owns everything and that I am a steward of God's wealth.

_____ I believe that Scripture mandates me to bring my first fruits and my tithes to God to demonstrate that I believe that God owns everything. I covenant today to weekly bring my tithes and first fruits into God's storehouse.

_____ I believe that according to the teachings of Jesus, I am mandated to grow and increase God's wealth.

_____ I covenant this day to effectively manage God's wealth.

_____ I covenant this day to grow God's wealth.

_____ I believe that God desires to prosper me.

_____ I will sow financial seed in the Kingdom of God, and I will expect a harvest.

_____ I will expect miracle provision in my financial stewardship.

_____ I covenant to leave an inheritance to my children and grandchildren.

_____ I believe that God will give me the creativity to grow His wealth.

Section 2

This Is Our Father's World

The Worship of God Puts Money and Its Use in Perspective

Chapter 13

UNDERSTANDING MONEY— THE MEASURE OF VALUE: THE ESSENCE OF WORSHIP

How do you define money? Does it have value or is it a measuring system of value? Money in our culture really has no actual value. The currency that we call money is no longer established on the "gold standard." In reality, the things it can purchase determine the value of money. A dollar bill or a thousand dollar bill has no actual value. It is no longer worth a certain amount of gold. What gives our currency value, is what it can buy.

How much is a college education worth? How much is a medical degree that makes you a medical doctor worth? How much is a Volkswagen worth, or a Cadillac, or a Ford, or a Mercedes Benz, or a Rolls Royce? How much is a 10,000 square foot house worth, or a mansion on a beautiful cliff overlooking the Pacific Ocean? Or, how much is a 900 square foot apartment worth, or a 700 square foot mobile home?

The truth is that money has value because we give it value. Perhaps what we are really talking about is value rather than money or currency. That brings me to the real foundation of this book: we must address the real meaning of money, i.e. the value we place on "stuff."

So, what is money? I believe that money is really a measure of value. A house has value, and the amount of money that it is sold or purchased for is the measure of its value in our economy. Money is neither good nor bad. It is simply the value we place on things that we purchase.

We say, "If I only had that much money, I would be happy." Yet money or the stuff it buys does not purchase happiness. That "stuff" can enrich or destroy our lives. Some wealthy people I know have been destroyed by their access to money, and others have been enriched by their resources.

So, you want to get rich? Why? You want money? What do you want your money for? Do you want money because you think it can buy you security in your old age? What if you get sick or have an accident? Will it secure you?

Money has another purpose. All money belongs to God, and is specifically for the purpose of God. Money will feed the hungry, heal the sick in our hospitals, and provide us with highways and parks and an unending list of things. Perhaps the most important thing money can do is assist you is in fulfilling the dream that God has placed inside you.

Your Checkbook and Your Value System

Recently in a sermon I said, "Your checkbook will tell God more about your true faith than your tattered Bible." That is true. Your tattered Bible may suggest you spend time in the Word and what scripture verses you like the best, but it does not say anything about the priorities of your life. Your checkbook tells about the priorities and the value system that determines the way you live. Our checkbooks identify the value system of our lives.

It is impossible for me to approach a worship service without realizing the real meaning of worship. The word worship comes from an old word, which really means "worth-ship" or the attribution of worth. Worship, by its very nature, is the placing of worth upon the God we worship. That is why I say that our checkbook will tell us more about our worship life than our tattered Bibles.

Establishing a System of Values

Every one of us lives out of a "value system." Your checkbook will show what is important in your life. What is important to you, your stuff or your God? Is it a beautiful home and car, or supporting missions? Where you spend your money will tell me whether you worship stuff or God. The register in your checkbook will define where you ascribe worth. Worship means to ascribe worth to God.

This book has to be about worship, because the most important and spiritual thing about money is how you ascribe worth to your wealth. That is the essence of true worship. Therefore, all of our worship comes out of what we attribute worth or value to in our lives. Because of that, I must give a lot of thought as to my value system.

It would be appropriate that, at this point, I tell you about my core and important values. I will let you judge if they are right or spiritual. I believe they assist me in giving proper attribution of my worth to God.

I want to suggest that every one of us first of all look at ourselves in the mirror and discover what we truly value in life and what system of values makes us tick. Let me share with you a little of my own system of values. Here is a listing of my ten most important values in the order that I place value on each of them:

Value 1: God - My relationship to my Heavenly Father, His Son Jesus Christ, and my personal intimacy with the Holy Spirit is where I attribute my highest worth. This is why about fifty to sixty percent of my income is always given to God. The worship of God is always my number one value.

I pastored one of the fastest growing churches in America in the 1980s, and I never accepted a salary much above poverty level. The last fifteen years of my pastorate, I accepted a salary of $400.00 a week. God has abundantly blessed me as I have lived by faith, but I knew in my heart that to keep my values straight, I had to never put value on the money that was in my pocket or in the bank. I would never suggest any other pastor do what I have done, but it was the way I needed to keep my priorities straight.

What I am saying by this is that the worship of God or the placing of value on my relationship with God is my number one value.

Value 2: Relationships with Significant People in My Life – It is out of relationship that Jesus came and died because Scripture says "For God so loved." Jesus highly valued relationships. Therefore, the value that is the central core of my life is first, my relationship with God and second, with others. This is a driving motivation to lead people to Christ.

I cannot have "control over others" or "demand to be a leader" as a high value because that would conflict with valuing relationships with people. When I lead, I must be a servant leader...never a served leader!

Value 3: Intimacy – Jesus had one disciple with whom He was most intimate and three with whom He was also in close relationship. I want to be like Christ and highly value intimacy with those with whom I am related.

Value 4: Corporate Worship – I love church! I love church services! My favorite time of the week is our Sunday night service because it is a time of intense worship. Sometimes when I speak in New York City, I leave right after the morning service so I can drive the 400 miles to get back to worship with the people of God at my home church on Sunday night. The value I place on corporate worship places demands on my time and my schedule.

Value 5: Fun – This may surprise you, however, in order to have friends and intimacy, I am an emotional being and fun is an emotion that makes me intimate with the people I enjoy. Therefore fun is important to me. I love using the things God has given me: my cars, my boats, my motorhome. I love biking on the Niagara Parkway bicycle path, Niagara Falls, Lake Erie, and most of all, having "fun" with my wife, my daughter, son-in-law and grandchildren. I love the emotion that is produced by having fun so it's a priority in my value system.

Value 6: Creativity – I was born to create things. I love creative people, and I love the feeling that permeates my entire being when creative juices flow out of my inner being. I have created ministries, television productions, buildings, and huge religious gatherings. I sat in my office one day and dreamed of an alcohol-free New Year's celebration for the city of Buffalo. Three of us sat in my office and dreamed. We planned and organized, and today First Night Buffalo is the second largest New Year's Eve Ball Drop celebration in America. I love to create!

Value 7: Nature And Creation – I love the outdoors and feeling the air, smelling the wonder of nature, and with Abraham counting the stars and the sand. To me, the open air is the world's greatest "cathedral" or place where I am closest to God. I have driven a convertible for over fifty years because

I love the open air and God's cathedral. My first convertible was a 1949 Chrysler. A picture of that car is on the wall beside my present convertible. I drive that open car, because I love nature. I love the trees, the mountains, the lakes, the ocean, the rivers, the flowers. This world is a garden, and I love God's garden.

I could go on with my value system, but if you took a look at my checkbook, that is where I spend my money. My beautiful red Toyota convertible is now fifteen years old, so I don't need to spend a great deal of money to make me happy, but I love it. I don't want to part with it; it gives me fun and pleasure.

Conflict in Values

I must take a moment to note that conflict between values can be destructive in our lives. For instance, if you place a value on relationships and a value on control, those two values are in conflict with each other. You cannot have a close relationship with a person if you want to control them. These two values are in deep conflict.

If you place value on the acquisition of things, that may well conflict with your value on worship, for worship is the surrender of everything to God. Abraham had to leave everything: his home, his family, and his possessions and begin a journey to a place that God had promised to give him. For Abraham, it was a complete rearranging of his value system.

I believe my worship comes out of a highly developed system of values and priorities and enables me to come to God in worship with a heart that is open to His Presence.

In my estimation, no one knows more about worship than my daughter, Aimee Reid Sych. For that reason, I've asked her to write the next chapter of this book on her view of worship. In this chapter, she talks about placing our highest value on Jesus.

Before we can recognize the value system out of which we live and make the proper changes and adjustments, we need to reshape our lives in the image of God. So let us together examine worship, for out of true worship comes the value system that makes each life a God-success. Before we can see the "worth" of things, we must see the "worth" of Jesus. Only then can we live a successful life.

Chapter 14

True Worship Has Seen God's Worth

God Is Our Source

By Aimee Reid Sych

Imagine with me being caught up in worship, your eyes suddenly open to a new dimension. A door stands before you and a voice speaks, "Come up here, there's something you must see." Compelled by curiosity, yet drawn further by this overwhelming presence that is beginning to surround you, a song so complex, so beautiful, so harmonious, and magnificent. Your inner being begins to compulsively sing along, a song that comes not only from your lips, but from the deepest part of your spirit. You go further and further in, as your eyesight becomes clear. Around you are innumerable angels, living creatures, and millions of worshipers standing around a sea, so smooth and gleaming with light that it appears as glass.

As if on cue, they all bow in unison, their song being muffled for a moment. Across the bending backs of this myriad of worshipers, rays of manifold colors appear, a light so beautiful that you can't help but gaze deeply. Suddenly, through the light appears a throne with the form of one seated upon it. It is as if you not only see the light, but you feel it permeating the very core of your being. Tears fill your eyes and emotion overwhelms you, for you have just caught a glimpse of the Holy!

The worshipers lift their heads toward the throne. A flash of brilliance crosses their gaze. Their song swells in incredible tones and harmonious melodies grow in their intensity. All they can do is fall on their faces once again, as this new glimpse of Majesty has deepened their cry:

Worthy is the Lamb who was slain
To receive power and riches and wisdom,
And strength and honor and glory and blessing!

As they bow again, you see deeper into this majestic light the feet of the one seated on the throne. Just the clarity of this brief glimpse causes a new cry of worship to pour forth from your lips, one like you have never uttered. If just His feet bring cause to such a song, what would come if you were to gaze into his very eyes?

"Holy, Holy, Holy...."

Falling to the ground you are changed forever, for you have just seen His worth! How you think, what you feel, your priorities, your values, your motives, your decisions.....are now all subject to **His Worth!**

MY QUESTION TO YOU TODAY IS SIMPLY, "HAVE YOU SEEN HIS WORTH?"

Knowing who Jesus is and drawing so close to Him that you truly **See His Worth** are two very different things. There are so many endless truths we can know about Him, for the Word is full of such complex insight into His character and person. Yet without the intimacy of His embrace, do we really see His worth? Worth that is so weighty it alters our entire life?

Dr. David Jeremiah said something so deeply profound, "We never truly know God until we worship Him, and we never really worship Him unless we know Him." It is a continuous cycle, like in James 4:8, "Draw near to God and He will draw near to you." True worship comes out of full knowledge of God and knowledge of God comes out of true worship of Him....for we have seen **His Worth**.

We must mature into the understanding that His worth has nothing to do with us, whatsoever. His worth is not contingent upon His interaction with our human lives, nor is it limited to what we have seen Him do in history. In turn, we must not filter our view of His worth through our experience with

Him. His worth is not based upon what He has done for us, in us, or even through us. Not even an incredible miracle could enlarge His worth, just as no appearance of lack could lessen His worth. His worth stands alone. We must delineate these two matters if we are to see Him as He is.

When we see Jesus' worth based on our own experience in Him, we stand on shaky ground as victims of our circumstance. On the contrary, when we discover His worth based solely on Who He is as Lord we stand on solid ground where nothing can move us. Victorious!

The term "worth" denotes value; it is from this word that we derive the worship term, "worthy." To obtain something of great value, you must be willing to spend extravagantly. In the same way, to gain more and more of the fullness of His Presence and heart, we must be willing to spend ourselves extravagantly for Him.

Seeing His worth produces **godly extravagance** in every area of our lives! Mary of Bethany was such a person – an extravagant worshipper:

> *Jesus was at Bethany, a guest of Simon the Leper. While he was eating dinner a woman came up carrying a bottle of very expensive perfume. Opening the bottle, she poured it on His head. Some of the guests became furious among themselves. "That's criminal! A sheer waste! This perfume could have been sold for well over a year's wages and handed out to the poor." They swelled up in anger bursting with indignation over her. But Jesus said, "Let her alone. Why are you giving her a hard time? She has just done something wonderfully significant for me. You will have the poor with you every day the rest of your lives. Whenever you feel like it, you can do something for them. Not so with me. She did what she could when she could – she pre-anointed my body for burial. And you can be sure that whenever in the whole world the Message is preached, what she just did is going to be talked about admiringly. (Mark 14:3-9)*

One evening recently, I was listening to a Klaus' album, Glory. I became literally "wrecked" by something he said during this worship experience:

> *I think for a moment about the story of the woman with the Alabaster Jar that poured it all out! The religious people said,*

"It is too much! How can you waste this expensive fragrance in one moment? I want to say to you tonight that if you are still measuring out your offerings, you haven't seen His worth yet! You haven't seen his worth yet! Cuz, she saw His worth and she poured it all out in a moment! She said "Jesus you're worth it! I'll pour it out on You."

Mary of Bethany saw **His Worth** and poured out an extravagant offering! Mary did not just use a portion of ointment to anoint Jesus. She did not try to keep any of it for her own purposes; instead she broke the box and poured out all the ointment, eliminating any possibility of saving some for another occasion (Brian Lake, Romancing the King, 91).

She saw that He alone was worth it all! "Such a waste," the disciples complained, "It could have been sold for a price equal to a year's wages." But Mary saw only one thing, "He was worth it!" Jesus, moved by her worship, corrected the men and so beautifully honored her. He placed her in the history record books for the greatest act of worship of all time! Luke tells of a similar worship encounter:

Now one of the Pharisees invited Jesus to have dinner with him, so he went to the Pharisee's house and reclined at the table. When a woman who had lived a sinful life in that town learned that Jesus was eating at the Pharisee's house she brought an alabaster jar of perfume and as she stood behind Him at His feet weeping, she began to wet his feet with her tears. Then she wiped them with her hair, kissed then and poured perfume on them. When the Pharisee who had invited Him saw this, he said to himself, "If this man were a prophet, he would know who is touching Him and what kind of a woman she is – that she is a sinner." Jesus answered him, "Simon, I have something to tell you." "Tell me teacher." He said, "Two men owed money to a certain money lender. One owed him five hundred denarii, and the other fifty. Neither of them had the money to pay him back, so he cancelled the debts of both. Now which of them will love him more?" Simon replied, "I suppose the one who had the bigger debt cancelled." "You have judged correctly," Jesus said.

Then he turned to the woman and said to Simon, "Do you see this woman? I came into your house. You did not give me any water for my feet, but she wet my feet with her tears and wiped them with her hair. You did not give me a kiss, but this woman, from the time I entered, has not stopped kissing my feet. You did not pour oil on my head, but she has poured perfume on my feet. Therefore, I tell you her many sins have been forgiven – for she loved much. But he, who has been forgiven little, loves little."
(Luke 7:36-48)

What was the greatest point Jesus was communicating here? Was it about forgiveness? Was it about canceling debts? Was it even about love? I believe that the key point Jesus was communicating was about recognizing **His Worth**. He was basically saying that until you realize how much you have been forgiven, you will just not understand. You don't understand the gift that He is about to give you, for if you did, you would see His Worth!

This woman had a past, a thin past, and everyone in the room knew it! But somewhere along the way she met a man, a man like no other! A man who saw through all she had done, and touched her so deeply that she was changed forever! She saw **His Worth** and poured out an extravagant love upon Him! Paul saw His worth and it drove everything he did!

[For my determined purpose is] that I may know Him [that I may progressively become more deeply and intimately acquainted with Him, perceiving and recognizing and understanding the wonders of His Person more strongly and more clearly], and that I may in that same way come to know the power outflowing from His resurrection [[a]which it exerts over believers], and that I may so share His sufferings as to be continually transformed [in spirit into His likeness even] to His death, [in the hope] that if possible I may attain to the [spiritual and moral] resurrection [that lifts me] out from among the dead [even while in the body]. Not that I have now attained [this ideal], or have already been made perfect, but I press on to lay hold of (grasp) and make my own, that for which Christ

*Jesus (the Messiah) has laid hold of me and made me His own.
(Philippians 3:10-12 AMP)*

In a single sentence we find the Apostle's great goal for life, his determined purpose: That I may know Him:

PROGRESSIVELY BECOME MORE DEEPLY AND INTIMATELY ACQUAINTED WITH HIM...

PERCEIVING...
RECOGNIZING...
UNDERSTANDING
THE WONDERS OF HIS PERSON!

What did Paul know that caused him to have this intense passion to now Jesus? Prior to the above passage in the same flow of thought, Paul gives us a transparent look into his heart:

> *But whatever former things I had that might have been gain to me, I have come to consider as (one combined) loss for Christ's sake. Yes, furthermore, I count everything as loss compared to the possession of the priceless privilege (the overwhelming preciousness), the surpassing worth, and the supreme advantage of knowing Christ Jesus my Lord and of progressively becoming more deeply and intimately acquainted with Him (of perceiving and recognizing and understanding Him more fully and clearly). For His sake I have lost everything and consider it all to be mere rubbish (refuse, dregs), in order that I may win (gain) Christ (The Anointed One), And that I may (actually) be found and known as in Him....(Philippians 3:7-9 AMP)*

Paul saw **His Worth** and poured out **extravagant devotion** to Him! There was no end to His dedication to Christ. The passion that once drove him to persecute Christians was eclipsed by pure devotion because He encountered the love and glory of God. He saw Jesus' worth and everything changed one day on the road to Damascus. For the rest of his days, extravagant devotion marked Paul's worship. Philippians 3 shows us Paul's heart in a crystal clear way. He counted every human gain absolutely nothing compared to the "surpassing worth" of knowing Him, as the Amplified Bible notes in verse eight, anything this world has to offer, no matter how beautiful, cannot even rate on a scale in comparison to this utmost privilege.

In turn, seeing His worth must propel us to worship with extravagant devotion. Like Paul, how do we come to "know" Him intimately, our hearts becoming wholly His? We must become fed up with the superficial things of life and religion, and desire desperately to be, as Chuck Swindoll says, "Profoundly aware of His presence, in touch with Him at the deepest level, thinking His thoughts, gleaning His wisdom, and living as close to His heart as is humanly possible, operating your life in the nucleus of His will." **We all need a "road to Damascus"** encounter with God that will explode our entire life with the reality of His worth. David also saw **His Worth,** and it defined him forever!

> *O God, you are my God, earnestly I seek you; my soul thirsts for you, my body longs for you, in a dry and weary land where there is no water. I have seen you in the sanctuary and beheld your power and your glory. Because your love is better than life, my lips will glorify you. I will praise you as long as I live, and in your name I will lift up my hands. My soul will be satisfied as with the richest of foods; with singing lips my mouth will praise you. On my bed I remember you; I think of you through the watches of the night. Because you are my help, I sing in the shadow of your wings. My soul clings to you…. (Psalm 63:1-8)*

From the time David was a shepherd boy, he grew increasingly in the revelation of who God is. He was taught in divine moments, through his failures, his victories, and most of all through his worship! Psalm 17:15; "And I, in righteousness I will see your face; when I awake I will be satisfied with seeing your likeness."

One of David's greatest qualities was that in the midst of just about any situation, he broke out in (what Beth Moore describes as) compulsory praises... seemingly in the middle of anything he would cry out about the greatness of God. David both expressed and encouraged others to worship in the most visible of ways:

- Cried out (Psalm 40:1)
- Art of declaration (Psalm 24)
- Dance (Psalm 149:3)
- Raising his hands (Psalm 63:4, 134:2)
- Clapping (Psalm 47:1)
- Bowing (Philippians 3:19)
- Freely singing the written song (Psalm 4:1)
- Singing the unwritten song (Psalm 98:1)
- Playing instruments (Psalm 144:9)
- Shouting (Psalm 47:1)
- Jumping (Psalm 18:29)
- With exuberance in praise before Him (Psalm 22:25)

David's worship also came in the deepest innermost ways:

- His heart was glad (Psalm 26:9)
- He was devoted and dedicated to God (Psalm 22:27-28)
- He took refuge in God (Psalm 31:1)
- He continually sought guidance from God (Psalm 25:4)
- He sought secret place wisdom from God (Psalm 51:6)
- He lived in cooperation with God (II Samuel 7:10-11)
- He gave to God extravagantly (II Samuel 8:15)
- He relied on God as His champion (II Samuel 8:14b)
- He had integrity in leadership (II Samuel 8:15)
- He had a deep belief in the promises of God (Psalm 106:12)
- He had a passion for the Ark of the Covenant/the Presence of God (II Samuel 7:2)
- He placed his hope in God (Psalm 39:7)
- He learned to wait on God (Psalm 40:1)
- He set God continually before him (Psalm 16:8)
- He found rest in God alone (Psalm 62:3)
- He gave himself completely to God (Psalm 35:10, "My whole being will exclaim, 'WHO IS LIKE YOU GOD')

David saw His Worth and poured out extravagant worship upon Him! This is why his life was defined as "the man after God's own heart." In his lifestyle, he was constantly in pursuit of the heart of God.

David saw His Worth and poured out extravagant worship upon Him in every way he could possibly feel or envision. Nothing stopped David from worship, not even his own failures. In fact, his failures only drove him to deeper dimensions of worship...worship that emerged from a humbled heart of total dependence upon God.

> *Better is one day in your courts*
> *than a thousand elsewhere*
> *I would rather be a door-keeper in the house of my God*
> *than dwell in the tents of the wicked. (Psalm 84:10)*

Throughout every era of time people have seen HIS WORTH...and it has transformed them forever. Tommy Tenney calls these people, God Chasers. God Chasers transcend time and culture. They come from every background imaginable. They come from every era of time that has existed; from Abraham the wandering herdsman, to Moses the adopted stutterer, to David the shepherd boy. As the parade of time continues, the names keep popping up; Madame Jeanne Guyon, Evan Roberts, William Seymour of Azusa Street fame - until we reach today. Really, only history can tell us the names of God Chasers, but they're there. Are you one?

God is just waiting to be caught by someone whose hunger exceeds his grasp. God Chasers have a lot in common. Primarily, they are not interested in camping out on some dusty truth known to everyone. They are after the fresh presence of the Almighty. Sometimes their pursuit raises the eyebrows of the existing church from a place of dryness back into the place of His presence. If you're a God Chaser, you won't be happy to simply follow God's tracks. You will follow them until you apprehend His presence.[1] (Tommy Tenney: 2011-07-28 - The God Chasers Expanded Edition. Destiny Image. Kindle.)

GOD CHASERS, THOSE WHO HAVE DISCOVERED HIS WORTH, AND PLACE HIM AS THEIR NUMBER ONE VALUE IN LIFE, POUR OUT EXTRAVAGANT HUNGER FOR HIM!

I have seen His Worth and it ruined me for the ordinary.

I have seen **His Worth...**

- Every time I hear the stories of my family's miracles crusades.
- When I see the lost coming to Jesus at our altar.
- When Jesus met me as a child and covered me with His Presence.
- When the Holy Spirit filled me as a teenager.
- When I saw amazing healings in the Philippines.
- When I looked into the eyes of the children in the Philippines.
- When He called my name and I heard His voice.
- When we, as a corporate body, began to pursue Him together in a new dimension during renewal.
- When I was in personal devastation and He met me there.
- When His Glory filled my home like a cloud.
- When He healed my marriage.
- When my six-week-old baby lay in a hospital with IV's hooked up to her, and I was too scared to breathe.
- When a group of 3D Women started seeking Him in the early morning hours together.
- When my covenant sister, Delia got up out of a wheel chair and walked.
- When I was in a hospital room with a six-month-old leukemia patient and we felt His life and joy takeover, healing this precious little girl.
- When I have been overwhelmed with confusion and hurt.
- When He meets my song at the piano.
- When He fills my time with Him with His beauty.
- Every time I look into my children's eyes.
- Every time I feel my husband's embrace.

- Every time I recognize His abiding Presence in my life.

I am ruined for the ordinary because of **His Worth**! When you catch a glimpse of **His Worth…**

- You pour out an **extravagant offering** on Him (Mary of Bethany).
- You pour out **extravagant love** on Him (Woman in Luke).
- You pour out **extravagant devotion** to Him (Paul).
- You pour out **extravagant worship** on Him (David).
- You pour out **extravagant hunger** for Him (the God Chasers).

Recognizing **His Worth** could determine how much of God you will truly discover!

ENTER IN. FIND HIM. DISCOVER HIS WORTH. BE CHANGED FOREVER.

Chapter 15

DISCOVERING AND ALIGNING

YOUR VALUE SYSTEM MUST BE GOD-CENTERED

So, you need money. You desire to create wealth. Do you know how many people in our world have been destroyed by their wealth? I have known wealthy people who have been very happy and fulfilled. I have also known wealthy people who have had their whole family destroyed by their wealth. It destroyed their happiness. It destroyed their relationship with their children. It destroyed their ability to function as productive members of society.

But you do need money to fulfill the purposes of God for your life. I want to suggest that before you create wealth, you need to create a value system that will enable you to make wealth serve you and not require you to serve your wealth. So let's create a value system.

Here's my story. By the time I was thirty years of age I already had experienced a very successful ministry, but I was a financial wreck. I had little if anything in the bank, I had several credit card balances that were seemingly beyond my ability to pay and almost nothing to show for over ten years of ministry. Then there was a "suddenly" of God in my life and our church exploded in growth as a direct result of a great move of the Holy Spirit. The income of the church began to grow beyond the $250,000 mark and one day the board of the church sat down with me and "voted" that my salary would be based on 10 percent of the yearly income. They thought that since the "tithes" in the Old Testament were to be designated for the support of the Levitical leadership, that a tithe of the tithe would be scriptural.

Now for the first time in my life, it looked as if my salary would have the ability to get this preacher out of debt. As God began to bless the church and bless me as a result, I began to slowly climb out of debt. Then God began to deal with my heart. During the next season of growth, I never once asked the church to give me that increased amount of money. As our finances began to grow, I realized that when they would reach the seven-figure level that my salary would become excessive. So, I made a decision to change everything and limit my salary.

As we brought three other Senior Associate Pastors on staff, I sat down with them and told them that God had spoken to me about "sharing the wealth." I told them that I wanted to go to the board of the church and tell them that this 10 percent of the church income that had been designated as the "Senior Pastor's salary" must become a "Common Purse" to be an abundant supply for all of us jointly. From that point on we would share it jointly. All four of our salary packages would be equal and the 10 percent designated for my compensation would become a "Common Purse" and would be designated to augment our income for emergency situations that would occur in all four of our families.

The board accepted our suggestion of the "Common Purse" and set our four equal compensation packages for this senior pastoral team. My salary was to be first designated from the 10 percent and the remainder would be placed into that Common Purse for emergency purposes for all four of us. If, for instance, there was a major repair on one of their homes or another emergency, we would meet together and fund that emergency from the Common Purse. The story of the "Common Purse" is told in a former best-selling book that we wrote in the 1970s, The Exploding Church. Because of church growth and an expanding staff of pastors, we eventually phased out the "Common Purse" idea.

I felt as if I must continue to live on the same level as the other pastors. Eventually, I reduced my salary far below the other pastors in the church. By the time I reached my 60th birthday, my salary was reduced to $500.00 per week with 20 percent of that being placed in a retirement fund. I have lived on a $500.00 a week salary for over twenty years. During this period of time the church also has provided the utilities on my home and for a limited period of time, a vehicle. Within ten years we reduced the amount again and I provided for my own vehicle. Yet in spite of that very limited income, I have experienced the blessing of God.

This may sound sacrificial, however, in reality it was a door to the blessing of God. Miracle after miracle has happened and our lifestyle has enjoyed the abundance of God. During these years of ministry, we had acquired a very lovely home with forty acres of property. Our first home was acquired before the days of the common purse.

Our family moved several times, each time selling a home and making acquisition of another piece of property. Every time the growth in real estate values caused the value of our real estate to grow. Eventually, God gave us this amazing forty acres of property in the country where Aimee and Jay and our beautiful granddaughters live in a wonderful old farmhouse built in the 1880s. Wanda and I have built a lovely home on the same acreage. Much of this is a result, not of my salary, but as a direct result of the miracle provision of God.

In the past few years we gave this beautiful home to the church as a "Life Estate" that enables us to live there without cost for the rest of our lives. When we go to be with the Lord, the house will become the sole property of the church and Jay and Aimee will continue to live in their beautiful farmhouse. However, they will not inherit our home. God gave us our beautiful home, and God will also bless Aimee.

If you came to my house, you would see that it is a house of abundance. God's miracles have given the Reid family a life that would make others envious. We live next door to our daughter and son-in-law who work with us in ministry. I don't think any family in the world has a better relationship than ours. Around us is our forty acres, golf carts to ride so we can watch the horses that Aimee and Jay own, a beautiful pond with paddle boats and a row boat, two lovely antique cars, of course, my fifteen-year-old convertible and Wanda's three year old SUV. It is truly a house of abundance. My spiritual children often take care of us; we minister with them and we are family. I wonder how life can be as good as this.

But here is the problem with most people. They know that there is a covenant promise from God to bless them. I know that and have experienced that in my own life. But what is it for? Abundance is not to provide us a bigger house or a more opulent car as a symbol of success. I ask a simple question: Just why do we want "stuff"?

Mother Theresa and Princess Diana died the same week. Who had the greatest wealth? Was wealth the money they had in the bank? When they died they both were on the front page of every newspaper in the world. They both had the adulation of the multitudes. So...what is wealth? Was it the mansion the Princess lived in or the Rolls Royce she rode in with a chauffeur? Or is true wealth something else?

If we could get our values straight, our lives would truly succeed. The way I suggest you do this is through worship. Place your central, number one value on Jesus. Pour the alabaster box of ointment (a full year's salary) over His person. Fall in love. Do what Aimee instructed in the previous chapter. Place your first and foremost value there. It will help you align your other values.

It will also keep you from the mistake so many people make. As you begin to list your values, align them to your worship. I guarantee that once you realize the values you have lived by are right or wrong and work on a revised value system, then, you will be a true candidate for the blessing of God.

Here are some of the values you should consider:

- Always, PUT JESUS FIRST! You cannot develop a proper value system unless He is first!
- Secondly, you must think of relationships with others as second: your wife, your children, your neighbor. Is your relationship with them clouded by your needing a bigger car or house than they have so they will respect you? Do you really care about them and desire to serve them?
- What about stuff? Does it consume you? Is it high on your value list? If it is, it will destroy you. That kind of an obsession will not only cause your own insecurities to rule your behavior, but will destroy relationships that can make your life rich.

My friend, Reverend Darius Pridgen, the most powerful civic leader in our city, tells me he always carries a camera with him so he can take pictures of the people around him. He says that if he carries a camera, his attention will always be focused on another person. Wow...what a way to live... focused on others! A proper value system will cause you to succeed in life.

SETTING MY VALUES

List the ten major values of your life in their priority sequence:

1. _____

2. _____

3. _____

4. _____

5. _____

6. _____

7. _____

8. _____

9. _____

10. _____

Carefully look at these values and then lay them before God. Are they right? Are they in "God Order?" Or, do you need to change them? Pray about this. Honestly seek God for a period of two weeks or more. Let God deal with your heart. Then, write a New Value System and began to implement this new system. Make certain that your first value is God.

MY NEW VALUE SYSTEM

1. _____

2. _____

3. _____

4. _____

5. _____

6. _____

7. _____

8. _____

9. _____

10. _____

Chapter 16

ABUNDANCE

CHANGING THE WORLD IS EXPENSIVE!

Iain MacDonald

My prayer closet was actually a closet. Under the suits and beside the shirts, was a dark corner where I spent time with God. I spent most of my time there wrestling with that small voice pushing me toward the call on my life.

For a few years, the Lord had been asking me to start a ministry in Fort Erie, Ontario, my wife's hometown, but business had taken most of my time. Things were going well, and His request couldn't be more poorly timed. I was pretty certain it meant the businesses would have to close and all our financial reserves would dwindle. On top of that, He was asking me not to take any pay from the ministry, hardly a comfortable place for my logical mind.

I had three adult children, all in, or heading to, university. I was just turning 40, this was not the time to change course. I had been a Christian all my life, and particularly so for the previous twelve years following after a mixture of the "word of faith" message and the resurgence of the prophetic ministry.

I had expected my life would be a process of steppingstones as the blessing of God continually increased, but my journey would more aptly be described as a war. There was no question I was growing as an individual, in my marriage, with my children, and in my desire to serve God and His kingdom. On the financial front, however, the supernatural flow others had experienced, had never materialized.

It was from here that we decided to step into the God-plan, but I was unprepared for what that would mean. Before this time, I would have said

I wasn't afraid of anything. What I was unaware of was that my obedience would force me to come face-to-face with what I believed about money.

As it turned out, the fear created by an uncertain financial future almost drove me out of my mind. Without the safety net, without a clear strategy through which my provision would come, I became all too aware that I had been deceiving myself. I had been doing all the right things on the outside, without first changing what I believed on the inside. I had been pretending to trust God, only able to do so when there was a bank account, a business, a backup-plan should God fail to provide. Remove these, and all that remained was my faith, which proved to be small indeed!

If I had the right beliefs about money, and my relationship to it, I would not be feeling all this fear. I would not have hesitated. All this doom and gloom wouldn't have been in my thoughts and wouldn't have come out my mouth. We had already decided to start the ministry, but it wasn't long before my world came crashing in around me. I only had two choices; pull it together, or perish.

My financial safety net had given me the ability to lie to myself, but that lie was about to disqualify me from my destiny.

Today, many of God's intended Kingdom leaders are caught in this same trap. Their talent, energy and charisma have allowed them to take advantage of economic opportunities. Through hard work and long hours, they produce what appears to a blessed life, only to discover that they sold their true inheritance for a bowl of porridge. Should God call them to their God-dream, as He always does, breaking away will prove impossible when faith in their assets is strong but faith in their God is weak. And should they be unwilling to disobey God, and naively jump in thinking their secular success proves they have the faith to get their destiny done, they will as I did, be trying to put up a tent in a storm.

I did my best to pull it together, and for the next few pages, let me share some of the transformation I have received going from a business person who understands the natural mechanisms of this world system, to a kingdom person who tries to live above that system, confident now in the abundant garden God created to grow all our dreams to maturity.

God was asking me to trade my dream for His Dream (capitals intended) but I knew His Dream was expensive and all I had was His promise that, "together we could do the impossible."

Introduction

What will it really take to transform the world around you? It will take few readers long to discover that one of the key realities to this process will be the financial requirements that a project of that magnitude would require. We quickly assume that there are only a few, if any at all, who can look at a mountain this big with any plausible expectation of successfully scaling it. "Perhaps Donald Trump, or Warren Buffet should have that job, but certainly not me."

What if I were to suggest that every person has the potential to accomplish great things like this? In all likelihood, your mind just dismissed that statement, as you would if I said you could lasso the moon. Your mind is telling you that this is only true in cartoons and self-help books.

When we hear Scripture tell us of the limitless potential within each of us, our minds react this same way and treat God's Words as religion-speak, which completely dilutes their meaning. How can we treat God's promises as anything more than pie-in-the-sky, when they espouse such limitless potential in a world where our personal limitations are so very real?

Like the warden bragging to a condemned inmate about the world outside their prison cell, little the warden says has any real meaning to the inmate who knows he will never again see the world outside the bars. While he hears the words, they are meaningless or even antagonistic. His mind will reject them and argue against them. Little the warden says will have any lasting effect on the inmate.

Our mind is designed to work this way so that we are not overwhelmed by the billions of bits of data and stimuli that bombard us in any given moment. The brain quickly sifts through all inputs, picks out the relevant stuff, and ignores the rest.

Consider instead the discussion with the warden if the inmate knew he was getting released the following day.

The most shocking and tragic reality of this allegory, as it applies to our financial reality, is that the inmate himself built and guards the prison. We decide what we believe, and what we believe determines what data our brain decides is important or relevant. What goes on in our brain, builds our future, for better or worse.

How, then, does each of us seize our rightful place as architects of the world around us? Whether it be our individual life, family, neighborhood, city, region, nation, or globe, we each have a place and a contribution, a divine assignment and authority to turn the world we see around us into heaven on earth.

How do you get the money you need for the dream in your heart?

Rather than discuss the common mechanisms that exist in our world to finance a dream: debt, equity, preferred or common shares, I'd like to look at the principles that govern the flow of money and how we can create a channel through which the needed resources confidently materialize. Once we possess the correct inner relationship with money, and particularly an inner confidence that everything we need is already waiting for us to place a demand upon it, we will courageously strap ourselves to the yoke and see our world transformed before our eyes.

When Jesus was here, He continually encouraged us with the power that is possessed when we believe something. This concept of believing has become quite diluted in our culture, particularly when we confuse it with something we merely "think in our conscious mind," or simply something we only aspire to believe. Certainly, we often use "believe" and "think" interchangeably in our culture, but these are two completely different concepts, and confusing them can deceive us when seeking to understand our true relationship to money.

You could meet three different people who seem to be doing the same thing as they each work hard at what they do: the first motivated by a dream they are convinced they can accomplish; the second motivated by the fear they will never succeed at anything and will end their life in humiliation; and the third numbed by the steady flow of meaningless success that has built a callus over their heart. All appear to be doing the same thing, only one will enjoy the journey, only one will be able to sustain the acceleration and weight of the fullness of what they chase.

An Abundant Heart

It is only by first gaining an understanding of our inner relationship to money that we will be able to assess ourselves. This inner relationship, then, will predict our lives on two levels. Firstly, our beliefs will either empower or destroy our ability to perceive our dream with any real expectation of accomplishing it. And secondly, once the dream begins to unfold in our natural world, our beliefs about money will give us the balance and stability to sustain the weight of the project as it gains momentum.

If our belief about and relationship to money and resources is so foundational to our ability to even step toward our God-dream, let's take a few moments to do an inventory of these inner realities. "What do I really believe governs the flow of resources toward or away from my life and Dream?"

The answers to the following few questions can identify and establish the foundational financial principles upon which great Dreams are built.

1. Is the world, this natural, physical environment, working with me or against me?
2. Is the flow of money and resources simply an economic equation, with only my natural ability and qualifications as variables?
3. What forces do I believe govern my ability to increase financially?

The answers to these three questions form the basis upon which all our financial expectations are built, so I challenge each reader to consider them carefully. In the next few pages, we are going to discuss these three beliefs from a Biblical viewpoint, particularly how God spoke to us with wisdom hidden inside His instructions regarding offerings.

As Paul, the apostle, wrote his letters to the Corinthian church, he was careful to explain that God is far more interested in our attitudes toward any offerings we give, than in the offerings themselves. While we tend to focus on the actual dollar amount of each offering, he warns us that it is, in fact, our understanding of the offering and our heart's agreement with it that will determine its octane.

As we move through the discussion, each chapter will try to discover these foundational financial principles and then compare them to three different Biblical offerings and the inner reality contained in the meaning behind each. My hope is that this will bring each of the offerings to life for you, empowering you to begin, or continue, to steward the financial resources God has given you with far greater purpose and intention.

As well, by turning up the octane level of each, you will dramatically increase the harvest potential of your offerings and build an indomitable expectation for ever-increasing harvests as your God-dream grows to not only bless you richly, but transform your world.

Before considering the pages to follow, set your heart to "OPEN", so that these concepts can engage your mind. Pray this simple prayer:

LORD, my heart is open to understand these principles; I will not allow my preconceived ideas to blind me to the possibilities contained within these pages. I am willing to reason with the suggestions this book presents. I am willing to see beyond the natural order of things. I am willing to allow God to stretch my mind. I am willing to do the impossible. In Jesus' Name. Amen.

Each chapter will close with a simple prayer outline that will prove helpful as a tool for the reader to use. Scripture tells us that until we decide to believe something, it has no power in our lives. In fact, it merely puffs us up.

We begin the process of believing by weighing the information, deciding if it is, in fact, true. If we accept it, we must decide to receive it by declaring that decision with our mouth. This may seem like a mundane step, but Scripture stresses the importance of believing and confessing as the legal transaction we must use to "plant" seeds of truth into our heart. Finally, as we embrace it, it will simply become a matter of tending those divine seeds until they flourish automatically in our lives.

May God Bless your journey through these pages...

Is the world working with me or against me?

This section will discuss our fundamental understanding of the nature of the world around us. Is the world trying to provide for me, or is it trying to starve me out? Do I need to compete for a shortage of goods, or is the world ready and willing to supply any need I may have?

For most of us, our perception of the world around us has been given to us by people whose understanding of the world is that it's a bad and dangerous place, a desert with a scarcity of resources. Growing up surrounded by this worldview has given each of us this same perception.

What further confounds us as humans is that we live in the world we perceive, not the world as it actually is. Consequently, if we believe the world to be antagonistic, we interpret every negative financial experience as evidence that the world is against us, and every positive experience as evidence that we are finally learning how to maneuver the world for our benefit. As each experience passes, we become increasingly convinced that the world is as we perceive it to be, and our soul becomes less and less willing to consider alternative viewpoints.

Consider instead the mind of someone who perceives the world as a good and safe place, an oasis always ready to provide whatever is needed. When I believe the world is cooperating with me, I perceive every positive financial experience as evidence that the world is working for me and every negative experience as evidence that I still have something to learn about how to align myself with the world's desire and willingness to provide abundance for me.

Scripture repeatedly tells us that "the just shall live by faith," and while we most often interpret this for our religious lives, it has much broader application.

Each of our lives is determined by what we believe. Proverbs says it like this, "as a man thinks in his heart, so is he." What you think in your heart, or believe, determines the life you live. Not only does it initiate your perception of the world around you, which has profound impact of the quality of your life, but it also forms the building blocks of your hope.

Hope defined means "what you really expect is about to happen" and what you believe about the world around you has a dramatic effect on this expectation of the future. Consider then, that Scripture tells us that "faith is the substance of things hoped for." As you transform your expectation of the future, this changes the blueprint being used by your faith to build your life.

Our belief about the world around us is a primary factor when determining the financial requirements of our Dream. The antagonistic perception will see any financial uncertainty as an unwelcomed adversary possessing the ability to decrease or destroy the Dream. Contrarily, the cooperative perception will perceive uncertainty as a welcomed opportunity to grow into greater levels of abundance, and by doing so, increase the scope and potential of the Dream.

When we consider this fundamental perception of the world around us, each of us finds ourselves on one side or the other, with the majority having to admit that they are most aware of their need to fight against or protect themselves from an antagonistic world.

Both people in the original paragraph experienced exactly the same financial situations, one positive and the other negative. Each is convinced that their perception is the accurate one, and while they hold opposite opinions, each can point to the same evidence to validate their belief.

These contradictions are the reason God gave us Scripture to help us understand the true nature of the world around us. We humans perceive our world through the filters of our preconceived understandings, rather than perceive it as it actually is. Therefore, we benefit so greatly by having the Scriptures to act as our plumb line.

Our humanity, mistakenly convinces us that our perception is true simply because we have spent so much time analyzing the intellectual and emotional data we have been receiving since birth. "I have come to these conclusions after much thought and careful assessment. How could I possibly be wrong?" This is THE trap Jesus warned us about throughout His teaching ministry. Therefore, we need to make the effort to recognize this human bias and develop a purposeful openness to perceive and understand Truth. We must overpower our natural tendency to automatically see what we've always seen, hear only what we already agree with, and ignore everything else.

The world is a good place.
And God saw that it was good... Genesis 1:25

Genesis tells us that God made the world, and that He said it was good. We all know that not long after creation, Adam and Eve's rebellion against God changed the world's ability to produce abundance in their lives, but we have wrongly assumed that creation changed also.

Instead, we should have understood that their sin simply interrupted creation's ability to serve the needs of Adam and Eve. Because of Adam's decision to reject God's Words and believe those of another, the earth would now grow wild with thorns and thistles. To get anything better, would require Adam's determined toil and sweat.

Rather than creation becoming a bad place, our perception should be that sin changed us and misaligned us from the abundance mechanism designed into this world. Since our world is built upon the things we believe and expect, when sin changed our perspective from a cooperative to an adversarial relationship with creation, we inverted our belief, filling our expectation of the future with uncertainty and lack. Creation didn't change, it is still bringing forth what we believe and expect only now our beliefs and expectations are contaminated by sin and fear.Let me explain using a familiar metaphor. We have such an advantage in our age to understand this reality. Anyone owning a computer, and possessing even a basic understanding of how they work, knows that if a virus infects the computer, it does not mean the computer is broken. In fact, the virus only works if the computer is functioning properly. Even though the unusual manifestation on the monitor appears to mean there is something wrong with the computer, simply removing the virus, and restarting the computer will prove that the computer hasn't changed at all, only the software has. This is not unlike our natural experience.

By observing the world around us, we have thought there must be something wrong with creation, but all along the real problem has been our perception of creation. The problem is not what shows up in our life, the problem is in what we believe. Miraculously, by simply changing the software we will automatically change the output. Creation has been working perfectly all along.

Imagine a person floating downstream in a canoe, and another running along the bank of the same river. The boater is effortlessly moving toward the destination with the river doing all the hard work, while the runner is having to work hard to reach the same goal. One person is in the flow, and one isn't. We have, perhaps, thought that sin dried up the river, that there is no longer a destination to reach, or that we do not possess the ability to reach the destination anymore.

None of these are true. The river is there and so is the destination, all we need to do is figure out how to get into the river. Experiencing the force of the river will further empower confidence in any personal strength or ability required to reach the destination. All we need to do is point the canoe, and let the river take us there, easy enough! This certainly runs contrary to the way most humans perceive the world in which they live.

My business training concentrated on the principles and disciplines needed to contend with an unruly and often adversarial world. Prescribing that ambition, coupled with a significant level of risk and fear, would sufficiently motivate me for the fight required to reach my goals. I was the runner, always aware of the effort needed to reach the goal, reminded with each stride that just one misstep could disqualify me. Torment in body and mind.

Scripture seemed to be describing a different system: "seek first the Kingdom and His way of doing things, and all the things you need will be added to you" (Matthew 6:33). Concentrating my attention on Biblical principles and disciplines as a lifestyle, beyond religious doctrine, qualified me to be the man in the canoe. All I needed to do was change what I believed. Peace in body and soul.

As we consider the Dreams God has placed in our hearts, we know that our understanding of the world around us deeply and profoundly affects our expectation to ever fulfill our destiny.

If we believe the world around us is at war with us, the likelihood of accomplishing our purpose is slim. Contrarily, if we believe creation is rooting for us, and standing ready to provide everything we need, the expectation of completing our destiny is quite different. This belief system, then, is the foundational principle that will govern whether or not we aggressively move toward our Dream. This stance, most often, decides whether our Dream lives or dies.

Let's step into the world as God created it, a world of abundance, where the garden and all its variety produced harvest after harvest for Adam and Eve. Consider their reality, waking up each day with unlimited potential.

All the resources we have discovered today were, in fact, on the earth at that time, waiting for someone to harvest them and understand how to transform them into the resources needed to complete our Dreams. God made trees and let us decide if we wanted to turn the tree into a house, a hockey stick, or an arrow. Regardless of what we made and the moral value of it, the world has been supplying abundance for us to use since its creation.

Adam's reality must have been vastly different than ours today, waking up knowing that he could do anything he could dream. The world was working with him. It seemed that no matter what he dreamed about building, the world would always have the materials he needed.

He dreamed about a house for Eve, looked around to find trees, and before long, the dream was manifested. It seemed that creation was waiting for him to just dream something. In fact, creation was so excited about the opportunity, that there were millions of acres of trees, even though Adam only needed one or two.

Our world is not much different today, in spite of all the reports of a stripped earth, there are as many trees on this planet as there ever have been. No doubt, we have used a few, but creation and its relentless desire to have the resources needed for our dreams, continues to fill every crack with a seed that will one day be a tree.

I'm reminded of creation's abundance mandate each spring when my war against dandelions is renewed. It seems that creation's desire to produce abundance in everything is a formidable opponent. It would seem that if there is any work to be done on this planet, it would not be a war against shortage, but rather the vigilance to contain the abundance that will otherwise overrun us.

Why, then, if creation's abundance is so evident, do we each have such an overwhelming expectation of shortage and lack? The answer comes from an understanding of our economic system. Each of our lives is so intertwined with the business systems of our world that we have come to believe that this mechanism is creation's mechanism, but it is not.

Our economic system is primarily built upon the forces of supply and demand. Supply is the amount of a product or service that is available, and demand is the amount of that product or service that the market desires. Theoretically, the price of that product or service is the intersection of those two forces.

So, in one instance, as the demand increases and the supply remains the same, the price for that item increases. Conversely, if demand decreases and the supply remains the same, the price decreases. Alternatively, if supply increases, the price decreases, or if supply decreases the price increases. While this may be a bit confusing, it offers understanding on why we believe the world is full of shortage. Simply put, shortage creates profit.

As you see from the example, businesses are very interested in creating a higher demand than there is supply, or failing this, a lower supply than there is demand. Either of these empowers a business to charge more for their product or service, and so a foundational part of their business plan is a mechanism to constrict the availability of their product or service. This will, in turn, enable them to charge a price sufficient to produce a profit. While this sounds insidious and conspiratorial, it is simply the economic theory that has run our world since time began, or rather, since Adam ate the apple.

What does that look like from our perspective? It appears that everything we have a demand for is in short supply, but this is not real, it's a manufactured reality. Each of our minds must break through the mirage constructed around our lives. As we grasp a true picture of the world around us, our Dreams will go from a fanciful wish to an inevitable expectation.

As we consider each of the foundational realities of money, let's look at a parallel reality contained within God's instructions to the Israelite nation. As you know, Old Testament instructions are pictures and parables to us today, God infusing a deeper and more profound wisdom within each of what may appear to be mundane rules and instructions.

My most favorite is God's instruction to Moses to have the Israelites build their toilets outside the borders of their campgrounds. While this seemed like an extraordinary bother, to travel such a distance to relieve oneself, we now know that this instruction prevented the spread of disease. Inside that inconvenient instruction, was the hidden reality of germs.

Similarly, let's look at the first of three of the offerings God commanded to see what profound reality they contain.

For this point, we are going to look at the First Fruit Offering. We will need a bit of clarification here because we've lost a bit of understanding of this offering in modern days. We have lumped the First Fruit offering in with the Tithe, and consider them to be the same offering when historically and scripturally they are significantly different.

Leviticus 23:10-14 describes a two-stage process for the First Fruit offering. Stage one is when the wheat harvest first begins and the farmer takes his first sheaf of wheat and brings it to the temple. When he does so, he is to take a lamb, some flour and oil, and some wine and give it all to the priest as a burnt offering. God tells them not to even take time to eat or drink that day until they have completed this first part of the First Fruit offering. Stage two happens fifty days later at the end of the harvest, when there was a specific offering to be brought to the temple: two loaves, seven lambs, one bullock, and two rams as the First Fruit Offering. (We can see then that since the tithe is specifically ten percent of all the increase, that is, the whole harvest, the First Fruit offering was an entirely different event.)

Scripture uses many examples of the First Fruit offering:

- The tree of the knowledge of good and evil was one tree amongst hundreds or thousands of trees in the garden, and God told Adam that this first tree was His tree and Adam was not to eat of it.
- God asked Abraham to sacrifice his son Isaac, Sarah's firstborn.
- God instructed Joshua not to touch the spoils from the city, Jericho. The first conquered city, and everything in it, belonged to God.

These all point to the first portion of the abundance God was going to bring forth. It is an offering that happens before the abundance arrives, and one that we have almost completely overlooked in our modern day. By mixing the Tithe and First Fruit offering together, we have lost the significance of its message: that God is the Source of our provision, and His creation is designed to provide everything we will ever need to bring our Dream to pass.

This offering played an important role in the mindset of the early Israelites. In Deuteronomy 26, God gave instructions about this offering, and while we mistakenly use this scripture to talk about the Tithe, it specifically refers to the First Fruit offering. It is easy to distinguish between these two offerings, as the tithe is every tenth piece and the First Fruit is just the first piece as their names describe.

The name, First Fruit, or perhaps for us, "first piece," gives us some insight that can speak to our foundational beliefs about abundance. We can draw parallels to other "first pieces," like the first piece of a birthday cake, to realize that God is trying to draw our attention to the internal reality He wants us to have when bringing our First Fruits.

Our hearts declare, God is the most important part of the harvest, the source of the increase. He's the Creator of the world of abundance from which the harvest flows. t points to my awareness of His abundant nature, that He would only create a world that would be good and a blessing to His greatest creation, me. It is from this heart, that we would rush from our harvest field, without hesitation or distraction, just to bring the first piece, the best piece, to God.

Picture the lesson that was visibly evident in the lives of the small children as they watched their parents grab the sheath of wheat and run with all their might to the temple. What would that child have understood about reality, as she watched the wisest and most significant people in her life treat God that way, to be so excited to give Him the choicest portion, the portion they had been waiting for since last year? She knew God got that piece because, when it comes to harvests, He is the beginning of it all.

If we revisit the original comparison between someone who believes this world is a bad place and someone who believes it's a good place, each of us can begin to perceive our world according to Scriptural truth and work to reject every other thought, until we feel our dreams coming alive within us. We'll begin to see the pieces of our dream, those pieces that seemed so impossible, coming into focus in our mind.

What may have been just fantasy, becomes real when we understand that we're not alone in its pursuit. That God and His entire creation are on our side, ready to cooperate with us anyway we need them to.

No, we should not expect to find people lining up to help us or to find big checks in the mailbox. While those may come, what most likely will happen first is that your perception of your world and your life's experiences will begin to change. Your future will begin to excite you. And your mission, to learn how to more closely align yourself with the mechanics of this world, should compel you to seek out an understanding of what those mechanics are.

Just as we spent years learning how to compete against a world we thought was against us, we must now spend the time to learn how to cooperate with a world that is for us.

Prayer

Heavenly Father, I can tell my heart has believed a lie. I know You love me, and that You were able to build the world any way you wanted to. And if that's true, You would certainly build a world that is good, a world that has in it everything I will ever need. I declare, My dream is Your dream, so I believe You have done everything imaginable to bring it to pass. I ask your forgiveness for believing You are anything but good, and for confusing what Your motives are toward me.

I declare a truce in the war I am waging against this world, and determine to learn how to work with Your creation, not against it, how to align my thinking and actions with its operating principles.

Fear, dread and selfishness are no longer what motivates me. Instead, I am going to learn how to use faith, hope and love to propel the Dream You have placed in my heart forward and build the life You promised I could have.

I declare God is for me. This world is for me. Everything I need for God's Dream to come to pass in my life is already waiting for me in my future.

This is the Truth and I will live out of this Truth and the blessing it creates for the rest of my life. For my cup of blessing overflows.

In Jesus' Name. Amen

Take a moment to imagine what your life will be like once the harvest of this Truth is ripe. How will it affect your personal wellbeing, your family, your finances...your Dream?

This can often mean a significant transformation in how you perceive your life and past events, but with the humility to begin dealing with all the false evidence that has presented itself as true, open your heart to the thought that they may only be facts or emotions based on a wrong perspective, a flawed perspective that has been handed down for generations.

"A lie told a thousand times is still a lie."

The World in the Keyhole

There once was a young girl who lived in an old Victorian house.

While she loved that place, she was continually drawn to the door but could only see through the keyhole what was on the other side.

Yes, her house was beautiful and hand-crafted, but the world in the keyhole was 'alive' with trees and flowers; bright in a different way than the candlelight of her room, warm in a different way than the fireplace she knew; ever-changing, unlike her world which remained ever the same.

She looked with wonder each time she gazed through the keyhole; she longed for the adventure of that world but withdrew knowing that she was better to stay where she was and leave the world in the keyhole to those meant for that life.

The more time she spent looking through the keyhole, the more comfortable it became and the less content she was with her own world, even to the place of frustration with the dreariness of her manicured room.

While originally content to merely peer through the keyhole and admire its beauty, she noticed that over time she began to imagine herself living in that world, and became aware of how "alive" she felt.

This feeling captivated her every thought, invaded every dream; until one day... she noticed that as she began to touch things in her room, those things came to life, artificial things became real, inanimate things opened their eyes, and dead things jumped to life again.

Awestruck, she looked around and noticed that her world was now full of the same Life she had once only known in the World in the Keyhole.

Chapter 17

Partnership – Overcoming Weakness

Iain MacDonald

Is the flow of money and resources simply an economic equation with only my natural ability and qualifications as variables?

From where does money flow?

None of us can deny that those who prepare to earn more money, using education, creative talent, business acumen, or the like, often find themselves earning a higher income. But neither can we deny that for every example of a successful PhD, there are 10 that are unsuccessful, particularly these days when only 1 out of 10 are not even working in the field in which they were educated. We all know 100 starving artists for every famous one. I can assure you there are more bankrupt business people than there are millionaires. If this was simply a mathematical formula: get education, get good job, get rich; take guitar lessons, write great song, get rich; think of idea, start a business, get rich; you'd think more people would opt to do it.

We all know the real keys to the flow of money are deeper, less quantifiable. At its deepest point, the main reason people fail is that they believe they are going to. I know this sounds cliché, and discovering all the individual realities that are contained within that one statement can be difficult. The solution, however, is not so hard to discover.

Let's look at what is at the heart of not good enough, not smart enough, not prepared enough, not creative enough; simply not enough. We as humans, while we put up as good a front as we can, are painfully aware of our own limitations. We all grew up in a world that was quick to point out our weaknesses. In fact, should we have been raised in the last 200 years, this is the premise upon which our education system was built. There are a few basic skills that everyone should have to be a whole person, and the job of the education system is to make sure each of us reaches a proficient level in all those basic areas. To accomplish this, our education system focused on identifying those areas that displayed weakness, so that these areas could become strong.

The problem was that it forced each of us to become aware that there are just things that we are not good at. "Yes, I can draw with excellence, but the main thing to focus on today is that I'm not good at math. And if I don't get better, I'll never have what it takes to be successful. No matter how hard I tried, I just couldn't get the whole math thing." In this equation, no matter how dominant your strength is, your weakness will eventually undermine it.

We not only learn this in school, it's everywhere we look. We try out for the baseball team, and the coaches start working on our weaknesses until we max our ability to strengthen them, and my inability places a ceiling on my professional aspirations. I keep moving up the dating pyramid, until I try to date the person who doesn't want to date me, having to admit I'm just not enough to get the one I want. The business earns good money, and we keep reinvesting it until one day we decide wrong, just like the gambler who doesn't know when to quit, it's all gone on one bad hand.

On and on the lesson goes until we are absolutely convinced we aren't enough, no matter how grand the dream is and how easy it may appear to accomplish it. Something will come up where I'm just not able to produce the excellence that's required, and I will eventually fail, and fail publicly.

Each of us has to admit that while we have some awesome strengths, they come with matching weaknesses. Strong left-brain people tend not to be strong right-brained. Logical people tend not to understand emotional matters. Masculine people have little understanding of feminine things. Extroverts tend to say things they don't mean, while introverts don't say the things they mean.

To be strong at one thing actually means to be weak at another, so none of us escapes our own awareness of the places we are weak. People often try to mitigate this problem by developing partnerships with others, in marriage, business, etc., and while this often produces greater success than going it alone, it can also multiply the weaknesses. The reality here is that none of us can predict what the future will bring, and few of us are fully confident we will have what it takes to meet every challenge.

So are we destined to take our best shot, if we shoot at all? What if I could find a partner who didn't have weaknesses, who knew the future, and who had the wisdom to turn every crisis into an opportunity? I know what you're thinking,

> *"The only person with that résumé is God, and He's certainly not interested in partnering with me."*
>
> *"Sure, God wants me to partner with Him, but that's a one-way street."*
>
> *"He has way too much to do to bother with my life."*
>
> *"He's working His big plan, and certainly doesn't have time to stop and play toys."*
>
> *"My stuff is so insignificant in the grand scope of things, it would be rude of me to even ask for help."*
>
> *"I asked God for help in the past, and just as I thought, He had so many other things to do, my thing was not important enough for Him to care about."*
>
> *"I don't think I've done enough for Him to warrant His attention, He only has time for the people who help Him with His stuff."*

We all realize that our perception of someone's attitude toward us greatly affects our attitude toward them. This is often what is in our way when relating to God.

Paul tells us in Romans 1 that we create God in our image. We try to understand God and His nature by thinking how we would think and feel if we were God.

So, if I were God and had to run the universe and keep everyone in line, I sure wouldn't have time to talk to little old me. If I could do anything, it wouldn't even occur to me to spend time trying to help an insignificant person. If I lived forever, I would be so busy doing the things I wanted to do I'd hardly even notice the things other people wanted me to do. If I was super-smart, mega-powerful and uber-rich, other people would become almost invisible to me, except where they could serve me and make my life better.

I think that's a pretty concise picture of how we believe God thinks? The only problem is, He never thinks like that, ever. Really, never! God has never had a self-focused thought. Not one.

I realize this is difficult to imagine because we are thinking about ourselves all the time. It will be useful, here, to delve into the mental processes that causes us to think about ourselves. We can then come to understand why God's experience is so different from ours.

When we experience something that is not the way we would like it to be; something is missing; we lack something we desire; something is not the way we would like it to be; we then consider doing something about it that would benefit "me." This is what selfishness is: any thought in the general direction of self.

God never experiences that in His consciousness because He does not lack anything. It's never too hot or too cold where He is. Everything around Him is exactly, perfectly, completely, precisely the way He would want it to be. So, He has never had an occasion to think about Himself.

At this writing, I have never been in a sensory deprivation facility, a tank that is specially designed to remove all conscious awareness of everything about your physical being so that you can relax and empty your mind, and "be" beyond the clutter of "me."

I wonder what this must be like, to be totally unaware of everything to do with your "self." After getting used to the environment, I think you would stop thinking about you and all the things you need and want, and start thinking about other things independent of how they affect you.

Certainly this can only give us a glimpse of what it might be like to be God. Nevertheless, it is useful to consider how different God's life is, without all the lack, discomfort, and annoyances that we experience every second of our lives. Clearly, He would be thinking of things quite different than the things we think about.

This helps us understand what it means for the Bible to say "God is Love." Because He never experiences a need, He never thinks of being served.

Rather, by seeing the needs of others, serving is the only thing that occurs to Him. This may sound trite, or even blasphemous, but Love is quite uncomplex. Love is just: others focused, simple.

Love is when someone is willing to sacrifice something for the good of another. Love believes so much in another person, that it is willing to give of itself to bless the other person.

This is God's nature, not just how He chooses to think, feel or act. When you do not experience any fear, lack, shortage, discomfort, confusion, or the like; when you are all-powerful, all-knowing and omni-present, you have nothing to think about except others, nothing to concern yourself with except the issues in other people's lives. When you don't need anyone to serve you, you become completely preoccupied with serving them.

Consider this: God loves you. Really, consider this: God loves you.

On a separate, but related note, God lives in eternity. That is quite different than living inside time as we mortals do. It's not just living inside time without end, like we will experience in heaven. Eternity is living outside time all together. Time does not exist in God's perception.

That means He can live my life, completely focused on me, and live your life, completely focused on you, simultaneously. You see, we don't share God's time. We all get 100% of His attention, 100% of our lives! Imagine what it must be like for Him when you go to sleep: He sits there waiting for you to get up so that He can interact with you again. He loves to be with you.

Finally, God can live the end before He starts the beginning. This is a profound reality in our lives and particularly in our understanding of the Dream He has placed in each of our hearts. Yes, God has a plan, but you "are" His plan.

God has seen the end of the world as we know it, whether that is in 10 years or 10,000 years. He is looking at it right now. Confusing, yeah, but when God created this universe, He was looking at every need of your life and made sure it was included and accessible in creation.

He knew exactly who, where and when you would be, and built into creation everything you would need. When He created Adam, he loaded you into his DNA. He mapped out your ancestors all the way back to Adam and

Eve, in order to design you with everything you would need to complete the Dream He would place in your heart. Every talent, ability, desire, every part of your personality, temperament, preference and passion, everything that evolutionists told you happened by some cosmic coincidence, was carefully and precisely crafted by God's intelligent design. You are perfectly aligned with your Dream and destiny, God made you that way on purpose.

Why am I here? Why do I exist? Why does any of "this" exist? The answer is remarkably simple, God had nothing to think about, nothing to care about, no one to express His love to. So, He created you. He wants to love you.

That's why He took the great risk of giving you His most precious gift: the ability to choose. In order for someone to love Him back, really love Him, they must first have the choice to reject Him.

A squirrel does not have the choice to reject God, so it does not really love God. Its consciousness is just aligned with Him by nature. Instinct has been programmed into the squirrel, and it can't think outside its programming.

Homo sapiens is not like this. We have been created by God in a completely different class. We have been given the freedom to reject our Creator. This same freedom gives us the ability to truly love God, and that is the reason God did all this in the first place.

Let's put all this together to try to understand what God thinks when He thinks about you. He is completely focused on you and your life. He is completely prepared for every need of your life and the Dream He purposely imbedded in your heart. He wants to be an active participant in everything you do. He wants to show Himself strong on your behalf to build greater courage in you as you go forward. He wants you to fear Him so that His words of Truth have extraordinary authority in your mind. He wants you to worship Him so that He can download His strength and vision into you through this intimate exchange. He wants you to pray so that He has a focused time to talk to you and help you see things you would otherwise overlook.

God is completely focused on what is good for you, what will allow Him to help you get to where you want to go. God wants to be your divine life-partner. In fact, that's the singular reason "In the beginning" even happened.

Let's look at how God has woven His desire to love us into the instructions He gave us in scripture. This spiritual reality of God's love affair with us is paralleled in a second of the offerings God instructed the Israelites to give: the Tithe.

By definition, the word tithe means "a tenth", or "ten percent." When God instructed Moses on the constitution on which to establish the Israelite Nation once they reached the Promised Land, He gave each of the tribes of Israel a portion of the land, except the tribe of Levi.

The tribe of Levi, known as the Levites, were those commissioned by God to work for Him. Instead of giving them a portion of the land, He instructed the other eleven tribes to give the Levites ten percent of their harvest each year, a Tithe of all their increase.

What was this reality in the mind of an Israelite in that day? They grew up knowing that God was going to give them a very special piece of land. However unlikely it may have seemed at the time for a vagabond tribe of desert nomads to defeat the highly trained warrior nations that presently occupied this coveted property, they marched forward with full confidence in God's ability to do what He promised.

If the Israelites had not become accustomed to God's provision and protection in their forty years of manna and quail, wandering across the Sinai, they certainly got the picture when they looked at the crumbled walls of Jericho. "God is on our side." "He's our not-so-silent-partner." Everyone, but that Achan fellow (Joshua 7), understood. That reality was cemented into the heart of every Israelite, young and old: God is my Partner.

It hardly mattered anymore that they were physically smaller than those who opposed them, that their weapons were vastly inferior, that their knowledge of war and strategy was incomparable to people whose life had been dedicated to its principles. What mattered was that God was with and for them. While they were still weak, vulnerable, naive, and inexperienced, all this paled in comparison to their recently understood alliance with El-Shaddai, which loosely translated means All-Mighty God.

Imagine the first church service in the promised land, when the priest gets up and tells them it's time to give their Divine partner His dividend check. Imagine being the young child watching her parents calculating the abundance of their harvest, knowing that Heaven's accountants were doing the same, listening to them as they spoke of their appreciation of the strengths their Partner offers to their enterprise, and telling the stories of how things were in Egypt under their former master. Each child must have become intrinsically aware of how confident that made their parents as they spoke of future harvests. What an impression it must have made on them to watch the expressions of gratitude on their parents' faces as they offered the livestock laden with precious harvest, declaring "All Glory to God," as they did.

It was through this outward expression that an inward reality was implanted in the children for generations to come. Since God is with us, He is our Protector and our Provider. We can count on His active partnership as we pursue the Dream He has placed in our hearts.

Time and distance do not change this message as each of us reads the Israelite stories today. God is still looking to partner with you. People are concerned that their Dream seems well beyond impossible, not realizing that God made it that way so that He could secure for Himself a place in our lives.

He so much wants to live our lives with us, to be intimately involved in every facet, every battle and every victory, not for some egotistical reason, as these would never enter His consciousness, but rather to build within our lineage a heritage of faith, a self-perpetuating awareness in all our descendants that God is their faithful Partner, and no matter how grand their Dreams, He will be there to help overcome every obstacle, defeat all opposition, provide every need, and supply all wisdom. Failure would never be an option. Why would they ever quit when their inner reality screamed, *"Victory is Inevitable!"*

Changing our world can seem like a formidable task riddled with obstacles and powerful forces with opposing agendas, not unlike Joshua's perspective when he was first given the task of leading his band of nomads toward their God promised Dream.

There are few humans that have known what this must have felt like, who do not also know the value of the synergistic partnerships from which the courage to venture forth comes. Each of you reading this book is being called into this same arena, perhaps to build a family, or perhaps also to rebuild a neighborhood, a city, or a nation.

Know this: God wants His presence and His promises to reside as living realities in your heart. He would have them to be felt-realities as you rise each day. They will feel like courage, bravery and creativity, where none existed before; optimism when there seems no reason for it; and hope even on the darkest of days.

As you weigh the harvest and calculate His dividend, you will stand, tithe in hand, bloodied and bruised, dripping with sweat, declaring all the while, "All Glory to God!"

Prayer

Heavenly Father, I know I have believed a lie about You, I now understand that You are completely loving, and that Your thoughts toward me are only good. I ask Your forgiveness for believing You would want to put any distance between us, and for anything I may have done or believed that caused any separation.

I know You are cheering for me, I am Your child, and You want to be my Partner in everything I do. I know You have put a Dream in my heart. Help me to discover what that Dream is, and grant me courage to fearlessly pursue it together with You.

I declare: God is my partner. His strengths are now added to my Dream. His partnership strengthens me, and I know that while adversity and opposition may come, we are well prepared and well able to overcome them all. I know this is the Truth, and I will live out of this Truth and the blessing it will create for the rest of my life and for generations to come.

In Jesus' Name. Amen.

Again, take a moment to imagine your tomorrows with the Truth of this prayer actively working on your behalf. Truth, once planted in the heart of a human has the Divine power to bring itself to pass. As you continually draw these images to mind, you are watering and fertilizing the seeds you just planted, encouraging and multiplying the magnitude of your harvest.

Dance...

Patiently He waited as He watched her every move.

Twirling here and spinning there, 'til her worth one day she'd prove.

"Would He like it?" how she pondered, "Would the look upon His face

Be of joy and celebration or one filled with such disgrace?"

'I will dance, yes, I must go! for its all I have to give.

just to show Him how I love Him and without Him I can't live'

Off she goes to please His heart, after all "it's all I've got"

So she played the song and danced along, 'til her worries she forgot.

He watched and so did marvel, with a smile upon His face,

As she danced and leaped before Him, knowing with Him she had a place.

"How He loves me" she could see it, "I know now I belong."

Yet little did she know, He was watching all along.

Elizabeth MacDonald

Chapter 18

Increase

The Mechanism for Limitless Resources

Iain MacDonald

What forces do I believe govern my ability to continually increase financially?

From whence does increase come?

Scripture tells us that wisdom stands on the street corner crying out for all to hear, "hey stupid, how long will you stay stupid?"MSG. Solomon's imagery here is that the wisdom of God is visible in all creation, that each of us can see Truth before us every moment, if we would but stop to perceive it. I can't help but think this is the reason Jesus always spoke in parables. He used a children's story filled with familiar imagery to express a Truth so profound it required God Himself to tell it.

Consider a priceless painting, hanging in a gallery. Rather than look at the painting, consider what must have been in the heart and mind of the painter. The canvas was once snow white. It displayed nothing. Beside it was a brush and palate filled with puddles of paint. Everything you see in that painting came from the heart of the painter, every stroke, carefully selected. Everything about that picture was totally under the control of the master's hand and heart. Perhaps he painted for a while, but didn't like the result. All he needed to do is paint over the top. He was free to change whatever he wanted until the image on the canvas exactly matched the image he had in his mind. There was no limit to his creativity, no right or wrong color or stroke. Bound to no exterior standard, he was completely free to express on canvas what he felt in his heart. The painter had taken a three-dimensional image and created a two dimensional painting.

This is not unlike the process of creation, when our four dimensional God "painted" a three-dimensional world. Everything about creation is the way it is because it has come from the heart of God.

Most of us have been so influenced by our modern evolutionist agenda that we have trouble observing the Truth that has been painted into the world around us. We have been taught that the forces of this world are a product of chance, of coincidence. Our inner reality, as a result, is to see natural things and spiritual things as separate and distinct.

But this is not any more true than the painting is separate and distinct from the painter. The painting is as perfect an image of the heart of the painter, as his skill would allow him to make. Paul warned us that none will have an excuse for not finding God, or discovering Truth. His heart and nature were all around us from the moment we were born to the moment we die, right before our eyes.

It's useful here to push this metaphor one step further. There is a familiar story that emerged after the Second World War. One of Hitler's mandates was to seize all the priceless artwork from the cities and towns he conquered. As his forces would draw near to a town or village, the locals would try to hide their paintings and sculptures so that he would not be able to find them. One of the ways they did this was to paint another painting over the top of the masterpiece. They were careful to use materials that would be easily removed at some later date without harming the true painting beneath. Once the war ended, they were able to recover their masterpiece, hidden in plain sight, by simply wiping off the counterfeit image.

This is not unlike the image we have of the world as it stands today. So much of what we see, so much of what captures our attention, is actually the counterfeit. Once God finished painting creation, He handed the brushes over to Adam and Eve and their descendants. It was God's intention to be the only One to instruct Adam and Eve on how to paint, but alas, another began to whisper his techniques into the ear of God's protégé. As the canvas unrolled each day, and Adam and Eve set out to paint, more and more of the intruder's techniques became visible in the landscape. Nevertheless, creation still occupied a majority of the canvas.

Each of us, as we peer at the canvas, must use a level of discernment. What has come from the Master's brush, and what from the corrupted protégé? Which images are rooted in a heart of faith, hope and love and which have been painted with fear, dread and selfishness? Once we have developed this discriminating eye, we can admire the strokes of the Master and peer into His heart, then, confidence will replace confusion.

It is from this vantage point that we discuss this final chapter, as we discover what forces govern the increase and decrease of resources. Each of us is hindered in our ability to Dream with true expectation and anticipation while we are unsure of the forces that will take our dream from its present lowly state, to its grand and rightful place. As long as these forces seem haphazard and unsure, we will be troubled and hesitant to employ them, when doing so would create any significant risk.

Humans are by nature risk-averse, and while it would seem that history rewards the few who have foolishly risked all and won, it has only done so by forgetting the countless who have done so and lost.

Risk is only risk to someone who does not understand the forces that control the outcome. Gambling at the roulette table is a risk to everyone, except the thief who set the magnets in place to cheat chance and force the ball to land in a specific spot. His wager is not at risk at all, he confidently bets on an outcome that he knows is sure because he understands the forces that control it.

Consider the awesome responsibility of an architect or engineer designing a bridge across a large river. How terrible their task would be if they had no understanding of the physical forces that would determine whether the bridge could hold the traffic load, wind load and water current once it was built. I wonder, would anyone dare invest the millions of dollars to finance the construction? Or, would anyone load their family into a vehicle and cross the bridge, if they were not first confident that the architects and engineers designed the structure with a thorough understand of, and confidence in, the forces that govern the success of the project?

Many people set forth building their Dream without first possessing an understanding and confidence in the forces that produce the resources they will need as the Dream grows. Without this knowledge so many Dreams collapse under the weight of debt and compromise as the Dream grows beyond the available provision, and the dreamer is forced to contaminate their vision to keep it alive. It is not long before the purity and passion that once drove the vision is lost and the Dream fades to dust.

To gather a glimpse of this wisdom, let's look to creation to see how it produces increase. There are three main things the tree outside my window is producing: leaves, roots and fruit: Leaves to gather sunlight to use as energy, roots to absorb water and nutrients from the soil to sustain the tree, and all this to finally produce fruit. Within the fruit are seeds, that procreative force that initiates increase. The future of that species of tree is contained within its seed--no fruit, no seed, no future.

Widen your view, everything you see in all of creation that grows or increases, does so using this same mechanism. Every plant and every animal, mammal, reptile or amphibian, were all divinely designed with this same "increase" mechanism.

When God initiated creation, He didn't need to plant 100 apple trees in the garden. He planted one, with a secret code programmed into its DNA. That secret code was its God-inspired mechanism of increase.

As if by magic, the first harvest season came and strewn across the ground beneath that tree were 100s of apples, each containing seeds that possessed within them the DNA to create another apple tree, nay a whole forest of apple trees, nay a whole planet full of apple trees! Limitless increase, within just one seed, because within each seed was the divine code to produce more seeds.

This is the miracle of creation. Eternity was implanted into every living organism, plant or animal. Lack and shortage were never the problem. If anything, God needed someone to tend the abundance. Creation already knew how to produce limitless increase.

On the crowning day of creation, God made man, a being designed to function on Earth as God did in Heaven. While he looked like an animal on the outside, equipped with this same ability to fill the earth with billions of humans, God gave Adam a distinct gift, an independent consciousness, a soul.

This soul was unlike the soul of other animals, it was not hardwired to a God-given instinct. Instead, each soul was designed with the ability to dream, and then at conception, God imbedded the Dream. Similar to the instinct given to animals, this Dream would guide their every thought and emotion, decision and action. This Dream was the DNA that, once discovered, embraced, and realized, would be the visible production of the human's life, their fruit. Surely, that fruit would be good to eat, but like the apple and the peach, hidden within that fruit lay the seeds of boundless increase.

Similar to creation's process, each Dream starts out small, each species of tree started with only one tree. As we look at the output of one man's Dream, the enlightened eye would never despise small beginnings, for hidden within their fruit no matter how limited it may appear to be, is unlimited potential.

Dominion

God couldn't wait to tell Adam why He created him, He could only wait two verses to say, "I am giving you dominion over all creation, go increase, multiply, subdue the earth."

God was well aware of the abundance mandate already programmed into every living thing. In order to give Adam a fighting chance against this flood of abundance, God knew He needed to explain to Adam how to guide the abundance toward the things he wanted and away from the things he didn't. God had already planted a Dream inside Adam, now Adam needed to know how to direct creation toward the fulfillment of that Dream.

God explained to Adam that within every living organism was a seed, and Adam could decide what increased and what decreased by deciding which seeds to sow and which ones not to sow. The ones he sowed would increase and the ones he withheld would decrease, simple.

While few of us are engaged in the agricultural industry, we all know that farmers still use this process to govern and improve their harvests to this very day. They exercise their dominion over their fields and livestock by deciding which seeds to sow, and, by exclusion, which to withhold.

Few of us struggle with this mechanism as it applies to farmers and shepherds, but it often takes a moment to consider that God is only using this natural process to show us a universal Truth. Jesus demonstrated an understanding of both worlds when He used this natural process as a metaphor to explain how God's Word is planted in the heart of a human and, if tended properly, will produce abundant fruit thirty, sixty and a hundred times as much. He was showing us that we could perceive a spiritual truth by observing a natural process in creation.

Let's look to see how God wove this third inner financial reality into the meaning hidden inside another of God's offerings, this one found in the New Testament.

Paul is writing to the Corinthian church talking to them about an offering his friend Titus was to receive from the church in the city of Macedonia and give to the people in the Jerusalem church to help them pursue the Dreams God put in their hearts for their city.

Of course, Paul was talking to them about the importance of the love and resulting generosity being demonstrated by the Macedonians. But a parallel reality is that the Dreams in each of their lives had produced fruit, and while this fruit seemed hardly sufficient for their own lives, these people, many of them farmers, understood something about how to make things grow. Eating all their harvest was exactly the wrong thing to do, no matter how hungry they were.

It seemed only natural to the Macedonians to conclude that the only way for their harvest to grow was to take a portion of their fruit and invest it into the Dreams of others. If they wanted their Dreams to grow and change a city, they needed to empower the Dreams within another city. This is just the natural rhythm of creation, distilled into Truth, and applied on a higher level: money is a seed, we just need to act like money-farmers.

What is money?

So many would answer that question by saying, it's the piece of paper in my wallet. It's what I use to buy things. Sure it's made of that and it does those things, but what is it?

It is best to understand money as containers of life-seeds. When we work, we transform our life, the minutes and hours of productive energy, into products and services, which we exchange for money. This money is then exchanged for the productive energy from other people's lives, the products they make or the services they provide.

Money is just a temporary storage container filled with life. We use money to transfer life energy from one place to another. When you take your container of life and give it to Levi Co. to purchase a pair of jeans, you are giving them life. That life empowers increase at Levi and they grow. Contrarily, you withheld life from every other jeans maker, and so they did not get life from you, and did not increase or grow. This is the simple productive flow of any economy, and how money facilitates the easy exchange of life from one person to another.

Money is a temporary storage for life, not unlike the seed that comes from a tree. All the activity of the tree, from spring to harvest, culminates in the seed it produces. The leaves gather sunlight. The roots gather nutrients and water which the tree uses to produce fruit. The fruit is the container into which the tree deposits its productive life.

Rich people have more life containers than poor people. Their Dream has gathered more people's productive energy than that of poor people. No one has a divine right to be rich. Everyone has a God-given Dream, and if that Dream is allowed to grow more and more people can find their dream within it. They are willing to invest their productive energy into it and the dreamer becomes what we call rich. A car, boat, house, etc. is considered expensive because it takes more productive energy to make it than something that is inexpensive. Rich people can purchase the expensive item because their Dream has given them enough productive energy, money, to make the exchange.

As well, when each of us discover and pursue our God-dream, we will be able to produce greater levels of excellence at lower levels of effort because we will be doing the thing that God specifically designed us to do. Like taking a Sherman tank onto a race track, or a Formula 1 car onto rugged terrain, when the vehicle is operating in the environment it was designed for, it's productive ability produces exponentially greater output. The Formula 1 car will put as much energy into going nowhere in the rugged terrain as it will into winning a race on the track. The difference is in the channeling of its energy toward the activity that best matches its design.

Further to this observation is the level of excellence we are able to create when our talents and abilities are applied to something we are actually good at. Few of us would buy a painting from someone who is not a gifted artist. If I could paint with similar excellence, I would only exchange a limited amount of money to have you do it for me. But if your painting displayed a level of excellence few could match, the amount of money I will exchange for it increases significantly. Consider how much you will pay for an average shirt, compared to one you perceive as excellent.

Where does excellence come from? Excellence comes from the degree of alignment of your talents and abilities with any given task, project or output. The rating you will give me when I sing a song, design a bridge, or have a baby, will depend entirely upon two things: First, my God-designed ability and talents, and second, the effort I put into maturing those abilities and talents.

Our evolutionist culture has taught us that only the second factor exists, that "we can be anything we want to be." This has wasted the lives of so many people. Trying to mature in an area that you are not Divinely gifted in will only ever produce mediocre output, and that only after much effort invested. The problem is, money never chases "average." Without first discovering your God-purpose, you are condemning yourself to a life of high effort, mediocre output, and average money.

By drawing all this together, we can understand why so few dreams experience sufficient increase to reach their God-intended fulfillment. Paul teaches us that the output of our lives is divided into two categories, two purposes: bread for food and seed to sow.

In the same scripture, he explains the increase mechanism of sowing and reaping. Part of the money we receive in exchange from our productive energy is used to sustain our lives (riches), and part of it is to ignite the mechanism that will automatically produce increase in our tomorrows (wealth). What happens if our productive energy is channeled into an activity that only produces a mediocre product or service? If our lives are only operating at fifty percent efficiency, sustaining our lives will require us to consume most, or all of the money we receive from selling our mediocre output. We will have nothing left to initiate the process of increase, and our lives will stagnate.

Understanding Increase

Albert Einstein declared, "Compound interest is the eighth wonder of the world. He who understands it, earns it; he who doesn't, pays it." This is the lesson taught to us by the tree, as it uses its productive output to increase each year, thus able to produce increasing amounts of seed. Some of which falls on the ground filling the soil with the nutrients its roots will gather next year, but some which fall beyond the shadow of the tree, germinate, and begin the cycle of increase all over again. Eventually, all other things remaining the same, the whole planet would be populated with the offspring of that one tree.

As well, an understanding of this mechanism moves our attention away from the portion of our harvest that we intend to consume, and toward the portion we designate as "seed to sow." With the growing awareness of God's intention for the Dream in our heart, that He wants it to continually increase, even beyond the boundaries of our lifetime, our attention also shifts from consuming seed to contributing that seed to the Dreams in the hearts of others. Not out of some altruistic pity or religious compassion but from a vision of the world, as God intended it to be: each person discovering, pursuing, and fulfilling the God-dream for their lives. Everyone believing in everyone else, and sowing continually into each other's Dreams. Everyone doing that which most efficiently transforms their passion and ability into productive output. Everyone experiencing the meaningfulness that only comes from doing that which your Creator intended when He knit the fabric of your life.

God never intended we would pursue our Dreams without first understanding that His creation, our playground, was a good place, a place ready to bring forth abundance, regardless of how much was required. He never intended we would even think to go it alone. His dream is to be our Partner, and for our hope of the future to be smeared with His presence and power.

Nor did He expect that we would have to be motivated by the fear of failure, lack, or insignificance; that without these forces propelling us forward, we would find no reason to persevere in the face of adversity, sacrifice when confronted with hardship, advance when overwhelmed by opposition. He expects we will be confident in His creation's ability to bring forth whatever is needed, confident in His committed partnership, and confident in the mechanism that governs the flow of resources to and from our Dream, no matter how grand its scale.

Prayer

Heavenly Father I know I have believed a lie about creation and the way You created it to work. All this time I have thought it was my adversary, when, in Truth, You created it with an abundance mechanism. I ask Your forgiveness for believing this lie and for anything I have done because I believed it.

I know You set the seedtime and harvest mechanism to bless me and empower the Dream you placed in my heart. I now know that our Dream is no longer impossible. In fact, it is Inevitable. You are on my side, creation was built to work with me. As I cooperate with its mechanism and separate a portion of my harvest to bless others, nothing can stop our Dream from coming into reality.

I declare my intention to use the seedtime principle to bless others. I commit to do this because I can see the power God built into this Truth, to not only empower our Dream, but also to sow into the Dream He has placed in others. I believe this mechanism works with exponential power. Not only will my Dream continually grow, but the Dreams around me will also.

I know this is the Truth, and I will live out of this Truth and the blessing it creates for the rest of my life and for generations to come. In Jesus' Name. Amen.

Each of us are now armed with the Truth. Knowing the secret code we are able to build a plan that opens the door to increase, no matter how small that seed may be at first.

Before you turn the page, allow your imagination to paint a picture of your future with the harvests of all three of these Truths in it. As this image grows more real in your mind, it is replacing the image created by the lies you once believed. The more this inner transformation happens, the more Hope you build. Hope is the blueprint that God needs you to determine. By deciding what you believe, and allowing that belief to build your real expectation of the future, you are giving God more and more to work with as He, and His creation, sculpt your world.

May God Bless your Dream...

Section 3

How Buffalo, New York Was Rebuilt by Dreamers

How Dreamers Found the Resources to Rebuild a City

So, you think you have dream, and you wonder where you will get the resources to fund that dream. Of course, the power to create the wealth to finance the dream is inside of you. But what if your dream is to change a dying city, a city that used to lead a nation? Now it is dying and thousands are moving elsewhere. The industry had created its wealth now stands in ruins and All around you, are voices predicting doom. What do you do?

In the 1980s when a new mayor assumed his office, he looked up and saw a huge billboard that read:

"WILL THE LAST PERSON TO LEAVE THE CITY PLEASE TURN OFF THE LIGHTS."

In that same time frame, a friend of mine, Rev. Dr. Bennett Smith, was the Senior Pastor of St. John Baptist Church in downtown Buffalo. He also had a dream to rebuild a dying city. He sat down at his desk and dreamed. After all, the huge church he led was the product of the dream of another man, and he was living in that man's dream. Now it was time for another dream, and Pastor Bennett Smith dreamed a big dream- a dream of rebuilding his city.

The dream began to take shape. First of all, there was the dream of a new housing development he would call McCarley Gardens after the man who had created the church he now pastored. He built 150 beautiful townhome units that would become the icon of the new Buffalo. He dreamed and built

St. John Tower, a beautiful modern Senior Citizens high rise that would become another demonstration of how a city can be transformed.

Political and business leaders also joined with the church and built a new harbor front area, including beautiful new apartments and over 1,200 subsidized homes to assist the population in home ownership. The rest that was accomplished will be told later.

But, today we stand forty years later in a city that has been rebuilt through the dreams of pastors and other leaders. The story is an amazing one. It is an iconic story of how to dream and how to finance the dream.

It will be told by a man who several years ago received a call from God at the renewal altars of the church I pastored and the prophetic words that were spoken over him: "You will disciple the leaders of this city." That prophetic word came true. Al Warner built relationship with and began to disciple and lead men and women who would join an army of people who believed in a dream--that their city could be rebuilt.

This is the story of their dreams and how they created the resources to finance the dream that God had given to the servant leaders of our city.

Buffalo, New York

Past - Present - Future

Beautiful Erie Basin Marina with Buffalo in the background

"Erie Canal in 1891: Shipping and distribution hub for the expansion of the West."

"Collection of Buffalo History Museum."

"PanAmerican Exposition at the turn of the last century, Buffalo's City of Lights."

"Collection of Buffalo History Museum."

"Buffalo City Hall erected in 1929, which was the largest city hall in America to date. It is a symbol of the Art-Deco era."

"Collection of Buffalo History Museum."

"Bethlehem Steel, a symbol of the industrial revolution."

"Collection of Buffalo History Museum."

"American Grain Elevators: 90% of the grain in the United States was shipped through Buffalo."

"Collection of Buffalo History Museum."

New U. S. Federal Court House, a return to creative architecture

Photos Courtesy Blake Dawson

Aerial View of Buffalo's Main Street

Photos Courtesy Blake Dawson

Delaware North International Headquarters under construction

Photos Courtesy Blake Dawson

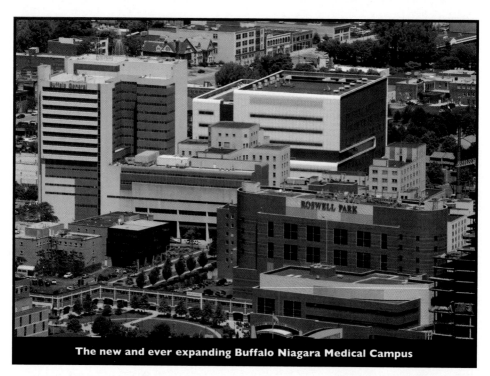

The new and ever expanding Buffalo Niagara Medical Campus

(Derek Gee / The Buffalo News)

The new **HARBORCENTER** that brings over 1/2 million visitors to Buffalo every year.

(Robert Kirkham/ The Buffalo News)

A winter scene at the new Canalside

(Derek Gee / The Buffalo News)

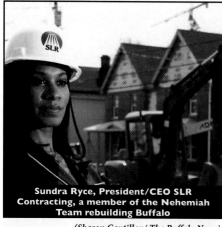

Sundra Ryce, President/CEO SLR Contracting, a member of the Nehemiah Team rebuilding Buffalo

(Sharon Cantillon/ The Buffalo News)

Pastors of the city join with Senator Anthony Nanula, Al Warner, Tommy Reid and Cliff Benson to pray over the construction of HARBORCENTER

Photo courtesy of Deb Warner

Nick Sinatra, President, Sinatra & Company; a member of the Nehemiah Team rebuilding Buffalo.

(Sharon Cantillon/ The Buffalo News)

Pastors gather to pray and bless the newly completed HARBORCENTER at the invitation of the Chief Development Officer of the Buffalo Sabres

Photo courtesy of Michelle Moser

Bishop Darius Pridgen, Pastor of True Bethel Baptist Church and President of the Buffalo Common Council

(Mark Mulville/ The Buffalo News)

Canalside during summer concert

Photos Courtesy Blake Dawson

Chapter 19

RESURRECTION!

Al Warner

A study of leaders in the Bible could lead one to believe that when God desires to change history, He raises up a great leader. However, when He desires to turn the world upside down (Acts 17:6)[2]; He chooses a whole team of leaders and calls them His disciples. The disciples of Christ today are as diverse a group as one could find—extroverts, introverts, preachers, writers, blue collar, white collar, etc.

God heard the prayers and cries of His people in Buffalo, NY. Buffalo was a desperate city in an accelerated death spiral. As God chose to turn Buffalo upside down, He assembled a team of servant leaders—men, women, insiders, outsiders, inner city, suburban, quiet, vocal, and multi-racial. This is their story both individually and collectively.

An important disclaimer: My wife, Deb and I, have lived here since 1989, more than a quarter of a century. We stand on the shoulders of those who have gone before us. Our way has been paved by the earlier sacrifices of those who preached, prayed, and built His Church in our region. The leaders I will highlight are only a fraction of the faithful leaders whom heaven recognizes as essential to the resurrection of Buffalo. If you are one of those or know one of them, we thank, honor, and bless our counterparts who stood their ground in refusing to let Buffalo turn off the lights. Many sowed in tears so that a harvest of rejoicing might come.

We seem an unlikely choice to work with such an august group of leaders. Part of our preparation was renewal services at the Full Gospel Tabernacle, Orchard Park, NY, under the direction of Pastor Tommy and Wanda Reid. Pastor Reid[3] was the loving father of the house.

Ken Horn, editor of the Pentecostal Evangel, wrote about our renewal experience at the Full Gospel Tabernacle, Orchard Park, NY, in 1997,

> Al and Debbie are former missionaries who had pioneered a number of churches for their denomination. They watched everything in their lives crumble: they endured a church split, lost their health, money, friends, and almost their marriage. They were rejected when they embraced the renewal movement. As I spoke with them, I felt a mixture of joy and sorrow—joy that God touched their lives, sorrow that some churches stubbornly resist renewal. It has so impacted their family that when their son, an avid sports fan, found out they had gotten tickets for the National Hockey League playoffs, he said, "If it's on Friday night, I can't go. I'd miss youth meeting."[4]

At the altars of renewal at the Full Gospel Tabernacle, we were internally transformed. A deep inner healing took place that we couldn't explain, but we knew that we would never be the same again. But the internal transformation was simply a set-up for our external call that was prophetically spoken by Pastor Reid: "You will disciple the leaders of this city."

For those of you unfamiliar with prophetic words, Pastor Reid's declaration took longer to manifest than I hoped or expected. This "delay" lines up with Ex. 23:20-31, especially verses 29-30. "But I will not drive them out in a single year, because the land would become desolate and the wild animals too numerous for you. Little by little I will drive them out before you, until you have increased enough to take possession of the land." The Lord began preparing us to steward the Word. We needed to build up our spiritual muscles, and then God would enlarge our territory. I compare this to training in a gym. To build muscles, a trainer determines the weight of plates to slide onto the bar. As you master one level, resistance training demands heavier plates are put on to take you to the next level. God has been building and conditioning our spiritual muscles. When we have increased enough, God will give us possession of our land.

The first leader whom God entrusted me to disciple was Anthony Nanula, City of Buffalo Comptroller. Anthony came from a family of entrepreneurs who built one of the largest chains of grocery stores in New York. At the time (1999), I was serving as Chaplain to the Buffalo Common Council, so I was in Buffalo City Hall at least twice a month. Randomly, I would stop by the offices of city officials, offering to pray for them. Comptroller Nanula's response was transparent: "I have never had a member of the clergy stop by unless he or she was armed to criticize me for a position I took, or ask for money for a project they were building. You mean you don't want anything!?!" Our simple prayer time began a lifelong spiritual relationship as Anthony moved from City Comptroller to Deputy State Comptroller and finally back to the private sector as a gifted businessman.

Before I let Anthony and other servant leaders tell their stories, let me introduce a foundational theological question (don't get nervous but it turns out theology is important)—does God hate cities?

Chapter 20

DOES GOD HATE CITIES?

Al Warner

"**A**lso, seek the peace and prosperity of the city to which I have carried you into exile. Pray to the Lord for it, because if it prospers, you too will prosper" (Jer. 29:7).

Big cities. What image comes to your mind? Crime, pollution, congestion, disease, sinners tightly clustered together? Is the city the invention of sinners (Babylon) or God (Jerusalem)? Countless of our cities groan today under the curse of urban blight. But, could our cities simply be waiting "in eager expectation for the children of God to be revealed" (Rom. 8:19), leaders who have God's eyes and plans to rebuild?

Ray Bakke gives food for thought in his urban classic, A Theology as Big as the City. During his urban ministry in Chicago, Ray recognized the rural bias of evangelicals: "... the Bible is a very rural book about a very rural God who makes gardens and whose favorite people are shepherds and vine growers, and whose least favorite folks are urban dwellers."[5] But when Ray fast forwards to the end of the Book of Revelation, a contrary reality leaps off the page: "Now it is all over and we all live happily in a rebuilt Garden of Eden, right? ... The trumpet sounds, the curtain opens and it's ... it's ... it's ... another city! An urban future forever. And what a city it is!"[6]

Eric Swanson and Sam Williams build on Bakke's concept:

Cities are strategic to God in the working out of his plans. Consider how often God addresses specific cities by name— Jerusalem, Babylon, Tyre—warning them, chastising them, loving them, and lauding them. Paul's letters in the New Testament are addressed to cities—"To the church at Rome," and Philippi, Ephesus, and other cities of Asia Minor. Though there were many house "churches" in each of those cities,

> *Paul wrote to them as one church, addressing his teaching*
> *to the broader context of the city and not just to individual*
> *congregations.... The story of the Bible begins in a garden and*
> *ends in a city. In many ways that we may not fully understand*
> *or grasp, cities are irrevocably tied to the eternal plans of God.*[7]

What a thought. God Himself is on a journey from the rural Garden of Eden to the heavenly City of Jerusalem. God Loves Cities! God shows Jonah His love for Nineveh. Jesus wept over Jerusalem. The missionary journeys of Paul take him from one influential urban hub to the next.

What is the role of the Christian in the city in which he or she resides? Look again at Jer. 29:7, "Also, seek the peace and prosperity of the city to which I have carried you into exile. Pray to the LORD for it, because if it prospers, you too will prosper." Our assignment is to effect spiritual atmosphere ("peace") and economic atmosphere ("prosperity"). Whether I arrived at my city reluctantly or not, this city is now my assignment. It's time to unpack the suitcases, settle down, and make an impact for eternity. Too many Christians are looking to escape rather than embrace the city that holds the key to their own destiny. Most of the leaders highlighted in the following chapters could have fled to other cities, but God had a plan to reveal if they would stay and give themselves to a hurting city.

What is the role of the church in the city? Bakke draws on the biblical story of Abraham negotiating for the salvation of Sodom. Bakke concludes, "The presence of godly people is beneficial for the salvation of places."[8] The "righteous remnant" acts as salt and light within their communities.

What can the church in the city learn from Nehemiah? Is there a biblical example of bringing together clergy and laity to develop and implement a common plan to rebuild a city? Dr. Bakke imagines this very scenario in a meeting of what he calls the Persian Urban Committee[9] made up of two lay leaders, Esther and Nehemiah, and one clergyman, Ezra. This committee is more than a think tank. Most of us are weary of yet another church committee appointed to "study" something. Nehemiah weeps, mourns, fasts, prays (Nehemiah 1), and then fearfully approaches the king to present the plan God gave him (Nehemiah 2). In many of our broken cities, church leaders, both lay and clergy, are still weeping, mourning, fasting, and praying, but have yet to develop a God plan and take the risks necessary to implement it. Bold action involving friends in long-term relationship is usually required to transform cities.

Maximizing the role of the laity is essential to city rebuilding. As Dennis Bakke enumerates, "Most of the heroes of the Bible are people called to secular vocations. Abraham developed real estate. Jacob was a rancher. Joseph was a high government official.... Esther won a beauty contest. Lydia manufactured cloth. Many heroes were military men."[10]

WHAT STEPS NEED TO BE TAKEN TO CONNECT PASTORS AND INTERCESSORS WITH BUSINESS LEADERS TO BUILD A COMMON CITY VISION ACROSS ALL SECTORS?

There is still more to learn from Nehemiah. Robert Lupton summarizes the Book of Nehemiah: "It is the firsthand account of a high-level government official who takes a leave of absence, secures a government grant, organizes the largest volunteer mission project in biblical history, transforms a dangerous ghetto into a secure city, and then repopulates it by inducing suburbanites to move in."[11] Nehemiah arrived in Jerusalem assuming that his call was to rebuild broken walls only to find that his biggest challenge in Jerusalem would not be its broken walls but its fractured people. **Application:** *As with Nehemiah, I thought the call of godly leaders was to rebuild walls, but could it be to rebuild people who in turn will rebuild the walls?*

How important are leaders who hear and implement the Word of the Lord and catalyze the masses? Robert Linthicum pinpoints the value of Nehemiah: "... it is easy for us to overlook the fact that those walls had been demolished for 141 years! ... Why did the Jews not say, sometime during those 141 years, 'We're not going to take this anymore'? ... The answer is simple. They lacked a Nehemiah."[12] I am reminded of Ezek. 22:30 "I looked for someone who might rebuild the wall ..." (NLT). Application: Nehemiah was one leader, but God has given Buffalo a team of servant leading Nehemiah's. It is time to bring together leaders with a Nehemiah call to develop economic projects that inspire new levels of creativity and entrepreneurship.

Still, more direction comes from Nehemiah; this time it is from the repeated use of the phrase "next to him" in Nehemiah 3. The phrase or concept is used forty-three times in a single chapter. Nehemiah came to Jerusalem with a group of outsiders to help restore hope to the insiders who had experienced the pillaging of their city for generations. Together these groups rebuilt walls and resurrected the city of Jerusalem. **Application:** *I cannot rebuild my hurting city alone! Who am I connected to who will build beside me? Are we regularly communicating with each other and God? Have I listened long enough so that it has become OUR God-given vision for Buffalo rather than asking others to follow MY vision?*

Before I share the story of my city of Buffalo, you should consider two key concepts summed up by Ray Bakke and Jon Sharpe as you evaluate your own city. First, "The answers to the city's needs are found in the city …"[13] Second, "We do not start with the needs of the city but rather with the signs of hope."[14] The longer an urban leader serves his or her city, the darker it can appear. Encourage yourself—today God is writing living testimonies of His activity in your city.

GOD LOVES CITIES! SO SHOULD WE!

Chapter 21

BUFFALO: THE GOOD, THE BAD, THE UGLY, THE FUTURE

Al Warner

I mentioned earlier that my city of Buffalo was in an accelerated death spiral. What elements came together to cause this to happen? Was it governmental, economic, spiritual, physical, or emotional? Let's turn the clock back further. Few outsiders understand the vicious economic roller coaster that is Buffalo.

Buffalo/Niagara Falls – On Top of the World

It's time to take a reader poll. When you hear the words "Buffalo, New York," what is the first thought that comes to mind? How many of you said, "snow"? How many of you said, "Lost Super Bowls"? How many of you said, "Buffalo wings"? (Yes, Buffalo wings originated in Buffalo in 1964.) To many, both locals and those who live far away, Buffalo has a negative stereotype.

The story of Buffalo is a tale of three cities: the first at the turn of the last century (1900), a second in the period 1960-1990s, and the current chapter being written since the turn of this century (2000).

A Powerful Past. In 1900, Buffalo had the most millionaires per capita of any city in America, and had already produced two U.S. presidents – Millard Fillmore and Grover Cleveland. Architects Frank Lloyd Wright and Louis Sullivan created many of their signature works in Buffalo. It was a prosperous city, with a bright future. In 1901, Buffalo hosted the Pan-American Exhibition, a World's Fair. Nearly 8 million people came from around the world. It was dubbed "the City of Lights" because of the 240,000 seven-watt light bulbs that illuminated the Exhibition. These lights were powered by electricity generated 25 miles north in Buffalo's sister city, Niagara Falls. President McKinley traveled to Buffalo to view such an awesome display, and as his reward was assassinated in downtown Buffalo in 1901.

Buffalo was a manufacturing hub—a port city on Lake Erie, the western terminus of the Erie Canal, and gateway city to the Midwest through the Great Lakes. 49 percent of the population of the United States and 51 percent of the population of Canada lived within 500 miles of Buffalo. Grain mills, steel plants – jobs, jobs, jobs. Niagara Falls – a wonder of the world, a producer of hydro-electric power, an international tourist destination, a place where the marriage covenant was sealed for honeymooners from around the world. What place could be better for a business or a family to build a future?

As a side note, during these decades of success and prosperity, there are no records of a revival move of God in Buffalo. This is in sharp contrast to Rochester, our sister city to the east. The greatest revival in North American history occurred there in the 1830s and 1840s under the preaching of Charles G. Finney. By contrast, Buffalo credited her achievements to the hard work of man rather than the gifts and favor of God.

Buffalo/Niagara, the Fall from Grace: A Blighted Chapter of History

A traveler to Buffalo/Niagara in the late 1900s might have found it difficult to recognize the glory of her past given the distress of a region in the midst of a death spiral. A drive through downtown Niagara Falls, only a few thousand feet from one of the great wonders of the world, would have revealed a business district largely boarded up and nearly empty, with an 80 percent commercial vacancy rate.

The decline of Western New York was statistically startling. At the turn of the last century (1900), Buffalo had the largest number of millionaires per capita of any city in North America. As recently as 1959, Buffalo's population was nearly 600,000. Today, the City of Buffalo is below 275,000 with Niagara Falls simultaneously experiencing a similar nosedive. During this same period, other American cities have experienced revitalization and increased property values, while those in Western New York plummeted.

What factors brought about this massive reversal of fortune? In the physical realm, the completion of the St. Lawrence Seaway in 1958 largely eliminated Buffalo's position as a shipping and transportation hub. As a result, major industries began to close or relocate. For example, the relocation of Bell Aerospace (1950s) along with the closing of Bethlehem Steel and Republic Steel plants (1970s and 1980s) eliminated over 75,000 high paying jobs. Other jobs were moving south, west, and overseas. Locally, incompetent and often corrupt leadership added to our woes. Because of toxic waste, the earth became poisoned in the Love Canal neighborhood of Niagara Falls and beyond. [15]

But could there be a deeper, less obvious, spiritual cause for this malaise? Could it be that the dark cloud that hung over our region had less to do with snowfall and sports teams, and more to do with principalities and powers that had been fed and multiplied in terms of strength and power?

Buffalo/Niagara, Redemption and Resurrection: A Hopeful Future

Fortunately, God is not intimidated by principalities and powers. In fact the Bible suggests that He does some of His best work in the dark. That is good news for Buffalo/Niagara.

The turnaround in Buffalo during the last decade may qualify for the designation "miraculous." Specifics will be shared in the leaders' testimonies to come, but signs of hope and life must include the following:

- For years, Buffalo has been blighted. But during the last construction season Buffalo had six different construction cranes in the air.
- Since 2012, over $5 billion worth of development projects have broken ground. During the next three years, expectation is that 12,000 new jobs will be created.
- The eight counties of Western New York account for $16.6 billion of economic projects that have been completed or are in the pipeline.

In our city, there is a battle for atmosphere. If we come under the existing atmosphere—**we lose!** But His Church is assigned by God to change the atmosphere and together **we win!** As Deb and I shared with the mayor of Buffalo several years ago, Buffalo is more prepared for a dramatic move of God than Atlanta, Dallas, or San Diego, because the felt need here is greater. Historically, the greatest moves of God have occurred in places of great felt need.

My desire is to encourage you to intentionally seek God in a desperate way for your desperate city. I recognize the darkness, but I do not accept that this darkness is permanent. This same God said, "Let there be light" in Genesis 1. The same Christ said, "I am the light of the world" in John 8. That same God also said, "You (all) are the light of the world" in Matt. 5. Our cities may be like the patient with cancer. God and we, His Church, are the surgical partners to take out the poisonous tumor, and replace it with God-given life! This is gap-standing, wall-watching, gate-keeping, and city-reaching.

What do you see in your own city? Corrupt politicians? Unrighteous business leaders? Rebellious high school students? A dirty bride as His Church? If this is all you report, then you are no different than your local newspaper or secular news station, simply reporting what you see in the physical realm.

GOD DID NOT APPOINT HIS CHURCH TO REPORT HISTORY, BUT TO MAKE HISTORY AND CHANGE DESTINY.

A thermometer registers the temperature at a particular time in a particular place. On the other hand, a thermostat controls the temperature at a desired level in that same place. Are you tired of reporting about the dead, dry, disconnected bones of your life and your city? Then get into God's presence, hear His word over you and your city, take charge, and Prophesy Life! Then watch a vast army in the supernatural, just like the one pictured in Ezekiel 37:10, begin to walk out of their tombs, throw off their grave clothes, and walk into their divine destiny.

ARISE, ARISE, ARISE!

Chapter 22

SERVANT LEADERSHIP: SHEPHERDING STALLIONS

Al Warner

We are using the phrase "servant leaders" in this section of the book. For those unfamiliar with the term, Robert Greenleaf coined the phrase in his groundbreaking book Servant Leadership: A Journey into the Nature of Legitimate Power & Greatness (1977). Greenleaf has an acid test for the servant leader, "Do those served grow as persons? Are the served becoming healthier, freer, wiser, more autonomous and more likely themselves to become servant leaders?"[16] Pause and ponder that statement. If you are feeling brave, ask those whom you serve to read these statements and share their thoughts.

Greenleaf expands the idea from a single servant leader to creating teams of servant leaders as groups of equals. He believes that there is an inherent flaw in the model that establishes a single chief sitting atop a hierarchy, "... the demands of the office destroy these persons' creativity long before they leave office."[17]

Greenleaf develops the discussion further to include not only individuals, but also institutions—businesses, education, foundations, and churches. His words to churches are prophetic: "But the dynamics of leadership—the vision, the values, and the staying power—are essentially religious concerns, and fostering them should become the central mission of the growing edge churches. Where else can it be done?"[18] He challenges churches to build future leaders: "Will not the growing edge church become a chief nurturer of servant-leaders, institution builders for the future?"[19] In case you are waiting for the "right" leader to come along, Greenleaf argues, "We are the leaders we have been waiting for."[20]

In his younger years, Greenleaf considered becoming a pastor. Instead he embraced God's call to a career in business, specifically AT&T. It was there that he developed the concept of servant leadership that reframed both the language and the definition of who should lead as well as how one should lead. Because Greenleaf followed God's call to corporate America, the book was not released to the smaller Christian bookstore market, but to the mainstream business community, and it continues to have global impact.

Contrast this idea with the secular images of leadership that too often permeate the church. John Stott proposes:

> Our model of leadership is often shaped more by culture than by Christ. Yet many cultural models of leadership are incompatible with the servant imagery taught and exhibited by the Lord Jesus. Nevertheless, these alien cultural models are often transplanted into the church and its hierarchy. In Africa it is the tribal chief, in Latin America the machismo (exaggerated masculinity) of the Spanish male, in South Asia the religious guru fawned on by his disciples, in East Asia the Confucian legacy of the teacher's unchallengeable authority, and in Britain the British Raj mentality—the overbearing pride associated with the period of British rule until Indian independence in 1947. It is easy for Christian leaders to assimilate one or other of these models without realizing it. But we need to determine that there is no place in the Christian community for the guru or the Confucian teacher or the African chief, for British Raj mentality or Spanish machismo. These models are not congruous with the spirit of love and gentleness.[21]

Up to this point, we have reviewed the foundational principles of servant leadership. But how might it look in a city? Too often the term "servant" is associated with weakness, a follower, having no opinion of his or her own. To the contrary, I believe servant leaders are powerful leaders with servant hearts.

Jesus was the ultimate servant leader who, "made himself nothing, taking the very nature of a servant (v. 5) … he humbled himself and became obedient to death (v. 8) … Therefore God exalted him (v. 9) …" (Philippians 2:5, 8-9). Jesus led from a heart filled with love and compassion rather than power and control. One of the terms that Jesus used in the Beatitudes is the word "meekness." The concept of meekness does not indicate weakness, but rather submitted strength. It is best illustrated by the Arabian horse.

The Arabian is neither the largest nor necessarily the strongest horse, but its strength is derived from its total obedience to its rider. It is this strength derived from obedience that enabled Jesus to humble Himself and become obedient to His Father. Out of this comes the power of the cross and the redemption of all the universe (Colossians 1:20).

When I consider the servant leaders that Jesus referred to as His disciples, may I suggest that Jesus was shepherding stallions. Although Jesus spoke a lot about shepherds and sheepfolds, the twelve He handpicked looked more like stallions than sheep. They did not blend into flocks; they led herds of horses. They were entrusted with planting churches, raising up leaders, writing much of our New Testament, establishing the presence of the Holy Spirit in the church, "going into all the world." They would reshape history with their boldness—teaching, casting out demons, performing signs and wonders, etc.

The disciples accomplished everything the Master had mentored them to carry on once He left. Yet near the end of their time together, Jesus prophetically modeled a servant taking a towel to wash their feet. What a contrast—servants yet stallions.

Stallion Christians are history shapers, destiny seekers, and world changers. They are reproducers. They do not accept things the way they are, no matter how long they have been that way. They are not weak or wimpy. Neither are they arrogant or proud.

They do not think like sheep. They do not do well on boards or committees that put stamps of approval on established ideas and processes. They do not want to just support an idea or just fund an idea. They want to be involved in the process. In fact, they have ideas of their own.

Listen to these words from Job describing the war horse found in Job 39:21-25:

> *He paws fiercely, rejoicing in his strength,*
> *and charges into the fray.*
> *He laughs at fear, afraid of nothing;*
> *he does not shy away from the sword.*
> *The quiver rattles against his side,*
> *along with the flashing spear and lance.*
> *In frenzied excitement he eats up the ground;*

he cannot stand still when the trumpet sounds.
At the blast of the trumpet he snorts, 'Aha!'
He catches the scent of battle from afar,
the shout of commanders and the battle cry.

A properly trained stallion has awesome power submitted to the control of his or her rider—power under submission, power that is properly harnessed. In the rodeo ring, with all the noise, smell, and distractions, the rider's health and safety depend on being able to focus the stallion on the rider's voice, the slightest movement of the knee, light pressure on the reins. So too, must the Holy Spirit harness the stallion leader who is required to be intimately acquainted with His voice.

Resurrecting cities requires stallion Christians who have an apostolic call and gifting married to a servant heart and spirit. They cannot be renegade stallions. They must carry a servant spirit and be willing to mutually submit. That might be the reason Jesus sent the disciples out two by two, and Paul always took a partner.

Leading in Buffalo requires a servant war horse mentality, much as Job described. Because of decades of downturn, our godly leaders are following the words the Lord gave to the prophet Jeremiah: *Then the Lord reached out his hand and touched my mouth and said to me, "Now I have put my words in your mouth. See, today I appoint you over nations and kingdoms to uproot and tear down, to destroy and overthrow, to build and to plant." (Jeremiah 1:9-10)*

The role of God-given leadership during certain seasons is primarily a "negative" rather than a "positive" one. All of us want to build and plant, but what if God recognizes that my city for now needs godly leaders to focus on uprooting, tearing down, destroying, overthrowing. Have you ever done demolition? It's hot, dirty, sweaty work that makes a mess. It's much harder to remodel than to build new. Nothing level or plumb. You have to make up for the last guy's mistakes. Welcome to my city! These same principles may apply to your city and your situation. Embrace the day! The testimonies that follow from the faith-based team are more than good stuff. They are tools for spiritual warfare. "They triumphed over him (the devil) by the blood of the Lamb and by the word of their testimony" (Revelation 12:11a). Enjoy these triumphant testimonies!

Chapter 23

THE SON RISES OVER BUFFALO

Al Warner

There is power in a story—power to encourage, power to amaze, power to challenge. Our most memorable stories follow the pattern of God's first story with humanity—creation, fall, redemption, and living out the destiny of God in the person's life. As the authors, our prayer is that the following pages will come alive for you with the power of the story of men and women who are on an incredible journey with God to resurrect and rebuild Buffalo.

Realize these stories are not meant to be isolated models. Rather, as is the case with the creative efforts of any master weaver, the beauty of the finished tapestry is realized in the joining together of diverse colors and patterns.

Therefore, these stories are meant to do more than entertain, more than convey facts and history, even more than inspire or exhort. These stories are meant to awaken your spirit to believe for greater things for you and those around you. Agree with God that these stories will lead you to the discovery of YOUR STORY. Let your soul listen as the dreamers speak of their dreams. Let your soul drink deeply as the Master Dreamer breathes His dream into you.

I. A DREAM TEAM

Anthony Nanula
Sundra Ryce
Nick Sinatra

Anthony Nanula[22]

Anthony's words of encouragement to fellow dreamers:

"RECOGNIZE THERE ARE TIMES WHEN GOD WANTS YOU TO
SPEED UP OR SLOW DOWN.
BE WILLING TO SLOW DOWN AND LISTEN."

For most of you readers who do not know Anthony, you cannot imagine how far "slow down and listen to God" was from the old Anthony's vocabulary. Imagine the story—a boy destined to dream, being birthed into a home with a Spirit-filled mother and a hard-working father who were both dreamers. So the journey began. Like many of us, Anthony did not recognize the Dream Giver for years, but long before Anthony was searching for God, God sought out Anthony and prepared him for his destiny.

Anthony Nanula's spiritual journey began with a praying and Holy Spirit-filled Catholic Charismatic mother. Eileen had a heart for hurting and disenfranchised people. She opened a little storefront space where she served what she called "good people who fell on hard times."

The Nanula family is best known in Buffalo as one of the owners of what was then Buffalo's largest chain of supermarkets, Tops Markets. Something connected this family with food: Dad built supermarkets while Mom fed the poor, eventually helping found a noteworthy mission for the Buffalo homeless, St. Luke's Mission of Mercy.

From this upbringing, Anthony went to college and upon graduating, returned to Buffalo with a vision. He saw Buffalo in history as the Queen City at the genesis of the Erie Canal, the major distribution center that catalyzed the growth of all of America. Goods were transported over the 500-mile length of the Canal to the docks of Buffalo and then distributed to the growing towns and cities throughout the Great Lakes. For decades Buffalo would be the Grain Storage Capital of America from which 90 percent of the grain that fed America moved through the Port of Buffalo. The young twenty-two-year-old Anthony looked back at what Buffalo had been and envisioned the re-creation of his city as a revived distribution center.

As with all dreams and dreamers, birthing the dream requires pieces of the puzzle to connect. Some call it luck, others call it fate, but we call it God's blessing. Coming home, the visionary dreamer Anthony had a chance encounter with Bob Rich, Jr. (Chairman of Rich Products, a multi-billion dollar food company based in Buffalo). Bob was forty-eight and Anthony was twenty-two. Bob Rich was building a large manufacturing plant and needed a third party to do distribution.

Anthony recalls, "I got this divine download in my bathtub. We could build a distribution center and transportation hub." Anthony found a developer, a property, and with the support of Bob Rich, he built what has turned into North America Center with one million square feet of occupied space on over 200 acres of developed lots. It was a fruitful project, and its success launched Anthony on his winning political career.

He first became our New York State Senator, then City Comptroller for Buffalo. During his tenure as comptroller, New York State experienced 9/11. The bottom fell out of Buffalo's finances, and Anthony was wrongly blamed for the crisis. Although eventually exonerated, the local newspaper viciously attacked him. It was at this point that our co-author, Al Warner, led him to a personal faith in Christ. Anthony encountered the Lord in a dramatic way. It was more than a crisis conversion—it was the beginning of a journey of discipleship with the man who led him to Christ. God taught Anthony to forgive those who attacked him and immediately the flood of God's mercy raced into his heart. Although the attacks did not immediately stop, Anthony's thoughts of revenge turned to feelings of forgiveness and healing.

Anthony is part of the faith-based team for the new Buffalo. But he is more than a dreamer—he is also a doer. Currently, he and his partners on our faith-based team are planning an extremely significant development on Buffalo's decaying East Side. This project is expected to be a detonator that could leverage hundreds of millions of dollars of new construction.

In describing his success in business and his approach to the rebuilding of his city, he uses three amazing words to express his philosophy of success: seeking, submitting, and yielding! Intriguing words for a doer, but these are foundational words for a God dreamer.

Sundra Ryce[23]

Sundra's words of encouragement to fellow dreamers:

"BE QUICK TO TAKE FULL ADVANTAGE OF ONCE IN A LIFETIME OPPORTUNITIES."

Sundra's words are impressive—her presence more so. For a woman of so few years she speaks with a wisdom and maturity far beyond what the calendar would indicate. But to know her story is to know that such qualities have been developing since before she was born. Indeed, she has always been "ahead of the curve." Yet, even for someone like her, perhaps especially for someone like her, ahead of the curve often leads closer to the edge of the unknown. For the dreamer looking at the Egyptian army behind and the Red Sea dead ahead, the paralyzing fear may be the nagging question, "Did God give me this dream?"

Sundra Ryce is an African-American woman brought up in a Pentecostal pastor's home. She had a prophetic word spoken over her life while still in her mother's womb. When she was three years of age, she came running to her parents with a paper written in her own handwriting even though she could not yet read or write. Her behavior confirmed to her parents the prophetic word that was given over her life—"She will go to the world."

Sundra confirms that from the time she was a very little girl God spoke to her and she grew up hearing God's voice. She came to know that her identity was connected to God. Sundra credits her parents with preparing her to dream bigger than Buffalo as they raised her as a "Global Citizen." Since her father was both a pastor and a businessman, she chose to join her dad in his plumbing and construction business as a teenager. Upon graduation, her parents gave her a seed gift of $10,000. Sundra recalls, "My dad told me, 'You are a leader. You need to start your own business.'" She used this money to fund the startup of SLR Contracting & Service Company, Inc. (SLR), her own construction firm at age twenty-two. Sundra had a vision to build and lead a multi-million dollar construction and development company for God.

By 2001, SLR was on the road to becoming the business that Sundra had dreamed. Unexpectedly, a crisis came to Sundra and her company after 9/11. She reflects,

> *9/11 was a turbulent season for SLR. Due to 9/11, government contracting and spending was at a standstill. Our sales dropped 67 percent. The U.S. government—federal, state and local—was our largest client. My CPA warned that if I did not close the doors in six months, I would be bankrupt. SLR was my dream. I asked myself the question, 'Did God give me this dream?' The answer was yes, so I decided not to close the doors. I knew I needed to rebuild my company and hold fast to my dream after the devastating hit, and I did. Remarkably, a year later, the same CPA declared to me, "I believe you have a billion-dollar company. I want to leave the CPA firm and work for you."*

Today, Sundra is known across the world for her success. She is President and CEO of SLR Contracting & Service Company, one of the largest general construction firms in America owned by an African-American woman. Under her leadership, SLR has completed over one-third of a billion dollars in construction, including $80 million in K-12 and university-level projects. Sundra states, "Our mission is to be 'Best in Class' and deliver value to our clients and the communities in which we live and work. That is the mission of my personal and professional life as well. That has always been my dream."

Recognitions include:

- Essence Magazine, "Rising Stars: Why She's One to Watch," (Nov., 2014).
- Ebony Magazine, "Dream Builder," a profile of Sundra (Dec., 2013 issue).
- Black Enterprise Magazine, "Rising Stars, 40 and Under" (2012). Also ranked SLR No. 87 of Nation's Top Largest Black Businesses (2011).
- ICIC and Inc. Magazine ranked SLR No. 6 of the Top 100 Fastest Growing Inner City Companies in America (2008).

Sundra is a member of a partnership that is targeting the East Side of Buffalo for development. The significant project is expected to leverage hundreds of millions of dollars of new construction on the East Side. She is one of the most impressive leaders we have ever met. This interview would be incomplete without letting her tell us about her philosophy of life and how she has made it through great difficulties.

> *I dealt with many challenges, including financial hardships, loss, self-acceptance and fear. One of my best leadership habits is to always make the choice to be powerful in the face of fear, challenge or obstacles. I am a servant leader and a dreamer at my core. My passion is to inspire other dreamers to achieve their highest success and actualize their dreams. My favorite motivational quote is "What would you attempt to do if you knew that you could not fail' (author unknown)."*

Nick Sinatra[24]

Nick's words of encouragement to fellow dreamers:

"IF YOU ARE NOT MAKING ANY MISTAKES, YOU ARE NOT TRYING HARD ENOUGH."

The setting was prophetic as we interviewed Nick in a building he had just acquired, an architectural treasure from Buffalo's glorious past. E. B. Green built the Market Arcade building in 1892. The building, much like the city around it, fell on hard times. But when old things die, sometimes God sends sons to breathe life into the dead, dry, disconnected bones. Remember Ezekiel and "dry bones, now hear the word of the Lord." 25 At his core, Nick at thirty-four years of age is a life-breather. Where others run away from urban blight, Nick runs toward opportunity. This visionary is contagious—he creates enthusiasm wherever he goes. Nick represents the next generation of world-class leaders in Buffalo.

Nick graduated from Yale University, Wharton School of Business, and worked in Governor George Pataki's economic development agency in Buffalo, The Empire State Development Agency. Following that, he became the Associate Political Director at the White House under President George W. Bush.

If there is a word that describes the success of Nick Sinatra, it is the word passion. Well, perhaps passion mixed with an abundance of hard work. He affirms, "I have a passion for Buffalo. I have traveled to over twenty nations and have found little passion for community, but in Buffalo I have found passion for the community." Nick's hard-working Italian family came to Buffalo in 1906 with a love for work and food. In 1981, the year Nick was born, his father opened their family's Italian restaurant.

These qualities made Nick decide to return to Buffalo from Washington D.C. in 2009 to found Sinatra & Company Real Estate, a real estate investment firm. He desired to return to his home city and to help re-build Buffalo. Today, Nick owns over one million square feet of commercial space and over 1,000 housing units, making him one of the leading owners of real estate in Buffalo. With backing from Colony Capital and the Pritzker/Vlock family office, he has invested over sixty million dollars in Western New York.

To expand, Nick partnered with a group of real estate developers in Southern California to form American Coastal Properties to reposition and redevelop residential real estate in that market. CNBC News produced a news story about the growth and impact of his Southern California venture. Nick now oversees over $150M in commercial and residential real estate assets.

These are impressive statistics! But a story illustrates the journey Nick is on. My wife and I are chaplains to Nick's companies. He asked us to pray for an out-of-state meeting with several key financiers. We prayed together. The afternoon of Nick's flight, he called from the Buffalo Airport runway to say his flight was delayed and he would be arriving in New York City late which would put him into rush hour traffic. He would be late for his key meeting. He was nervous as to how businessmen he had never met would perceive this. We prayed and put the whole matter into God's hands. Nick did indeed arrive late, but his financier friend who had called the meeting with his colleagues had already sown up the deal. Nick said if he had been there on time he could not have done any more than was done. Nick saw evidence of the supernatural God fighting battles on his behalf. Let this story sink deep into your spirit.

Nick has little interest in pursuing business as usual. He constantly seeks to raise the bar both for himself and others. One example was so newsworthy that the Buffalo News, our local newspaper, penned,

> *Developers pledge 10 percent of profits from luxury apartments to Say Yes: The unique partnership represents a novel form of community charity that capitalizes on the surge in redevelopment activity in downtown Buffalo. "We're making big bets on Buffalo. You also have to make big bets on the children in Buffalo, because you can't have a successful city without a successful school system," Sinatra said.*

> *...In turn, the partners have now agreed, in writing, to contribute 10 percent of their monthly profits to Say Yes Buffalo, the educational initiative that pays to send Buffalo high school students for a college education. ...And both Lewis and Sinatra hope that will provide a model for other developers and business leaders to follow as well.26*

Nick's philosophy of business is expressed in these significant words, "There are 100 ways to invest capital, but two things guide my investments:

1) What keeps me grounded is looking at the long term. I am building a company AND rebuilding a community.

2) I have to give back to the city and community that has given me so much."

He adds, "As long as you are going to dream, DREAM BIG," and he has. This member of the team believes that their Buffalo initiative, a $35-40 million detonator project, is a catalyst for the rebuilding of Buffalo's East side. In spite of contrary voices from his friends in other cities, Nick chose to come back to Buffalo and is using his success to rebuild our city.

II. TOUCHING THE HEART OF GOD
FOR A CITY

Buffalo has been a city of immigrants for generations. Buffalo is a prime example of a community that succeeded because of the Industrial Revolution. At the first part of the 20th century, Buffalo exploded with growth as thousands upon thousands of immigrants came from Poland, Ireland, Germany and Italy to work the huge factories. There were little cities within the big city where each of these people groups from Europe established their own individual expressions of the American dream. In addition, significant numbers of African Americans moved from the South to Buffalo.

Today, much of that has changed—Buffalo has become a city of refuge with people coming from diverse cultures and ethnic backgrounds well beyond Europe. These include the new refugee communities from Southeast Asia, Central Africa, and the Middle East. Jesus command for us to go into all the world may be followed simply by crossing the street in a downtown neighborhood. Too many of these contemporary Buffalo refugees have fled political and ethnic persecution in their former countries. Many of them speak little if any English. What would Jesus do? You are about to encounter a handful of the countless leaders who are bringing God-breathed creative solutions to the specific needs of these people groups.

EMPLOYING THE NEW COMMUNTY OF REFUGEES:
A PASSION FOR LARRY SZRAMA[27]

Larry's words of encouragement to fellow dreamers:

"WHATEVER YOU BIRTH FROM THE FLESH, YOU MUST SUSTAIN BY THE FLESH; WHATEVER YOU BIRTH BY THE SPIRIT IS SUSTAINED BY THE SPIRIT OF GOD. WHEN THE SPIRIT BIRTHS IT, IT IS NOT UP TO ME, SO MY STRESS IS LOWERED."

Willy Wonka. You know who I mean—that crazy magical genius who loves making candy. May I introduce Buffalo's Willy Wonka, Larry Szrama. Although the chocolate Larry makes is sweet, several chapters of his life could have produced toxic bitterness. Larry endured seasons where God's dream lived more like a nightmare. However, because Larry refused to quit dreaming, the chocolate river is flowing and the day of harvest is here.

Larry Szrama comes from a very successful family who began their family business when Larry's grandfather established Szrama's Deli in what was the Polish section of Buffalo. The family philosophy was expressed by Grandpa who said that if you did not have money, you still got your food at Szrama's. Later, the family owned three Bells supermarkets.

Larry enjoyed making chocolates. When he was twenty-five, he founded his own candy company, Landies Candies, which initially grew, but then flat lined for fifteen years.

Larry admits, "Things took longer than expected, but deeper roots take time to grow. I did not quit; I kept tithing and sowing even when it was difficult." A committed believer, Larry came to Christ in the 1988 Billy Graham Buffalo Crusade. He was discipled at the Bread of Life Church by his pastors, Dominic and Lucia Schipani.

So, why was the business flat lining? As Larry grew in his faith, the counsel of godly friends, biblically-based sermons, books on leadership principles, combined with a word from the Lord revealed to Larry multiple business relationships that were wrongly aligned. Larry repented, and things began to turn around. God gave Larry literal dreams during the night hours of new chocolate products, including a unique type of chocolate pretzel. Today, partially because of QVC's shopping network, Landies Candies is one of the fastest growing candy companies in America. In fact, from June-December 2014, Larry sold 1.4 million made-in-Buffalo pretzels to QVC customers. Imagine the divine acceleration of a product moving from the dream stage to 1.4 million pretzels sold in a few months!

Larry Szrama walks out his faith by almost exclusively hiring unemployed refugees to man his candy factory. When you walk through Landies Candies, you encounter the world—Africa, Asia, the Middle East and more. Although most of the employees speak little English, they are learning rapidly to communicate and they have proven to be one of the major assets of this growing company.

Again, the dreamers in Buffalo are serving the diverse people groups among us in our city. Everyone is important to the new Buffalo faith-based team.

The Medical Needs of a Refugee Community

Dr. Myron Glick[28]

All doctors take the well-known Hippocratic Oath—"Do no harm." But Dr. Myron Glick reports to a Higher Authority. Jesus taught, "'I was sick and you looked after me… When did we see you sick or in prison and go to visit you?' The King will reply, 'Truly I tell you, whatever you did for one of the least of these brothers and sisters of mine, you did for me'" (Matthew 25:36b, 39-40). Myron feels called to the last, the least, the lost. As a doctor, Myron looks after his patient's bodies. As a Christian, he prays with patients, touching their souls and spirits.

What do you do with a large building that formerly housed the NBC affiliated television station and the local PBS television station? Dr. Myron Glick had an answer. He bought the building and established the largest (40,000 patient visits per year) and most successful medical clinic in Buffalo, dedicated to serving the most vulnerable and poor, including refugees. As Dr. Glick writes, "Our mission is to provide a culturally sensitive medical home, especially for refugee and low-income community members, facilitating wellness and self-sufficiency by addressing health, education, economic and spiritual barriers in order to demonstrate Jesus' unconditional love for the whole person." Dr. Glick is truly being the hands and feet of Jesus on the West Side of Buffalo where a majority of the Hispanic population and most of the refugee population lives.

SERVING THOSE WHO COULD BE DISPLACED
BY CITY TRANSFORMATION

Rev. Michael Chapman[29]

Pastor Chapman's words of encouragement to fellow dreamers:

"NEVER STOP DREAMING.
THERE WILL BE OBSTACLES.
ALL THINGS WORK TOGETHER FOR GOOD."

Still waters run deep, so the saying goes. Rev. Michael Chapman is quiet and reserved on the outside, but a deep river of creativity and entrepreneurship is constantly flowing from deep within. He is an introvert, yet leaders come to his office to seek his wisdom. He enjoys the monastic life but is often drawn into the whirlwind of church activity. He shies away from the limelight, yet the current Mayor of Buffalo is part of his church. Dreamers come in all flavors.

Rev. Michael Chapman wears many hats in our city. Although a pastor of one of Buffalo's largest African-American churches, St. John Baptist Church, Pastor Chapman is at the same time one of the city's most successful business entrepreneurs. Heading fourteen not-for-profit and for profit corporations, this talented man and his church literally began the rebuilding process of Buffalo as the neighborhoods around them began to decay. In 1977, St. John bought land and built McCarley Gardens (150 units), one of the most successful housing complexes in Buffalo. With the Gardens doing well, they built St. John Tower (150 units), a major housing development for Senior Citizens. Michael Chapman followed the example of his predecessors, Rev. Burnie McCarley and Rev. Dr. Bennett Smith and built a Charter School, a successful Hospice Facility, a Life Center, a Child Care Center, plus other projects. St. John Baptist Church has completed $40 million of construction projects with another $70-80 million in the planning stages.

Matt Enstice who heads the Buffalo Niagara Medical Campus (more on Matt to follow) recalls that Pastor Chapman helped to teach him about the neighborhoods that surround the Medical Campus. As the Medical Campus was growing and expanding, Matt Enstice called on his friend Pastor Chapman to bring people of the community together to talk and develop lines of communication. Too often when cities turn around and rebuild, the existing population that has typically endured the downturn for years is displaced. Matt and Pastor Chapman did not want to see that happen.

Many of the younger generation had already moved elsewhere, but there were a substantial number of aging homeowners who were living with the growing Medical Campus on one side and the deteriorating and neglected neighborhood on the other. These community residents could be displaced from their lifetime homes. In addition, most of the needed community services had moved, and there was no quality market even to buy their groceries. Who would advocate for them?

As St. John Baptist Church had done in the '70s, Michael Chapman and his congregation responded immediately and have at this writing already built seventy-seven townhomes, five single-family homes, and a site has been approved by the city for a much-needed supermarket. In the process, the present homeowners are not being displaced but will continue to live where most of them were born and grew up. To pastors of inner city communities, Pastor Chapman proposes, "It is your role to prevent gentrification from taking place."

This outside-the-box thinking reflects Pastor Chapman's view of creation theology. He believes, "Humanity creates and in this way shares the image of God. Because of Him, we can create and have creative thought." Pastor Chapman closed our time together just as he had opened it, giving God all the glory. "The only way this faith-based initiative and social justice model could have transpired is because God has been with the current as well as the previous pastors."

III. ENTREPRENEURIAL DEVELOPMENT

Looking back, Buffalo was truly a birthplace of entrepreneurial dreamers, including:

- The first successful skin graft
- 13th President—Millard Fillmore; 22nd and 24th President—Grover Cleveland
- American Express
- The father of punch cards, H. Hollerith and machine data processing
- Mark Twain and the great American novel
- The nation's first Day Care program
- The world's first movie theatre
- Martha Matilda Harper, the mother of business franchising
- The first large scale hydroelectric power plant, the city of lights
- Louise Blanchard Bethune, the nation's first female architect
- Fisher-Price toys
- Air conditioning
- Bell Aircraft, the first plane to break the sound barrier
- The fingerprint scanner
- The implantable pacemaker and inventor Wilson Greatbatch

Buffalo also becomes a flavor enjoyed around the world because of Buffalo wings! [30]

What a great walk down memory lane. However, what lies ahead for such a historically entrepreneurial city?

Glenn Thomas[31]

Glenn's words of encouragement to fellow dreamers:

"LET THE LORD BE THE LORD OF THE DREAM;
MAKE SURE IT IS NOT YOUR DREAM BUT HIS;
FAILURE IS NOT THE END, BUT A STEP ON THE WAY."

Pause to re-read Glenn's quote: "Failure is not the end." At age fifty-seven, Glenn's story is powerful as you are about to read: success, recognition, reward; as Shakespeare wrote, the world is his oyster. Yet behind Glenn's "overnight" success is a lifetime of preparation along with a mixture of failure and success. Glenn's journey demonstrates that God's way up is often down. In God's eyes, failure never disqualifies the dreamer nor cancels the dream. Perhaps this is the story that will breathe life into your dusty and dormant dream. Wake Up!

Buffalo is raising up a whole new group of creative people who are changing our world with their innovation. On Oct. 30, 2014, 43 North, the world's largest business idea competition, was held in Buffalo. One of these creative people, Glenn Thomas, a leader in his Buffalo church, won the one million dollar grand prize. There were 7,000 applicant inventors from ninety-six countries and all fifty states, yet an inventor from Buffalo captured first place.

Glenn is a remarkable man. By education, he is an engineer. We think of engineers as left-brained people who are prone to rationalize everything. Not so with Glenn. He is an engineer who dreams and creates new things. Yet on the road to success lay potholes of failure. After he was betrayed in one of his business ventures, he repented. After another company seemed to fail, the Lord corrected Glenn. After his wife Pam died in early 2014, Glenn grieved and then pushed on. Pursuing the dream was more costly than he imagined.

This award going to a man from Buffalo proves that Buffalo is once again producing dreamers. It is no wonder, given the breath-taking majesty of Niagara Falls, the magnificent Lake Erie that looks like the ocean but is in reality one of the largest lakes in the world, the magnificence of several Frank Lloyd Wright signature homes, and the beauty of the Pierce Arrow automobile, one of the most stunning automobiles ever built. This city still produces the dreamer and the creator.

Glenn's company, ASi, was given this prestigious award for a business plan based on revolutionary rapid metal forming technology. ASi's process impacts metals at very high velocity which softens the metals for only a fraction of a second, but long enough to enable the softened metal to be pressed into a shaped die to form the part. The speed and precision of the ASi process can reduce manufacturing costs by 25 percent or more while providing improved part quality and performance.

In 1997, Glenn started journaling in earnest. Leading up to the competition that took place in late October 2014, Glenn's journal included the details of what God was about to do in his life. One example:

20th July: In prayer, after the Lord gave me Proverbs 18:16 as encouragement ("A man's gift makes room for him, and brings him before great men" NKJV), He then gave me a direct prophetic word: "Before this year is out, your gift, Glenn, will bring you in contact with several great businessmen, and you will be blessed in relationships with them." …these words really helped increase my faith and keep working and persisting with the businesses.

Glenn's example certainly teaches others to dream again. Glenn quotes one of his mentors, Wilson Greatbatch (the inventor of the pacemaker): "Nine out of ten things I've tried didn't work out. Don't crave success; don't fear failure. Do your best. Make sure your work is a good thing in the sight of the Lord."

IV. FATHERS, FRIENDS, AND THE FUTURE

*"**WHERE THERE IS NO VISION, THE PEOPLE PERISH***" (**PROV. 29:18 KJV**).*

*"...**YOUR YOUNG MEN WILL SEE VISIONS; YOUR OLD MEN WILL DREAM DREAMS***" (**ACTS 2:17**).*

The preceding testimonies were meant to inspire the reader as well as provide some "thumbnails" to help discern the awakening of a God-move in any given region. Be awake, be alert, for there is a seismic shift that God is bringing to the cities of the nations, including your city.

In the following stories, we witness the impact of what God does as we pray, "Thy Kingdom come, thy will be done in earth [in my city], as it is in heaven" (Matthew 6:10 KJV). God produces a "new thing" beyond anything of which the earth is capable. Spirit-empowered momentum and acceleration are moving beyond earthly expectations.

As you meditate on these examples, see the subtle impression of the Seal of the KING on the men, the means, and the majestic outcomes.

Matt Enstice[32]

Matt's words of encouragement to fellow dreamers:

"IF YOU BELIEVE IN SOMETHING AND HAVE A PASSION, YOU CAN DO IT."

Did you hear the one about the guy from Saturday Night Live who came home to help rebuild Buffalo? Crazy as it sounds, that is not a punch line from a joke but the real-life story of Matt Enstice. Ecclesiastes reads, "a time to weep and a time to laugh..." (Eccl. 3:4a). Buffalo has endured a long night of weeping. Could it be that God's choice to bring our city out of weeping might be a leader who specialized in making others laugh? Isn't that just like God?

Matt Enstice is the only leader we interviewed who is related to one of the families that led Buffalo at the beginning of the 20th century, but make no mistake about it—Matt is new Buffalo to the core. Matt is the Executive Director, President and CEO of the flourishing Buffalo Niagara Medical Campus (BNMC).

The BNMC began in 2001 when a group of community leaders, elected officials, and the heads of the region's health care and medical education institutions came together to create a not for profit organization, the Buffalo Niagara Medical Campus. The BNMC facilitates collaboration and planning among these institutions. The BNMC is continuing its exponential growth with projections that by 2017 there will be 17,000 employees and an additional 4.5 million square feet of development on the campus. Cliff Benson (more on Cliff to follow) believes that "The Medical Campus is the most significant creator for the new Buffalo."

Matt was certainly the ideal choice to lead this massive development. His philosophy of leadership emphasizes collaboration, collective vision, and teamwork. He confirms, "The core of what I do is to unite institutions with a purpose. Work hard, work together and good things will happen." Matt was looking for a dream of his own.... but he became the driver of the dreams of other people. The Medical Campus is a dream of a collective group while being led by a unique and gifted visionary who has submitted his creative talents to a greater purpose.

Matt prioritizes honoring those who built the foundations of our city. He gives credit to former Buffalo Mayor Anthony Masiello who planted the seeds for the BNMC and played a key role in what is happening today. Given that Matt is in his early forties, he honors the gifted leaders who paved his way. His own BNMC board chair proudly points out, "I'm Matt's gray hair." He listens to the counsel and wise advice of those he respects. At the same time, Matt had to fight through the spirit of the "Old Buffalo" that repeatedly declared, "Good luck, it will never happen here." Matt exemplifies the miracle of a man who knew how to balance forces around him and make bold yet wise decisions.

As the former Production Coordinator for Saturday Night Live, Matt enjoys fun. Lest one think that this huge undertaking has stolen his sense of humor, one need only hear Matt proclaim that the BNMC is and will continue to be "A Playground of Innovation." He believes that on a playground boundaries are pushed and established rules are challenged—what was impossible becomes possible!

Matt's story is a still unfolding adventure of a visionary who is building one of the leading and most innovative dreams in the world today. This may not be your dream or call, but Matt has thoughts for you.

- Small wins are important. They build momentum. Celebrate small victories.
- Don't overpromise anything. False promises leave many hurt.
- In your city, work to establish mutual benefits for all and develop a mutual city in which everyone wins.

Cliff Benson[33]

Cliff's words of encouragement to fellow dreamers:

"DREAM BIG, WORK HARD.
UNDERSTAND YOU WILL HAVE SETBACKS."

Buffalo, NY, wishes to publicly express our gratitude to Bob Buford of Dallas and Reid Carpenter of Pittsburgh in light of the following testimony. Cliff Benson had his "Aha! Moment" as he read Bob's book Halftime. The result: Cliff shared the book with Terry Pegula leading to nearly $2 billion dollars being invested in Western New York. Reid talked Cliff out of going to seminary and becoming a pastor where he might have touched hundreds or at the most thousands. Instead, Cliff stayed in the marketplace and used his gifts to help transform a city and touch millions. Bloom where you're planted!

Cliff Benson is an example of a "servant leader." He is a true friend to two people who are best known as the owners of the Buffalo Bills and the Buffalo Sabres—Terry and Kim Pegula. Cliff serves as the Chief Development Officer of the Buffalo Sabres and President of the Sabres Foundation. The Sabres Foundation focuses on underprivileged inner-city children, the handicapped, and veterans as three of its main emphases. No job title can fully describe Cliff's role in rebuilding our city and restoring hope to its citizens.

Cliff is a CPA and an attorney who retired after 37 years with Deloitte (Pittsburgh). His life and perspective dramatically changed after he read the well-known book, "Halftime: Moving from Success to Significance" by Bob Buford. The theme of the book is that the first half of a Christian leader's life is invested in building success so the second half, the best half, can be enjoyed and devoted to significance. Cliff immediately knew God was speaking to him, but did not know what he should do. Perhaps, he thought, he should go to seminary and become a clergyman. But his friend Reid Carpenter, founder of the Pittsburgh Leadership Foundation, challenged him, "You are where you are supposed to be... you can walk into CEO's offices where I cannot." Realizing his new significant role, he became involved in Imani Christian Academy, an inner city Pittsburgh school, and at the same time started a hockey program associated with the NHL for inner-city kids, "Hockey in the Hood."

Later, Cliff began to develop what has become a close friendship with Terry and Kim Pegula. Cliff Benson says of his friend, Terry, "Terry is a devout Christian driven by faith and an entrepreneurial spirit." Cliff challenged Terry, a billionaire, to read "Halftime." Both men embraced the godly road to significance. Cliff helped Terry sell a significant portion of his business assets to turn the success of both of their lives into world changing significant actions. Their first project was to build the Pegula Ice Arena at Penn State. In 2011 Terry decided he wanted to purchase the Buffalo Sabres ice hockey team. Cliff asked "Why?" Terry told him that the Sabres were his favorite team for twenty-five years.

But, it had to be about more than just owning a sports team. The question they asked each other was, "Do you want to make a difference in Buffalo or not?" The man who became the owner of the Sabres said, "If we only win the Stanley Cup, we failed God's bigger plan for us in Buffalo. We need to be significant in helping rebuild this city." At this writing they have not yet won the Stanley Cup, but they are truly making a difference in Buffalo.

Terry's wife Kim completes the team that God has positioned for significance. Kim grew up in Western New York and her vision and energy for the renewal of Buffalo have been a critical part of the Pegula's ongoing efforts. Her attitude toward servant leadership was modeled before the 6:00 a.m. opening of the new Tim Hortons Café (similar to Dunkin' Donuts) at HarborCenter. There was a long line of customers waiting to initiate the new restaurant. In the cool dark of the morning, Kim in her Sabres jersey was serving steaming hot chocolate to the crowd. What a picture—the co-owner of the team serving hot chocolate. But do not underestimate the God creativity in Kim. Her gifts and talents are reflected in the beauty and excellence of countless facets of the HarborCenter complex.

Terry, Kim, and Cliff are walking out the dream of Jesus when He taught us to pray, "Thy Kingdom come, Thy will be done, on earth as it is in heaven." They are bringing this prayer of Jesus to this community; they have turned success into significance and are bringing great joy to our city. Since 2011, the Pegulas' total investment in Western New York is nearly $2 billion dollars. Glancing back, it is interesting to note that Terry's father drove a coal truck in Carbondale, Pennsylvania, never owned a home, and made an hourly wage of $3.00 an hour.

The biblical passage that has most impacted Cliff since he came to Buffalo and sums up why he is here: "Seek the peace and prosperity of the city to which I have carried you into exile. Pray to the Lord for it because if it prospers, you too, will prosper" (Jeremiah 29:7).

Rev. Darius Pridgen[34]

Darius's words of encouragement to fellow dreamers:

"NEVER STOP DREAMING AS LONG AS YOU WAKE UP IN THE MORNING."

This is such a powerful quote. Pause, take your pulse. Now, if you are still breathing, keep dreaming! Bishop T. D. Jakes preaches that we should beware of dream-killers. You know the type. In fact, a face may pop into your mind of a dream-killer who has crossed your path. For the young Darius Pridgen who had a pastor say "No" to his dream, that could have been the death of his vision. Instead, God allowed a pastor to say "No" so God could speak and young Darius could say "Yes" to serve God rather than man. As with Joseph in the Old Testament, what the dream killers meant for evil, God turned upside down for Kingdom good.

How did Darius' journey to leadership begin? When he was a young man, the violence on the African-American East Side of Buffalo started to escalate. Darius went to a pastor suggesting an anti-violence meeting. That pastor said, "No. I do not want the gangs to come and break the windows." The church was burying kids killed during the violence but wanted no part in the potentially messy solution. In hindsight, Darius believes this was the best "No" possible because it forced him into the community to take a stand and make a difference. This became his call to the city.

Eventually Darius became pastor of a small church, True Bethel, which he described as very parochial. With a job offer at the Sheriff's Department of Broward County Florida in his hand, he stood to announce his resignation and move south, but as he looked at the faces of his church family, he said to himself, "I cannot leave you." Today he pastors the largest predominantly African-American church in Buffalo with three campuses and is the President of the Common Council, the city's chief legislative body. Perhaps most importantly, he lives a life that is centered on pastoring not just the congregants of True Bethel but the entire community. He preaches the funerals of one-third of the homicide victims of violence, mostly youth.

Forty to fifty young people come to the altar at every funeral. However, burying this many kids has taken a toll on Darius which is etched on his face. Darius recounted the time when he came into the sanctuary to perform a funeral, but rather than dressing in his usual clerical robes, he dressed in jeans and sneakers and sat down to have a heart-to-heart with parents who have children engaged in gang warfare.

Darius is a risk taker. In 2010, he spearheaded an anti-violence campaign, Enough is Enough, during which thirty-six churches worked together to end violence, especially focusing on inner-city neighborhoods. October 2011, marked the one-year anniversary, at which time the city celebrated a 38 percent drop in homicides during the twelve months. As Darius reflected, "[Witnesses] are starting to come forward, because one thing that people are starting to realize is...if we protect each other as a community...that these thugs and the people wanting to commit crimes...they become the minority and the law abiding citizens become the majority."

Darius' family has caught the generational call "to act justly and to love mercy and to walk humbly with your God" (Micah 6:8b). The authors sat in a crowded courtroom as JaHarr Pridgen, daughter-in-law of Rev. Darius Pridgen was being sworn in as a City Court judge. Most of the sitting judges of our region filled the front part of the courtroom joined by the Mayor of Buffalo, other political leaders of our city, and the leading clergy in Western New York. Every inch of space was jammed with the movers and shakers of the City of Buffalo. The attractive former Assistant District Attorney who was about to become a judge commanded the attention of the room. Every speaker who addressed the body of leaders told of JaHarr's skills and talents. Frank Sedita, Erie County District Attorney, for whom she had worked for a decade spoke of her brilliance, her wisdom and her ability to be fair and caring. It was obvious that this was not just political rhetoric, but accolades to a woman who was highly respected by those who supervised her.

We watched the Pridgen family including proud father-in-law Darius present in the courtroom. We watched the gathering of the leaders of Buffalo and thought, Buffalo has a "Royal Family." Beloved by all sides of the political spectrum, this family is God's gift to our city.

Darius epitomizes the servant leader. Concerning his leadership style, he reveals, "I am not afraid of not getting my own way.... I read the Bible before I read the newspaper and pray, 'Put me where You want me today, say what You want me to say today'.... Start out with the Bible and when you watch the news you will have your mind on the Kingdom."

Discussing a leader's desire for power, he adds, "Ego comes with a perception of power. Although my contract as pastor is only for a single year at a time, I live with no fear about not being re-elected in my church. I am a better servant than a leader. Ego is so dangerous. I always carry my own briefcase."

> *My life was changed forever during a trip to Jamaica. The Jamaican kids hung around the McDonald's near my hotel, but they could not go in because they did not have shoes. I rented the children's section and brought the kids in. This incident changed my life. I came back home and got rid of my luxury car, my jewelry and bought a used Volkswagen Beetle. The Lord showed me how spoiled rotten I could be. When I am with people, I always carry a camera in my hand so I can make others my focus. I see greatness in being the least. I sit in the back at conventions. But I never stop dreaming!*

Needless to say, Darius Pridgen is the living demonstration of true Kingdom greatness. As Jesus portrayed, "Whoever wants to become great among you must be your servant..." (Matthew 20:26). We believe that in Buffalo, he is a man who is considered by both other leaders and the masses to be among the most remarkable leaders in our recent history.

Darius brings two worlds together—the rich and powerful alongside the down-and-out. He is as much at home in a room weeping with a mother who was just evicted from her home as with a multi-millionaire who seeks his wise counsel. As Darius sums it up, "I am called to be a voice to those who feel they are voiceless."

Section 4

THE KINGDOMS OF THIS WORLD SHALL BECOME THE KINGDOMS OF OUR GOD

Hallelujah! Hallelujah! Hallelujah! Hallelujah! Hallelujah!

For the Lord God Omnipotent reigneth.
Hallelujah! Hallelujah! Hallelujah! Hallelujah!

For the Lord God omnipotent reigneth.
Hallelujah! Hallelujah! Hallelujah! Hallelujah! Hallelujah!
Hallelujah! Hallelujah!

The kingdom of this world
Is become the kingdom of our Lord,
And of His Christ, and of His Christ;
And He shall reign for ever and ever,
For ever and ever, forever and ever,

King of kings, and Lord of lords,
King of kings, and Lord of lords,
And Lord of lords,
And He shall reign,
And He shall reign forever and ever,
King of kings, forever and ever,
And Lord of lords,
Hallelujah! Hallelujah!

And He shall reign forever and ever,
King of kings! and Lord of lords!
And He shall reign forever and ever,
King of kings! and Lord of lords!
Hallelujah! Hallelujah! Hallelujah! Hallelujah! Hallelujah!

-Hallelujah Chorus, Handel's Messiah

CHAPTER 24

HOW GOOD AND PLEASANT IT IS...

"AND THEY WERE WITH ONE ACCORD AND ONE PLACE, AND SUDDENLY...."

Would it surprise you to know that there is no shortage of people willing to take credit for the turnaround in Buffalo? Politicians, business leaders, educators, get in line! I am sometimes asked what I consider to be the key. I am certain there are hundreds of keys but as Bishop Reid and other spiritual leaders in our city stipulate, we must build an "Upper Room of prayer" before we have the strength of God and the wisdom of God to accomplish the herculean task of recreating a city.

We believe that this Upper Room of prayer and of Holy Spirit visitation is a part of the eventual rebuilding of our city. The correlation between the two cannot be separated. This entire manuscript will climax with a call to build an Upper Room of prayer that will catalyze a rebuilding of our cities, our culture and our nation.

Tommy Reid picks up his pen and tells the story....

In this amazing story we could mention so many spiritual Upper Rooms that have been the catalyst for the recreating of our city, however, I will only mention a few. The Buffalo area has literally "hosted" the Presence of God during the past few years.

It is my belief that you do not have the power or creativity to change a city, change a nation, or change the world without the power of the Holy Spirit. So let me first define what I mean by building an "Upper Room."

The biblical "Upper Room" is far more than a location where people pray. Jesus really defined that place when he told His disciples that they must go to a place where they would meet the Holy Spirit and be filled with His person and His gifts. We must remember that this was far more than a room where they would receive an experience that, so often, we simply regard as a liturgical encounter. Jesus defines it as being an encounter between those who had chosen Him and the person of the Holy Spirit. Remember, Jesus had prepared them for a dramatic time when He would leave them and return to His Father.

Jesus describes the reason for sending them to this "Upper Room" in that they would meet the "person" of the Holy Spirit who would take His place in their lives and in the world. Jesus further describes the encounter that they would have with the Holy Spirit. He said that the person of the Holy Spirit they would meet in this "Upper Room" would literally replace Him as a friend and a Counselor. He also told them that when they met this person that they would receive the "power" of the Holy Spirit, and with this power they would change the world. He indicated to them the God who had traveled with the children of Israel and who had dwelt in a little box called the Ark of the Covenant would actually invade their lives and dwell in them.

So, we define the Upper Room as Jesus said it would be. It is a place of meeting with God. Secondly, it is a place of His Presence.

THE "UPPER ROOM" IS A PLACE WHERE MAN ENCOUNTERS THE ACTUAL PRESENCE OF GOD IN THE PERSON OF THE HOLY SPIRIT.

In describing the future of the church, Jesus told them that when they gathered together "In My Name, I will be in your midst." The Upper Room is a place of "Presence." It is also a place of empowering. The very power that made the sun to stand still, the Red Sea to roll back, and even the dead to be raised would be in this place we call the "Upper Room."

Probably, most important of all, it would be a place where for the third time in the history of the universe, God would come to dwell "IN" a human being. Remember, He breathed His life into Adam in the Garden of Eden. He encountered Mary and "incarnated" Himself into a human being in the person of Christ. Now for the third time in the history of the universe, God would come and take His abode inside of a person.

Therefore, when we describe the term "Upper Room," I want you to see it is not just a place where people pray or go through the liturgy of church. This is a place where people meet God in intimacy and friendship

What follows is a brief listing of places where God has met with people in our city. This is not an exhaustive list. There are thousands of other places, but it describes some of the most important places where people in our city have encountered God.

In that dimension, let me tell you how I see the wonder of God coming to Buffalo and Western New York.

The Visit of Billy Sunday to Buffalo: This story would not be complete without noting the amazing Billy Sunday Crusade of another century that sparked the creation of the City Mission which is, to this day, the main mission to the homeless of Buffalo.

The Charismatic Renewal of the Late 1960s and 1970s: We cannot forget the monumental move of the Holy Spirit during the Charismatic Renewal in the Roman Catholic Church in which over 100,000 received what contemporary Bible scholars refer to as the "Baptism of the Holy Spirit." The years of 1972 and 1973 are significant in this renewal.

The Chapel: In 1962, a young preacher by the name of James Andrews pioneered one of the first mega-churches in the northeastern United States known today as The Chapel. A pioneer in the field of media, this church today is pastored by his successor, the Rev. Jerry Gillis. Under Pastor Jerry's leadership, The Chapel has had significant growth, and today has over 6,000 in attendance every Sunday.

I remember my first personal time with Jerry. I drove up to the huge complex of buildings known as The Chapel. Jerry came out of his office, and we drove to a restaurant. I remember saying to him, "Jerry, I believe the amazing growth of The Chapel is the result of how you understand the church." After asking him how he saw the church and his personal role in the church, he told me that when he came to Buffalo, he believed God had called him to pastor a geographic area in the city, not just a local church.

He described that geographic area as a five-mile radius from the physical campus of The Chapel. He told me that he was to partner with 110 churches in this area that preached the Gospel of Jesus Christ.

The story of how Jerry has been a steward of that vision and his calling to our city is what I term the story of a contemporary apostolic visionary who has truly not only impacted the thousands who fill his church every Sunday, but has impacted thousands in the lives of pastors and churches throughout our city.

My Senior Associate, Jon Hasselbeck joined our staff with a vision to open a church in the northern part of Buffalo that would serve the thousands of college students in that part of the city. Jon believed that his church would be planted not just by his home church, but by the "Church at Buffalo." He explained his vision to Pastor Jerry.

Within a few weeks, Pastor Jerry met with both of us and offered to become our partner. Shortly after this meeting, the amazing pastor of The Chapel met Jon and placed in his hand a large check. After receiving the check, Jerry and I met in my office, and I asked him if our church constitution agreed with his doctrinal position. He seemed not to be interested in our constitution as he looked at me and said, "Tommy, aren't you and I planting a Pentecostal church together?" I looked at the younger man, and as a man old enough to be his father, I thought, "I have truly met a man of God." Jerry Gillis and The Chapel are a manifestation of the church of the future, a true Upper Room of our city.

The Church I Served as Lead Pastor for over Fifty Years: The year that Dr. Andrews was pioneering The Chapel, I was still in Korea working with Dr. Cho in the establishment of Full Gospel Central Church. Although the ministry in Korea was the most successful I had ever experienced, my heart was burning with a passion for Buffalo. The Lord continued to make it very clear to me that His assignment for me was the city of Buffalo and not Korea. When Dr. Cho asked me to be a co-pastor of the emerging church, I knew that I must return to Buffalo.

I came back to Buffalo in 1963 and joined this amazing team of spiritual leaders that God would use to touch the city of Buffalo. In the next few years, the Holy Spirit would create a 'mega church' with ten branch campus locations.

Teen Challenge of Buffalo: One year, a young man attended a missionary convention in our church and gave two homes in Buffalo for the purpose of reaching the world for Jesus. He told us that we could sell them and use the money to preach the Gospel in any part of the world. We gave that home to a group of Jesus people in our church who established a half-way house for young people coming out of the drug culture. Their leader, Paul Edwards, led this little band of Jesus people as they renovated the house on Person Street and began to take in troubled young people. About two years later, Paul and I met with Teen Challenge, and gave the house and ministry to the Teen Challenge organization. They eventually moved to larger facilities and over the years, hundreds of young men have been given a new life as they encountered Jesus in that amazing Upper Room now called Teen Challenge.

Eagles Wings Is Birthed in Buffalo: My successor, Bishop Robert Stearns leads a worldwide ministry called Eagles Wings. They are specifically known for their support of the Covenant that God made with His people, Israel. However, perhaps one of their greatest accomplishments has been his vision to establish what has become the largest prayer meeting in the history of the church, the world-wide Day of Prayer for The Peace of Jerusalem. Today, it involves over 300,000 churches. This prayer meeting born in Buffalo, and co-founded by Dr. Jack Hayford, is an apostolic worldwide expression of the contribution that Buffalo has made in the prayer movement in the world today.

Saving Grace Ministries: When I think of Upper Rooms in our city, my mind immediately goes to a house of encounter with God for a forgotten segment of our population, men coming out of the prison system. Think for a moment of the growing community of men and women released daily from our prison system. Terry King did and built Saving Grace Ministries.

Because of the epidemic growth of the drug problem in America and other sociological problems in our culture, our prison population is exploding. What do we do with parolees—our family members, sons, daughters, moms, and dads—who leave prison, return to our neighborhoods, and cannot find employment, housing or basic human needs? The tragic truth is that our nation finds acceptable that the vast majority of them return to prison.

But not in Buffalo. Since Saving Grace was founded, it has become the most successful rehabilitation program in America to serve this group. Years ago, Terry was one of Buffalo's most successful businessmen. One night, driving back from building a summer home, he was involved in an accident, and a young person died. Terry went to prison, where he found Christ. While in prison, he developed an educational program to teach prisoners spirituality alongside skills to succeed when they re-entered the community. Upon Terry's release, God used his business skills, combined with his passion to build a restoration program for this growing population of men and women being released from prison.

Today, Saving Grace Ministries, Inc. owns fifteen homes in Buffalo and has literally created a new atmosphere of renewal and hope in a once deteriorating area of the city. The ministry serves in partnership with New York State Department of Corrections along with six strategic state, county, and city partners to assist over 800 men and women returning from the prison system. The ministry targets to service those individuals marginalized with horrific criminal histories and those who struggle with mental health diagnosis who would return to community with no other housing provider willing to assist, care, coordinate, and meet their basic human needs.

The ministry recently completed the build-out of a brand new long-term affordable housing eight-unit apartment building. In 2014, Saving Grace established a Café and a Bake Shoppe employing community members and affording opportunity for clients to access gainful employment. A thriving church has been established to serve the neighborhood including the hundreds of people coming out of prison and re-entering society. Formerly, 70 percent returned to incarceration. Today, those served by Saving Grace Ministries have turned that figure around; 70-80 percent of clients not only do not return to prison, but become successful citizens of Buffalo's new thriving community.

Saving Grace also has programs in Rochester, NY, Elmira, NY, Canisteo, NY and Tampa, Florida. A ministry birthed in a dream, became a vision within a man's heart, and today represents the Church alive. Terry King often shares that "Your life's dream will only become your reality when you live it out by faith." He adds, "Today's church is challenged. Will we act as the church is called and do the will of the father to change the people of a community?"

True Bethel Baptist and Pastor Darius Pridgen: Perhaps one of the most dramatic moments in my life was the day my co-author, Al Warner took me to the office of Pastor Darius Pridgen at True Bethel Baptist Church and introduced me to a man who has impacted the renewal in Buffalo probably more than any other person. There on a wall, I saw a picture of a little boy riding a go-cart in the parking lot of a large Twin Fair store. I recognized the store as the very building that now houses True Bethel. I said to Pastor Darius, "Who is that little boy riding that go-cart?" The handsome young Darius answered me with these words, "that little boy is me on this very parking lot."

And I realized that no city renewal takes place without the birth of a little boy who becomes a man and dreams great dreams. Today, Darius Pridgen is not only Pastor of the three- campus church known as True Bethel Baptist, but has also become the President of our Common Council. He is regarded as one of the men "who gets things done" in Buffalo, and has truly been a major leader in this re-creation of our city.

The Home Prayer Meeting Movement: I cannot write this part of the book without also remembering the day when Dr. Cho planted in my spirit that we must start home prayer groups. It was not long until our church had 246 prayer groups with over 2,000 people in attendance every week. We appointed district leaders in every section of the city. Later most of these district leaders would become pastors of campus churches. Soon we had built over ten campus churches.

This leads me to my next "upper room."

Pastors of those campus churches and others who joined us, decided to meet together approximately six to eight times a year in we call COVnet or Covenant Network of Churches. Tears and hugs dominated the room as all of those spiritual sons and daughters came back home to be with their spiritual dad. One of those men wrote the Foreword of this book. For over fifteen years, we have met, and now we meet monthly just to be the united body of Christ. No one could feel more fulfilled than this spiritual dad who meets with his family every month. That gathering today has been my upper room where we are truly in one place and in one accord. It is our "Upper Room."

The Healing of Delia Knox: There is one last "upper room" experience I must mention. This is not an Upper Room located in a specific building, but an Upper Room found in the heart of one of the greatest servants of God I have ever known, Delia Knox. It was about twenty years ago that I walked onto the platform of the Buffalo Convention Center where I was to introduce the guest speaker for a huge gathering of the African American Community who were raising funds to build Buffalo's first minority owned nursing home. That night, a beautiful young lady was seated on the platform in a wheelchair. She had been hit, head on, by a drunken driver on the Queen Elizabeth Highway between Buffalo and Toronto.

I watched as Delia began to sing the beautiful lyrics of that song, "He Is Able." I sat in entranced by her voice and mesmerized by her spirit and her talent. I wondered, "Is my God able to make her walk?" I was to find out.

Delia was to later become my second daughter in my heart. I took her to many venues to sing and testify. She also became a true sister to my daughter, Aimee. I had her sing for me in Atlanta where she met a handsome young Bishop whom she later married. I had the privilege of conducting the marriage ceremony for Delia and Bishop Knox.

You talk about an "Upper Room!" Let me tell you of the greatest "Upper Room" of my life. The telephone rang at my house one day and Delia's twin sister, Enid, said in words almost too emotional for me to understand, "Pastor, Delia's walking! Get on the internet and look!" I did, and watched live a revival meeting in Mobile, Alabama as she took her first steps in almost twenty-three years. It was the greatest miracle perhaps of our century.

I remember when she came back to Buffalo, no longer in a wheel chair, but walking. Her brother-in-law, Jim had signs placed all over the city, which said, "There is Joy In the City...Delia walks." Along with Wanda and Aimee, I went to the airport to welcome our daughter who had been crippled. Now, for the first time, I would see her standing on her feet! I will never forget the moment I saw her pushing her wheelchair, and I looked into her eyes face to face for the first time. This was truly an "Upper Room" for our city.

I stood on the porch at her parents' home as the car drove up bringing her from the airport. I watched as she got out of the car, walking as if she had never seen a wheel chair.

We must realize that this renewal was birthed in the fire of an Upper Room.

The Ministry of Benny Hinn: Many times, "Upper Rooms" make an impact not only on a city or region, but from them is born something that touches the entire world. I think of it as a place in history with global significance. An event took place in Buffalo that has world significance. Let me share this "Upper Room" with you.

My telephone rang one Thursday night. At the other end of the line was the president of the local chapter of the Full Gospel Business Men. He told me that the speaker he had scheduled for that Saturday had canceled and asked if I could help him get a speaker. My mind went to a conversation I had with my friend, Maggie, from the Kathryn Kuhlman Foundation. She told me of a very young and unknown Canadian evangelist and asked me to attend one of his meetings in Toronto. Although I could not attend, her words describing the anointing of the Holy Spirit that was upon this young man were etched on my memory. I said to the president, "Yes, let me call a young man in Canada that my friend, Maggie from the Kuhlman Foundation told me about.

He told me to go ahead and make the call, and so I picked up the phone and for the first time heard the voice of a man who would become my spiritual son, Evangelist Benny Hinn. The weekend Benny came, I also asked him to stay in town and preach our Sunday morning service. It was the beginning of a lifetime friendship. For the next two or three years, this young evangelist preached for me at least once every month for a citywide healing service. His visits became more frequent until he preached two healing services every month as well as one Sunday morning service every month. I had the privilege of introducing him to some of the major pastors on the West Coast.

Soon, we traveled together to California and the international ministry of Benny Hinn was launched.

My introduction to young Pastor Benny Hinn was the beginning of a journey. I was with him several times every month. I had the privilege of ministry at his father's funeral. Our church became his church for a monthly ministry in the United States. This Upper Room was a friendship between a pastor and a young evangelist. To this day, Pastor Benny calls me his pastor. We have become a spiritual family.

In those years, when Benny Hinn built an "Upper Room" in the city of Buffalo, thousands of people came to Christ. The pastor of our largest daughter church, Pastor John Tonelli, was one of the very early people who came to Christ. Today, I estimate there are at least two thousand people in our church and other churches in the area who came to Christ when Pastor Benny ministered in Buffalo.

Recently, I came to the realization that in the nation of Indonesia he ministered to over one and a half million people in a single service. This was the largest single gathering in the 2,000-year history of the church. Every time I hear about another great crusade in a nation around the world, I think about those foundational days. Benny built an "Upper Room" in our church that has reached around the world.

A Renewal Upper Room: Let me to take this moment to introduce one more "Upper Room." It was the spiritual birthing of the ministry of our co-author, Al Warner. On a beautiful Sunday night, this young Christian and Missionary Alliance Pastor from East Aurora, New York, walked into our church. Discouraged from the rigors and heart-rending problems that often arise in a church community, he and Deb were hungry for God.

That night, in an atmosphere strange to their traditions, they were prayed for by the renewal evangelist, Dennis Shearer. Not long afterward, as he and Deb were overwhelmed by the Presence of the Holy Spirit at our altar, God prophetically spoke that Al would lead and disciple the leaders of our city. Little did I know that the words prayed over them were so accurate, and would become reality, or the impact he would have on our city or its leaders.

From the "Upper Room" of that renewal altar was birthed a ministry that would touch our city in such a dramatic way. Al would bring the political and business leaders of our city to the same altar where he was touched by God. He would pioneer the National Day of Prayer in our city. He would lead the first regular city-wide "Pastors' Prayer Meeting" in the history of the city every week for over fifteen years.

I am reminded that the prophetic word from God is creative. And that night it created the ministry of my friend and co-author, Al Warner. I want him to tell you about the citywide pastors' prayer that has impacted our city for the last fifteen years.

Again, I define an Upper Room as a place where heaven touches earth and people have a dramatic encounter with God. Upper Rooms are amazing places where lives are changed. They can be home prayer meetings. They can be in huge cathedrals or small insignificant churches. The Upper Rooms that I have included in this chapter are, of course, an incomplete list. But, to me, they are some of the truly significant places where people have met with God and heaven has touched earth. I think of the words of Moses, "If your presence does not go with us...we do not want to go".

The truth that I would like to convey to you in this book is that we will never be able to be a Nehemiah generation who rebuild a city until we first build an Upper Room of prayer. May we truly be a generation who realize the importance of prayer and encounter with God, for without that foundation, we can never restore the foundations of a nation or rebuild our cities.

Chapter 25

SHOUT! FOR THE LORD HAS GIVEN YOU THE CITY!

Al Warner

What did God say to you as you read the last chapter penned by Pastor Reid? If you are not from Buffalo, you may not know the players. But Pastor Reid's account was like a master jeweler taking individual pearls from history and stringing them together to create an awe-inspiring necklace. However, this is not just the two of us inviting you to look at our Buffalo family photo album and tell us how beautiful our stories are. Instead, allow the Holy Spirit to speak deeply to your spirit. Pastor Reid's words filled our eyes with tears and our spirits with praise as a trusted regional father told his faith-filled stories of God's divine appointments in our city's history. This is what the Psalmist declares:

"Since my youth, God, you have taught me, and to this day I declare your marvelous deeds. Even when I am old and gray, do not forsake me, my God, till I declare your power to the next generation, your mighty acts to all who are to come" (Ps. 71:17-8).

"So the next generation would know them, even the children yet to be born, and they in turn would tell their children. Then they would put their trust in God and would not forget his deeds but would keep his commands" (Ps. 78:6-7).

The power of faith-filled story: This is the same Pastor Reid to whom the Holy Spirit spoke over 40 years ago as the second largest steel plant in the world was dying in Buffalo and asked, "Do you have enough faith to say to the dry bones of this CITY ... 'RISE AND WALK AGAIN'?" God is doing a transformation before our very eyes. Pastor Reid had the opportunity to grow old and bitter. Instead, he is still dreaming and releasing and building dreams in others.

This book is more than the pleasant reminiscing of Pastor Reid in his eighties and me at age sixty. Where are the ancient Upper Rooms in your city, dusty or rusted though they may be? Who are the fathers you need to honor and empower? Who are the fathers like Pastor Reid who can recall and release the faith-filled stories of your city's history? What are the new Upper Rooms God is calling you to build—Upper Rooms of worship and intercession, intimacy and friendship, His glory and presence, and empowerment for signs and wonders?

Is your God big enough to release you to "Shout! For the Lord has given you the city!" (Joshua 6:16)? Find a spiritual father or mother. Adopt a spiritual son or daughter.

IT IS TIME TO DREAM THE DREAMS OF GOD AGAIN!
IT IS TIME TO CHANGE OUR WORLD
AND REBUILD OUR CITIES!

God's dreams are blooming in Buffalo, and community leaders are inviting pastors to share a seat at the table. For the first time, leaders in the marketplace understand the significance of setting the right spiritual atmosphere. We are living in opportune times. A recent example in downtown Buffalo makes the point.

The HarborCenter, the largest private development in the history of Buffalo ($200 million) is being built by Terry and Kim Pegula, Christians who own both the Buffalo Sabres and the Buffalo Bills. Cliff Benson, Chief Development Officer of the Sabres and the driving force behind this project, asked me to bring a team of pastors to pray before construction began (October 2012). We prayed over an empty blacktopped parking lot. Our group came back two more times to pray at various points of construction. Finally in January 2015, Cliff invited our pastors to declare a blessing on the finished structure. The HarborCenter with its two NHL-size ice rinks will bring 500,000 people into downtown Buffalo each year. The pastors prayed and then collectively sang "To God Be the Glory." The sound was heavenly. This would have been impossible in the old Buffalo.

Once again, I am asking co-author Pastor Tommy to join me in sharing his reflections from that day at the HarborCenter.

HarborCenter Becomes a House of Prayer

I have attended more prayer meetings in my life than I could possibly count. Prayer meetings as a child growing up, prayer meetings while I was being trained for ministry in the Bible college I had chosen, prayer meetings in Korea, prayer meetings in the church I pastored for fifty years, as well as innumerable prayer meetings in other places.

However, in my memory as a Christian, not one of them, including the phenomenal prayer meeting of thousands of people in Korea, was as significant as the one I attended led by Cliff Benson and Al Warner at the just-completed HarborCenter in Buffalo.

It was significant because it was not a clergyman or a professional religious person who called us together. It was the builder of an exceptional sports facility in downtown Buffalo. Cliff and Al wanted the pastors to see and pray over the result of a vision conceived three years before.

I recall walking into the 716 Restaurant housed in the new hockey center with this sizeable group of pastors from many denominations. Cliff met us and invited us to pray with him and for the owners of Buffalo's two major sports teams, the Sabres and the Bills. When all the pastors arrived, we began to walk through the HarborCenter. We were escorted through two hockey rinks on the 7th floor of this huge building. We were taken to the world-class training facility and were amazed not only at the state-of-the-art facility, but also the enthusiasm of the strong Christian who oversees it.

Finally, we filed into the bleachers at one of the huge rinks. I knew we were a large and diverse group, but in that moment, almost every available seat in those bleachers was filled with a pastor, and some of us had to stand, and we spilled over into the overflow space near the bleachers.

At the invitation of Cliff, we first lifted our corporate voices in prayer. Then someone began to sing, "To God Be the Glory." The large group of pastors suddenly became a choir, and our voices echoed through the hockey arena. I knew at that moment that heaven kissed earth, not at a cathedral, not even at a small insignificant Evangelical or Pentecostal church, but in one of the finest and now best-known hockey complexes in the world, invited by the man who was changing not only a city but also the hockey world.

This was truly the church, various denominations united with a leader of the business/sports world ... praying ...what an amazing Upper Room.

Now that you know that a group of pastors stood at the epicenter of millions of dollars of development at the invitation of the stakeholders, you might wonder how the journey began. But first a question—how might God view the role of pastors in a city? Are we called to pastor a church, or to pastor a community? How do I balance the needs of those inside the four walls of my church, with the needs *"in Jerusalem, and in all Judea and Samaria, and to the ends of the earth" (Acts 1:8)?*

Years ago, at the conclusion of a meeting, a lady came up to me. "Rev. Warner, you know our region pretty well. How many churches are there?" I had done my homework, and proudly replied, "Over 1200." "That's funny," she responded, "I thought there was just one." For a moment, I was speechless. Then I replied, "Ma'am, I stand corrected. You are right, I was wrong. God sees just one church in our region." This fits with the theology of Paul who wrote most of his letters to a city or region (Rome, Corinth, Thessalonica, Galatia, etc.) House churches existed throughout each city, but they had to share a single letter written to THE church in the city. The same is true of the Apostle John, who wrote kudos and critiques to city churches in the Book of Revelation.

If there is but one church in a city, His church, how does it affect the day-to-day life of a pastor and a congregation? An obvious outgrowth is that I need to get to know my citywide teammates who pastor other congregations in the city to which God has assigned us all. It is, after all, easier to play a team game when I know my teammates. A second outgrowth is that I need to learn to love the city to which I am called, not just the people to whom I am called. These simple principles were about to change my wife's and my lives forever.

In 1999, we were growing increasingly troubled by the racial divide in Buffalo, especially in the church. What to do? My wife and I discussed our concern with Pastor Jon Hasselbeck. After thoughtful prayer, we agreed to invite Rev. Dennis Wiedrick of Hamilton, Ontario, Canada, to come to Buffalo for special meetings. To confront the racial separation, we asked him to speak for five days in five different area churches, two predominantly black inner city churches and three predominantly white suburban churches. Our plan was that each congregation would travel to other churches and cross-pollination would occur.

Weeks before the meetings, Dennis contacted us with a concern. He felt that although our plan was worthy, it was also risky. We were asking people to step out of their personal comfort zones and attend services in parts of our city and region where they had never stepped foot before. We were confronting the principalities and powers that drove racism in our region. Our actions were declaring we were going to war!

Dennis challenged us that we needed to prepare the way with prayer. So we invited a number of pastors and their spouses to come together and pray on the Thursday mornings leading up to the meetings. A relational bond began to form.

A few weeks later, when the meetings took place, the fledgling unity of the pastors allowed the Spirit of God to break through and "do a new thing" (Is. 43:19). God commanded the blessing (Psalm133) and changed many of our lives forever. Hundreds of people and dozens of pastors moved freely between each other's buildings. A statement was made in both heaven and on earth.

But perhaps the greatest lasting impact of these meetings was that the pastors who had gathered to prepare the way, decided to keep on praying together! That was October 1999, and our pastors' prayer group continues to meet every Thursday to this very day. From its birth, our group gathered pastors across racial and denominational lines. As is often the case, we did not even recognize the importance of this foundational piece the day we started.

Although this group started relatively easily, it has only continued with lots of sweat and tears. It is often easier to start something than to continue and finish well. The price goes up as the race goes on. Note Paul's word in Act 20:24 on his final trip to Jerusalem, "However, I consider my life worth nothing to me, if only I may finish the race and complete the task the Lord Jesus has given me—the task of testifying to the gospel of God's grace."

We call it a pastors' prayer group, but it is so much more. Prayer for personal as well as regional issues is foundational. Equally important, strong enduring relationships have been formed, tears of betrayal have been shared, offenses have been laid down, testimonies of breakthrough have been celebrated, and strategies for community transformation have been birthed.

I believe I have met some of the best teammates, and finest pastors, here in Buffalo/Niagara. Servant leaders, washing one another's feet, listening to the voice of the Spirit, leading the Body of Christ, and transforming our cities. We have become partners in prayer.

If the Spirit is calling you to build an Upper Room of praying pastors, here are some practical thoughts. Our group has very few ground rules:

1) The lead facilitator is responsible to guide and adjust the flow of the meeting.
2) Comments and prayers should be kept short. This is not the place to preach a sermon from last Sunday, no matter how excellent it was.
3) In order to build covenant relationships, it is important to maintain confidentiality at the table. The transparency of participants must be honored.

These guidelines help to create a safe atmosphere for vulnerability, a place where pastors can share about themselves, their marriages, their children, and their doubts and fears. It has become a healing place, where love and compassion are poured out between and among hurting pastors. The often-lonely journey of the leader becomes transformed through caring relationships with fellow gatekeepers.

This is not a closed group, but one that is ever changing. Pastors and regional ministry leaders have come and gone over the years. Some are with us for a season and leave to birth other similar groups. We welcome newcomers and bless those called elsewhere, knowing that God is ever expanding His Kingdom.

The Upper Room of praying pastors in the Buffalo/Niagara region has raised the vision for godly leaders, which in turn has raised the vision for congregations, which has raised the vision for our city. Hence, these pastors are pastoring not only their local congregations, but our city as well.

I have observed the dangers of "lone ranger" leaders. I believe in the leadership sandwich—those above me who speak into my life, those beside me as my peers who encourage me, and those into whose lives I speak. "An African proverb epitomizes the value of community in one's life journey: If you want to go fast, go alone. If you want to go far, go together." [36]

If you are not a pastor, you may ask, "What difference does it make to me whether my pastors and other pastors in my city gather to pray?" Glad you asked. Some of you may think of prayer as mystical and mysterious, which indeed it is. However, I believe it has a practical side—our God fights for us (Exodus 14:14).

In our city, pastors who came together to pray were excited enough by the results to promote corporate prayer to their congregations. This has resulted in hundreds of opportunities for regional intercession and worship. Recently there were seven different unity gatherings in a single weekend. The pastors have led the way, and Christians across racial and denominational lines have embraced and expanded the model. Team Jesus is coming together in Buffalo!

Over the years, the heavenly bowls of intercession have been filling with the prayers of our group, the prayers of hundreds of thousands of Christians throughout our region along with the heavenly hosts—Lord, bring Your Body Together! All of us desire to be the fulfillment of Ps. 133 (God's people dwelling together in unity) and John 17 (that we may be one as the Father and Son are one so that the world may believe).

Now to the practical side: Look at what God is doing in the Buffalo/Niagara area!

2002—A small group received a prophetic word that there were hidden terrorist cells meant for destruction in Buffalo, but that God wanted to uncover them. Our pastors group began to pray for mercy and exposure. Regional intercessors joined the fight. Six days later, Friday the 13th of September 2002, the "Lackawanna Six" terrorist cell was uncovered and the members arrested in Buffalo. The most praiseworthy part? The enemy's plans were exposed without any death or destruction visiting our city. Our God fights for us.

2008—Once again, a prophetic word was received that there was a hotbed of terrorism along the international (U.S./Canada) border at Niagara Falls. The call was for intercessors to gather from Canada and the U.S. to protect our nations. We responded to the call on Sunday, Sept. 28, 2008 when over 400 Christians from Southern Ontario and Western New York along with the mayors of Niagara Falls, Ontario, and Niagara Falls, NY, spanned the Niagara Gorge across the Rainbow Bridge and prayed. We prayed for protection on our borders and blessings on our twin cities of Niagara Falls. No problems ever surfaced. Our border continues to be safe and guarded. Our God fights for us.

2009—ABC brings Extreme Home Makeover to Buffalo. Church volunteers led the way turning out the most volunteers (6000+) in the show's history. In addition to the "hero home" being built, 29 homes were impacted with new paint, new roofs, new siding, and porches, with 109 trees being planted, and three new parks being established—a five-block radius was revitalized. God's compassion was poured out in tangible ways.

2012—Don't laugh out loud, but God moved outside my religious box. May I suggest that a high-wire walker was an answer to the prayers of our region? June 15, 2012, Nik Wallenda of the famous Wallenda family linked our two nations of Canada and the U.S. when he walked a wire over Niagara Falls. But Nik did more than wire walk. He prayed audibly to his heavenly Father to the amazement of 20,000,000 ABC and CTV television viewers:

> "Thank You for Your peace, Lord. Thank You for Your confidence, God. Thank You Jesus."

*"Thank You Jesus, my righteous King. Praise You, Father God. Praise
  You, Jesus."*
*"Oh Lord, You are my Savior, You are my King. You are my Jesus.
  You are my Counselor, You are my wisdom. Praise You Jesus."*

Nik took prayer walking to *new heights!* God's Word was shared with millions.

2013—In the last chapter, Pastor Reid mentioned our local churches coming together on Good Friday. The regional bowls of intercession tipped earthward during Good Friday Together. Many of the leading churches of Buffalo came together to lift high one name—Jesus Christ! No famous speakers or singers were flown in, just some of the best and brightest from our region. By actual count, 13,000 people gathered in the great sports center where the NHL's Buffalo Sabres play. A significant offering was taken to bless the city in the areas of sustainable housing, education, healthcare, and teen mentoring. It was obvious that night that the church was becoming one. Renewal started in the Upper Room of prayer and was now being modeled for the citizens of our city by the public expression of His Body. The fruit from Good Friday Together continues:

- Our unity commanded the blessing of the Lord.
- Our unity sweetened the soil of evangelism.
- Our unity released the power of the Holy Spirit.
- Our unity is transforming our region.

And your city? What are you waiting for? What is God's dream for your city? An intercessor friend, David Beam said, "Transformation is seeing things happen that we never imagined would happen in our city."

The testimonies of the faith-based team recorded in Chapter 23 reveal that these leaders are feet to the prayers of generations of those who have prayed and believed for a better and transformed Buffalo. I felt the Lord say that now our pastors prayer group needs to be covering to the feet of those He is calling to rebuild Buffalo. Because of this, our pastor's prayer group has prayed with and for each of these leaders.

The story of the New Buffalo is the story of people, not just of brick and mortar.

Chapter 26

THE NEW BUFFALO

Words alone cannot describe "The New Buffalo." After years of huge losses in our population base and the loss of almost every major realtor in the downtown area, Buffalo was a dying city. Entire neighborhoods were being torn down and becoming thousands of acres of vacant land. Buffalo was best described almost forty years ago by the sign I wrote about at the beginning of this book. This sign near city hall read, "Will the last person leaving the city, please turn off the lights."

To see this city literally come alive, to see sixteen billion dollars of construction either in the pipeline or actually being built, to walk through the new Canalside area and see thousands of people skating on several major ice rinks or strolling through Canalside built on the site that had been the western terminus of the Erie Canal is seeing a truly contemporary miracle. Buffalo is being re-born!

Where and how do you begin to describe it? Words are inadequate. Maybe the first place to begin is in perhaps the largest project in the city, The Medical Campus. Under the leadership of Matt Enstice, the Buffalo Niagara Medical Campus is what the Buffalo News called "a hotbed of construction." It is two million square feet of construction, equal to ten Walmart Super Centers. This development is becoming one of America's leading medical, research and education centers. It is an investment of billions of dollars. When completed within the next two years it will bring an additional 5,000 workers to the 120-acre campus increasing the Medical Workforce to 17,000 to 20,000 persons.

A few years ago, leaders seeing the potential for renewal, built one of America's premier sports arenas in downtown Buffalo. This beautiful new arena was undoubtedly an attraction to the new owners of the Sabres when they purchased the NHL Hockey team. Alongside the state of the art arena, Terry and Kim Pegula, new owners of the Sabres and Buffalo Bills, built the new HarborCenter. With an investment of nearly 200 million dollars, it contains two hockey rinks, two restaurants, an indoor parking ramp, a pro shop, and training centers. It also houses a 205-room Buffalo HarborCenter Marriott. HarborCenter attracts hockey teams, hockey fans, and hockey gatherings from all over the world. It is not unusual to look at a day's activities and see hockey teams from several nations. It is expected that HarborCenter will fill the hotels of downtown Buffalo with over 500,000 visitors every year. It is becoming truly the Hockey Center of the entire world.

Beside the phenomenal HarborCenter is Canalside. It may well be the major expression of the new Buffalo. In the winter, thousands fill several new outdoor hockey rinks, others walk through the Naval Park which has several large naval vessels, or simply enjoy the wonder of a beautiful snow-enhanced outdoor park. Nothing in America can supersede the wonder of Buffalo in the winter through the lens of this amazing Canalside attraction. From world class restaurants to the outdoor vendors with hot dogs, few cities in America can compare to the creative fun that Canalside provides for the people of America's renewal city.

When you walk through the new downtown Buffalo, either on the beautiful tree-lined sidewalks of Canalside, or walk back into time and stroll on the cobblestone of what is called the Cobblestone District, downtown Buffalo is one of the most amazing spots in the world.

With all of this activity attracting people from all over the world, today hotels are being constructed in new high-rise buildings in the downtown area. From Marriott to some of the more contemporary chains, we are becoming a vacation capital of the northeast. Who would have thought that in just a few years Buffalo would have gone from a city whose lights were about to go out to one of the most vibrant cities in the world!

Buffalo has been one of the truly great industrial and manufacturing cities in North America and home to huge factories which turned out thousands of Fords and Chevrolets. Retracing the automobile history of Buffalo, we were famed for being the home city of both the Pierce Arrow and the Thomas Flyer, the first automobile to cover a journey around the world. It was one of the truly great steel cities, home to the second largest steel plant in America. At one time, Buffalo was the Grain Capital of America with 90 percent of the grain flowing through the silos in downtown Buffalo. It was also the Queen City of the Industrial Revolution.

How do you top that? Well, I think we have. Talk about factories that employ thousands, Buffalo may well become the solar capital of America. Solar City, the largest of the Governor's Buffalo Billion projects is being erected on the site of the old Republic Steel plant; 5,500 pilings were drilled and the plant's foundation laid. At this writing, Solar City will provide nearly 1,500 jobs at the plant and an additional 1,440 jobs at suppliers and service providers. Buffalo has truly become a key city in the energy revolution in America.

Old abandoned buildings including warehouses are being re-born as middle-and high-income loft apartments. New office buildings are being erected. Construction is everywhere. Huge cranes have not been seen in Buffalo for decades. On a single day recently, we counted six dotting the skyline of this new Buffalo.

Typical of the construction going on, one local corporation, Delaware North is not moving to another city, as hundreds of companies have done in recent years, but is building their new Delaware North Headquarters. It contains a twelve-story Westin Hotel, office and retail space of 193,000 square feet, and is, for just this one company, a one-hundred-and-ten million dollar project.

Buffalo has truly been re-born. Today, as cranes dot the skyline, construction is no longer the exception; it is the norm. It is truly a miracle city of America. Literally thousands of new jobs, over 16 billion dollars of new construction, the host of what probably will become one of the most, and potentially the most significant medical campus in America--how can you describe this without using the word, "miracle!"

But, what happens to the poor, the people who lived in the decaying housing of an old city? The leader of the Medical Campus describes the amazing miracle that happened in the Fruit Belt next to the exploding Medical Campus. Matt Enstice, the President of the Medical Campus, called his friend, Pastor Michael Chapman and said that he must be the man to re-create the Fruit Belt. He told Pastor Chapman that we need hundreds of new homes for the new residents of Buffalo, but we do not want to displace the families who have lived there for generations. It has been a work of art to see these creators rebuild a section of the city to house both the new Buffalo population as well as serve the existing population. It was the church that was called to see this miracle of joining the new Buffalo to the old Buffalo.

The Buffalo News describes this re-creation of Buffalo in descriptive headlines like, "They're Back, Buffalo's Millennials." The vibrant young are moving back to downtown Buffalo. Their lives become exciting in an area where you can walk to a Broadway show or a world-class restaurant within blocks of your loft apartment. Life is easy and convenient when you can live in an apartment where you do not even need a car. The popular rail system comes by your house every ten minutes. Downtown Buffalo is becoming the "in" place to live. Another headline describes the "hot" housing market with these words, "Home Prices Where It's Hot." In the downtown zip code of 14422, prices for housing rose by 22 percent in the past year. The news describes Buffalo as "hot". No longer are people fleeing the city, they are moving back to the city by the thousands.

How did this happen. Miracles like this do not happen overnight. This has been a process, a spiritual process. You cannot re-create a city without a spiritual revolution. Jesus told us to "Disciple Nations." I believe that He meant what He said. He did not tell us just to get people ready for heaven. He did not tell us to just disciple individual people. He consistently provided a pattern for the church to impact the world by building a prototype of heaven on the earth.

When the disciples asked Jesus to teach them to pray, Jesus taught a prayer pattern that we often forget. He said to begin our prayer with these kinds of words, "Our Father which art in heaven, Hallowed be thy name, *THY KINGDOM COME, THY WILL BE DONE, ON EARTH AS IT IS IN HEAVEN!*"

Isn't it interesting that Jesus told us to begin by invoking the coming of a heavenly paradigm of life to be established on the earth? He then told us that we were to "disciple nations." I cannot read those words without seeing the concept that if we are to disciple nations, we are to create on this earth a people who can rebuild cities and cultures that have become dysfunctional and cause them to function like heaven.

Here in our city, the church is beginning to believe that heaven can come to earth, that cities that are dysfunctional can become functional. The church today that is the supplier of every bed that exists for the homeless, tomorrow will empty those beds by discipling a city to become a manifestation of the Kingdom of God on the earth.

The revolution that we are seeing today began with prayer. You cannot rebuild a city until you first build an Upper Room of prayer where people are challenged and changed to become personally and corporately an expression of the Kingdom. The rebuilding of Buffalo has been and still is a spiritual journey. How is the rebuilding of a city birthed spiritually?

This last understanding of using money, of unifying people, and of realizing God's dream is quite an amazing one for you and your city or the world around you. Let's review together what we have learned.

Chapter 27

BUILD AN UPPER ROOM AND RECREATE A CITY

We have just taken a journey of faith together. I have so enjoyed sharing my journey with you. Our journey began with a vision, a dream, and the discovery of the God-ordained destiny for each of our lives.

I believe that the destiny of our lives was written by God before the foundation of the world. This vision for destiny leads us to a question of where we will obtain the resources to fund our dream. Not one of us can even imagine where we will find the resources to fulfill our dream.

So we took a further step in our journey. We discovered that creating wealth was a spiritual process of finding the wisdom of God and discovering our own God-given gifts and talents. We discovered that the resources to fund the dream were already inside us.

Then we took the journey one step further. I shared with you an unbelievable dream I had over forty-five years ago. Buffalo had been the model of the industrial age. Now, as the American steel industry decayed and facility after facility was being closed, I looked down on the dying remains of one of the largest steel-making facilities in the world. I knew that within months it would be a decaying and rusting dinosaur.

With our co-author, Al Warner, we described the city of Buffalo as I knew it as a boy. It was one of the great port cities of the world with hundreds of ships from all over the planet making Buffalo a distribution center for all of North America. This great city was then the 9th largest city in America. Buffalo had been a distribution center at the terminus of the Erie Canal. As a distribution center it made America into a new nation.

At the turn of the century, it was called the City of Lights. From the city of lights, it became one of the centers of the steel industry and a center of automobile and aircraft production. It seemed that Buffalo was always a winner. It had been great!

But then, changes came in our culture. We had enjoyed the productivity of the industrial age, but the world had changed, and we had not changed with it. By the 1980s, Buffalo was a dying city, and a city largely without hope. As I have said, someone erected a huge sign by the great art-deco City Hall that read, "Will the last person leaving Buffalo please turn off the lights."

I came back to that city in 1963 with a dream. My first dream was to build one of the most significant churches in America. We had the privilege of enjoying a great move of the Holy Spirit, and Jesus did build His church and the world watched as God built one of the fastest-growing churches in America.

But I had a greater dream. As I saw the city falling into decay, urban blight, crime and unemployment, I heard a cry coming from deep inside of me, "Can you speak to the dry bones of this dying city, RISE AND WALK AGAIN."

Somehow, I knew that my life was about dreams, and no dream is too big for the nature that God put inside of me. So I preached about building a new Buffalo. Somehow, I believed that a partnership between God and His people could do exactly what Nehemiah did. We could rebuild our city. I believed that we could also find the resources and the money to rebuild this city and fulfill the prayer that Jesus taught us to pray, "Thy Kingdom come, Thy will be done, on earth as it is in heaven."

The story of the re-creation of Buffalo has now become a reality. I am grateful for dreams that we dream and dreams that we see come to reality.

But I want to say something that literally burns inside my spirit. Before the people of God in the book of Acts could minister to change the cities of the world, they first built an UPPER ROOM before they could REBUILD A CITY!

WE MUST BUILD AN UPPER ROOM
BEFORE WE REBUILD A CITY

In the late 1960s, I saw the beginning of one of God's great miracles. The Charismatic renewal had come to our city. As a child, I had dreamed of seeing a great revival come to Buffalo where I would pastor a large Pentecostal or Charismatic church that would grow from that revival. Little did I know how God would give us those two great miracles. I was totally unprepared that it would come through the Charismatic Renewal in the Roman Catholic Church.

I was an eyewitness to the renewal that took place in the Roman Catholic Church where over 100,000 people received the Baptism of the Holy Spirit. I questioned, "why there," because our little church had fewer than 200 people. But God sovereignly decided to build an Upper Room, not in the church I pastored, but rather in the Roman Catholic Church. However, in time, that great move of God overflowed into our church, and The Tabernacle literally exploded in growth. God truly visited His church.

This was a move of the Holy Spirit that covered our city as the waters cover the sea. I was there to see it with my own eyes. This move of the Holy Spirit was accompanied by the "Jesus movement" when thousands of youth were brought into the Kingdom of God. The late 1960s through the 1970s were truly the years when thousands encountered God. God had literally built an Upper Room for our city.

In the 1990s another time of spiritual awakening came to our city. It was called The Renewal. As the move of the Holy Spirit in Toronto and Pensacola began to spread across the world, God visited Buffalo in a dramatic way. The Buffalo renewal meetings lasted over two years and dramatically affected hundreds of lives. People from all over the northeastern United States came to our church to hear a young evangelist by the name of Dennis Shearer. One night, a Christian Missionary Alliance pastor came to the renewal meetings. Although the atmosphere of renewal was somewhat foreign to their religious practice, God touched both Al and Deb Warner in a remarkable way.

The 1990s were marked by many unique prayer and renewal movements. During this same period, on the east side of Buffalo another remarkable Upper Room was being built at the Calvary Baptist Church under the leadership of Senior Pastor Troy Bronner and his Assistant Ted Howard. This expression of renewal was the establishment of an early 5:00 a.m. prayer meeting. Every morning hundreds of people would drive from all over Western New York to fill every pew of the Calvary Baptist Church.

My first experience at this unusual urban prayer gathering began when my alarm went off at 4:00 a.m. and I drove toward the east side of Buffalo. I had heard there were large crowds but was not prepared for what I was about to experience. Arriving before 5:00 a.m., I approached the church and found there was not a parking place within blocks. I finally found one about three blocks from the church and walked toward Calvary Baptist Church. As I approached the door of the church, there were hundreds of faces from many different ethnic groups filling every available seat in the auditorium. There were white faces, black faces, Asian faces--all races and ethnicities, and I became overwhelmed by the spirit of worship. I wondered where I would sit. However, someone saw me and escorted me to a pew near the front of the sanctuary. I looked at the pew and wondered if there were enough inches left for me to fit in!

I thought to myself, "It's 5:00 a.m. This must be unusual." But it was not unusual. This is the way it was every morning ,and this would continue on for four years. I will always be grateful to my friends, Pastor Troy Bronner and Pastor Ted Howard for calling Buffalo to prayer at 5:00 a.m. every day. Over those years, thousands came to pray. I knew that morning that God truly answers this kind of prayer.

May I state irrevocably that, without thousands of Christians representing almost every major denomination interceding in prayer, Buffalo would never have been rebuilt. I know our hearts leap when we talk about rebuilding a city or a nation, but let me assure you that it does not happen without prayer. We cannot rebuild a city until we first build an upper room.

Whether that prayer is lifted in a beautiful basilica or humble African American church on the east side of Buffalo, God answers prayer. He answered the prayers of thousands of people who prayed and believed that God would change Buffalo. He did! So let us pray.

THY KINGDOM COME,
THY WILL BE DONE,
ON EARTH AS IT IS IN HEAVEN!

Final Word

DELIVERING A KINGDOM

Why did I spend hundreds of hours writing this manuscript and soliciting the help of others to write with me? When Billy Graham was asked at over ninety years of age what surprised him about life, he said, "That it was so brief." I agree.

It seems like yesterday that I was that little boy on Elm Street in East Aurora at an old handmade altar bench as God called me into ministry and showed me my future. It seems like yesterday that I was that young evangelist driving that baby blue Cadillac convertible to cities across America and later selling it to buy our tickets to Asia. It seems like yesterday that I met Dr. Cho, and he shared with me his vision about the future.

Now I face forward. What do I dream now concerning the future of the church and the change I believe God has called it to make to our world, our nation, and our cities?

I remember as a nine-year-old the day that Japan bombed Pearl Harbor and President Roosevelt called it "The Day of Infamy." I was a scared, little boy. Would my father be drafted and go to the battlefield and would I lose him? Would Hitler send his airplanes and bomb our city? I remember the invasion at Normandy and victory in Europe. I remember the day that the armistice was signed, and Japan surrendered and again our nation was at peace. I also remember the euphoria that came to everyone around me. We won!

We could now live in peace without fear of being bombed or the Nazi forces ruling our nation. There would be no more air raid practice times, and now, we would be able to get gasoline for our car without rationing. Most of all, my Dad could buy a new car.

When the war was over and we desperately needed a new car to replace our old worn out 1937 Ford, I remember an ad for the new 1946 Ford. Dad owned a Ford, and we wanted a new Ford. The ad showed a hand, holding a crystal ball and inside the crystal ball was a brand new 1946 Ford. At the bottom of the ad were the words "There's a Ford in Your Future." To keep our ten-year-old Ford running during the war, my Dad had installed two rebuilt 60 hp, V8 engines. I wanted what was in that ball. I believed that one of those beautiful shiny new Ford automobiles was in my future.

I feel like that advertisement today. There is something in the future I see for the church and for the world. Let me close this book by telling you what I see in that prophetic picture for our future.

There Is a Vision To Be Seen

Look at the future for a moment and the role you will play in the future of the church and our culture and our world. **Get A Vision!**

What kind of a vision did the Apostles see when they left the Upper Room? They saw a world where every person heard the Gospel. They saw a world where the believers were not just discipling individuals; they were discipling nations.

I pray that after you have read these pages God will give you a vision. The vision that God will give you is very different from the six o'clock news. It is a vision that Jesus described when He told us to be a people who would disciple nations.

Why did He say that? Because we have a Kingdom truth inside us that can disciple the leaders of the world to change the world.

Pray about the vision. Live in the vision. Think about the vision when you get up in the morning, when you work at your job, when you come home at night and eat your dinner, and before you go to bed. May you dream the vision that God has for His world.

There Is a Prayer To Be Prayed

We all remember the request of the disciples, "Lord teach us to pray." Jesus responded with some instructions and a model prayer. That model prayer is not just idle words. It is the prayer that Jesus asked us to pray because it is the description of what God wants to do on the earth. That prayer begins with addressing a God who is known by the endearing term, "Father." The first and foremost request is made in that prayer for something to happen on the earth. Listen to the words of the prayer of Jesus, "Thy Kingdom come, Thy Will be done, on Earth as it is in Heaven."

It is obvious that the first thing in the mind of Jesus was that the order and economy of the Kingdom of God would be manifest or come to the earth.

I would suggest that every time you pray that you pray that prayer. There needs to be a concert of thousands of believers praying that prayer. The Scripture says that "all of creation groans for the manifestation of the sons of God" (Romans 8). I am convinced that this is the cry of our world.

Our cities groan with something we call "Urban Blight." Whole neighborhoods fall victim to the horror of gang wars and homicide. But crime and violence is not confined to the city. Terrorists have threatened the peace of the entire world. The tormented world groans for change.

If we really believe in the power of prayer, and we pray as Jesus taught us to pray we can, and will change the world

There Is a Kingdom To Be Delivered

Just how do you deliver this magnificent Kingdom to a hurting world? Let me describe the delivery system of God's Kingdom with this story. There was a young aspiring Catholic missionary by the name of Teresa who had just arrived in the city of Calcutta, India. I believe she was asking God how she could deliver the love of God's Kingdom to the people of the city of Calcutta.

As she walked down the street she saw a little baby girl lying on the street dying. With love and compassion she picked the dying baby up. Knowing the baby had been abandoned, Teresa carried her home. Never before had this little human being felt the arms of love. Never before had the baby felt the caress of a soft bed. The missionary lovingly placed the baby on a bed and gave the baby her first bath. She put warm clothing around her little body and lovingly held the baby probably for hours. Eventually the precious little one died in her arms.

Let your imagination follow that baby girl as she entered heaven. She looked around and realized that it looked strangely familiar. She thought to herself that she had been here before. She realized that she had been here before. And she had! In the loving arms of that Catholic missionary, she had been embraced and loved. She had been bathed and clothed. Heaven was certainly familiar. The Kingdom she now experienced was the same Kingdom she had seen on the earth in the embrace of a loving missionary. She felt at home.

We have all seen talented and anointed servants of God deliver the Kingdom in so many ways. There was the young pre-teenager by the name of Jim Bakker, who sat beside me on the front row of First Assembly of God in Muskegon, Michigan and dreamed of being a preacher. He delivered the Kingdom through his creative talents in the field of television. The young successful evangelist by the name of Oral Roberts delivered the Kingdom by giving our world a University that would inspire students to be world changers. David Livingston delivered the Kingdom when he demonstrated the life of a true missionary to our world. The world honored his work by giving him a grave in Westminster Abby. The people to whom he had delivered the Kingdom in Africa said that England could have his body, but his heart must stay in Africa. So they cut his heart from his body and buried his heart in Africa. He had delivered the heart of God's Kingdom to Africa. My friend Reverend Dr. Bennett Smith, pastor of St. John Baptist Church in Buffalo delivered the Kingdom to his city when he designed and built the first new model of successful urban housing in Buffalo known as McCarley Gardens.

But my greatest example of delivering the Kingdom was an unknown lady by the name of Helen Rice Reid who shared the Kingdom with me. She delivered the Kingdom to me when I was young child as she read to me the story of the crucifixion every night. We never finished the story because both of us would burst into tears, but she introduced me to the loving Jesus who died for me. She delivered the Kingdom to me when she told me prophetically what God wanted me to do with my life. She delivered the

Kingdom to me when she took my hand at my graduation from Bible School and said, "I am very sick with cancer, but I am so convinced that you are to take the Gospel of the Kingdom to the world that I will travel with you."

For the next six months before she died, my Mom traveled with me. She wept when people came to the altar. She cheered when people got healed. She embraced me when I haltingly preached my first sermon, and she embraced me a few months later with her tears as she went to heaven. Helen Rice Reid delivered the Kingdom to me. Without her love, her faith, and her vision I would not be who I am today.

Our world is in the need of transformation. The Kingdom was designed to change the world. You are destined by God to be part of that transformation by delivering the Kingdom of God to our world.

That does not mean that everyone is destined by God to be a high profile person who delivers the kingdom by television or builds a university, but that you are still very important in this amazing proposal to change the world by delivering the Kingdom to the hurting people of our world.

The more of the Kingdom you learn, the farther your borders of influence will grow. You may start with the transformation of a neighbor, and then God will give you greater influence. That is what the Scripture means when it says to begin in Jerusalem, then Judea, then Samaria, then the ends of the earth. Start right where you are to deliver the Kingdom!

Little did the disciples know the importance of the words of Jesus when He said, "Follow Me." Their obedience to the words of the Rabbi called Jesus literally thrust them to the ends of the then known world. And they changed it!

MAY YOU HAVE INSIGHT AND GOD'S DREAM FOR THE WONDER OF THE KINGDOM, AND MAY YOU CREATE WEALTH AND CHANGE THE WORLD AROUND YOU WITH THE POWER OF GOD'S KINGDOM.

ENDNOTES

1 Tommy Tenney: 2011-07-28 - The God Chasers Expanded Edition. Destiny Image. [Kindle]

2 All Scripture quotations in this section, unless otherwise noted, are from the New International Version.

3 A note about my co-author, Pastor Tommy Reid. We are blessed in Buffalo to have several key leaders in their seventies and eighties. These are not leaders coasting toward Glory, but they continue to model cutting edge leadership. Much like Caleb in the Bible, they are asking God for their next mountain: "So here I am today, eighty-five years old! I am still as strong today as the day Moses sent me out; I'm just as vigorous to go out to battle now as I was then. Now give me this hill country that the LORD promised me that day" (Joshua 14:10b-12a). Pastor Reid, I have learned as much from your modeling as from your teaching. Thank you for the honor to work with you to change our world and rebuild our cities.

4 Ken Horn, "God's Presence Fills the Tabernacle," Pentecostal Evangel (June 8, 1997), 17.

5 Raymond J. Bakke, A Theology As Big As the City (Downers Grove, IL: InterVarsity Press, 1997), 22.

6 Ibid., 187-8.

7 Eric Swanson and Sam Williams, To Transform a City: Whole Church, Whole Gospel, Whole City (Grand Rapids, MI: Zondervan, 2010), 35.

8 Bakke, 40.

9 Ibid., 106.

10 Dennis Bakke, Joy at Work: A Revolutionary Approach to Fun on the Job (Seattle, WA: PVG, 2005), 249.

11 Robert Lupton, Renewing the City (Downers Grove, IL: InterVarsity Press, 2005), 9.

12 Robert C. Linthicum, Transforming Power : Biblical Strategies for Making a Difference in Your Community (Downers Grove, IL: InterVarsity Press, 2003), 110.

13 Raymond J. Bakke and Jon Sharpe, Street Signs : A New Direction in Urban Ministry (Birmingham, AL: New Hope Publishers, 2006), 258.

14 Ibid., 261.

15 "Love Canal: A Legacy of Doubt," New York Times, November 25, 2013.

16 Albert K. Greenleaf, Servant Leadership: A Journey into the Nature of Legitimate Power and Greatness (New York: Paulist Press, 1977), 27.

17 Ibid., 77.

18 Ibid., 94.

19 Ibid., 261.

20 Ibid., 359.

21 John Stott, Basic Christian Leadership (Downers Grove, IL: InterVarsity Press, 2002), 113.

22 Current: Regional Director and Founding Partner, American Coastal Properties with $75,000,000 worth of high-end real estate investment in Southern California.

President, Niagara International Capital Limited that performs investment banking and investment services.

Previous: NYS Senator, City of Buffalo Comptroller, Deputy Comptroller of New York State.

Credentials: Principal owner, Nanco Enterprises and Nanco Assoicates, two family investment holding companies. Family companies include Essex Homes of WNY, one of the largest homebuilders in the region. The family co-founded Top's Markets, a statewide chain of super markets.

Developer and co-founder of North America Center, a 425 acre industrial and commercial park, one of the largest public/private real estate partnerships in Western New York history.

23   Current: President and CEO, SLR Contracting, a construction firm with $20 million in revenue.

Motivational speaker, author and leadership coach.

24   Current: Founder, Sinatra & Company, real estate investment firm with one million square feet of commercial space and 1,000+ housing units.

President, Founding Partner, American Coastal Properties with $60,000,000 worth of high-end real estate investment in Southern California.

25   Old African-American spiritual song.

26   Jonathan D. Epstein, "Developers pledge 10 percent of profits from luxury apartments to Say Yes," Bufalo News (July 30,2014).

27   Current: CEO, Landies Candies, chocolate manufacturer.

Credentials: Winner, Taste of Buffalo food festival—2010, 2011, 2012, 2013, 2014.

28   Current: Founder and Chief Medical Officer, Jericho Road Community Health Center, 40,000 patient visits per year.

29   Current: Pastor, St. John Baptist Church; President, Board of Directors, St. John Fruit Belt Community Development Corporation; President, Board of Directors, St. John Community Development Corporation.

30   "Next Things Now: Innovation & Entrepreneurship in Buffalo," 43North, accessed Feb. 5, 2015, <https://www.youtube.com/watch?v=E-YgcN-en3U&feature=youtube>.

31   Current: CEO, ASi (Adiabatic Solutions, LLC), metal manufacturing company.

32   Current: President and CEO, Buffalo Niagara Medical Campus.

Previous: Saturday Night Live, Associate Producer.

33   Current: Chief Development Officer, Buffalo Sabres, NHL ice hockey team.

Developer, HarborCenter.

Board chairman, Imani Christian Academy.

Previous: Managing Partner, Deloitte Tax LLP (Pittsburgh).

34   Current: Pastor, True Bethel Baptist Church.

New York State Overseer, Full Gospel Baptist Church.

President, Buffalo Common Council (legislative).

Built Subway franchise store, first Subway located in a church in the U.S.

Co-owner WUFO, an AM radio station.

Built Family Dollar Store.

Significant housing initiatives.

35   John B. Hayes, *Sub-Merge* (Ventura, CA: Regal Books, 2006), 209.

A sequel to *How to Live out of a Dream*
See special pricing on page 228 when you choose to purchase
the package selection.

ORDER FORM

Quantity: _____ books x $23.95 ea. = Subtotal: $ _____

Shipping & Handling add 10% ($4 minimum): $ _____

New York State sales tax (if applicable) $ _____

Total $ _____

Make checks Payable to COVnet Ministries. U.S. Funds, please.

Shipping Address:

Name: _____

Address: _____

City, State, Zip: _____

Mail this completed order form together with payment to:
KAIROS Resource Center
3210 Southwestern Blvd.
Orchard Park, NY 14127

For quantity discounts and MasterCard/VISA, or international
orders, call 1-800-52wings, or order on dreammydestiny.com or www.kairosre-
sourcecenter.com

ORDER FORM

Tommy Reid DVDs and Books

DVD Order

How To Live Out of a Dream :   Qty _____ x $15 ea. = Subtotal: $ _____

Journal Of Life :   Qty _____ x $10 ea. = Subtotal: $ _____

Book Order

Create Wealth To Build God's Dream: Qty _____ x $23.95 ea. = Subtotal: $ _____

How to Live Out of a Dream: Qty _____ x $14.95 ea. = Subtotal: $ _____

Kingdom Now But Not Yet: Qty _____ x $10 ea. = Subtotal: $ _____

The Exploding Church: Qty _____ x $10 ea. = Subtotal: $ _____

SPECIAL: Save by purchasing ALL SIX Items

Both DVDs and four books: Qty _____ x $65 ea. = Subtotal: $ _____

Aimee Reid-Sych CDs

Release The Sound :   Qty _____ x $15 ea. = Subtotal: $ _____

Passion for His Presence :   Qty _____ x $10 ea. = Subtotal: $ _____

SPECIAL: Save $5 by purchasing both CDs

Both CDs   Qty _____ x $20 ea. = Subtotal: $ _____

   Shipping & Handling add 10% ($4 minimum): $ _____

   New York State sales tax (if applicable) $ _____

                  Total $ _____

Order today through:

KAIROS Resource Center

www.kairosresourcecenter.com

3210 Southwestern Blvd., Orchard Park, NY 14127

Make checks payable to COVnet Ministries. (U.S. Funds, please)

Shipping Address:

Name: _____

Address: _____

City, State, Zip: _____

Mail this completed order form, together with payment, to:

KAIROS Resource Center

3210 Southwestern Blvd., Orchard Park, NY 14127

How to Live out of a Dream   DVD - $15

This is an amazing docu-drama of the events in the life of a great dreamer. In these fast-moving forty minutes, you will see the healing of a boy crippled by polio. This boy learned to dream as he heard the voice of Jesus speak to him. and then took the hand of the One who would lead him through his life. See his mother as teaching him to dream, and the unbelievable story of ten-year-old Paul Crouch encouraging Tommy that he can do anything if he will just believe. Come take a journey with a dreamer as he teaches you to dream.

Journal of Life   DVD - $10

Tommy Reid is interviewed by his daughter Aimee, and shares with her the story of his fifty-plus years of ministry. You will see his early ministry in the Philippines, as the young 26-year-old Tommy becomes pastor of the great Bethel Temple in Manila. See 31-year-old Tommy, work with Dr. Cho spending their first year ministering together in what will later grow to become the largest church in the world. Revisit, with sight and sound, the tent meetings of the 1950's, the amazing miracles of healing around the world, the great Charismatic renewal, and the Jesus movement in Buffalo during the 1960's.

How to Live out of a Dream   Book $14.95

Your destiny was in God's heart before the foundation of the world! In *How to Live out of a Dream,"* Tommy Reid helps you discover how to dream God's dream to build God's Kingdom. In the sequel, *Create Wealth to Build God's Dream*, discover the resources God has placed within you and how to grow them to bring your God-given dream to reality.

Kingdom Now, But not yet   Book - $10

This is classic Tommy Reid as he shares the Biblical concept of bringing the wonder of the reign of Christ to the world in every day life. *Kingdom Now, But not yet* has inspired great ministries in many nations to change their world. If you want to be a world changer, *Kingdom Now, But not yet* is a must for you.

The Exploding Church   Book - $10

The Exploding Church is the amazing story of a church that grew from 120 attendees to over 800 in a single week. This was a runaway best seller in its day, making Tommy Reid one of the best known speakers in the world in the 1960's and 1970's. Hundreds of churches across the world were inspired by this story as it became a church growth classic in the 1970's.

Release the Sound

Imagine with us waves of sound arising from the hearts of the people of God. This sound is a Heavenly anthem, the sound of the Kingdom! In natural sound, two frequencies traveling toward each other from opposite directions will produce an amplitude twice their size when they meet. When our worship joins Heaven's song, the two become a single, pure, supernatural anthem with twice the amplitude, twice the reach! Our worship, joined with the worship of Heaven releases a sound over our cities, our nation, our world. We invite you to journey with us to Release the Sound of the Kingdom and become a partner with God as His Kingdom revolution takes place!

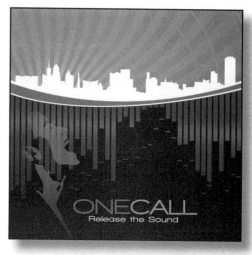

CD $15

Passion for His Presence

True worship strives to live at a level of perfect intimacy with the Lord of All - it is all that we are openly communicating with the Spirit of God! It is for worship that we were created. Once true worship begins to unfold in our lives, we develop a passion for God that burns in our heart of hearts! He so deeply desires to have an amazing and intimate relationship with you; true worship leads you into this intimacy. It opens the doors to heaven, to eternity. All that you long for in eternity can be born in your life today through worship.

CD $10

ABOUT THE AUTHOR

Tommy Reid

Tommy Reid is a dreamer and a teacher of how to dream God's Dreams. He began his ministry preaching citywide crusades, and at twenty-six became a pastor of Bethel Temple in Manila, Philippines, the largest church of his denomination. At thirty, he assisted Dr. Cho in what was to become the largest church in the world.

Returning from Korea, he accepted God's major dream for his life, building a world-class church in Buffalo, New York. The church exploded in growth and he wrote a best-selling book about its growth. As his dream continued, he built over 200 church-affiliated Bible Schools across America and Canada, a worldwide television ministry and twelve campus churches in Buffalo.

Primarily, Tommy Reid is a dreamer who has a passion to teach you to dream God's dream and help you discover the resources to fund that dream. This book describes the passion of his heart and life.

THE CONTRIBUTING AUTHORS

Al Warner

Al Warner builds bridges between leaders to transform their worlds. Through his ministry, God is assembling teams of servant leaders to rebuild, restore, and renew our cities (Isaiah 61:4).

Al and his wife, Deb, are founders of Set Free, Inc., a networking ministry connecting leaders to hear the word of the Lord, build relationships, and strategize for city transformation. Al has had over thirty years of experience pastoring local churches, including a term as missionary to Hong Kong. He currently serves as Chaplain of the Buffalo Common Council (Buffalo's chief legislative body). He and his wife also serve as chaplains to six businesses. Al is completing his Doctor of Ministry degree at the Assemblies of God Theological Seminar in Springfield, Missouri

THE CONTRIBUTING AUTHORS

Aimee Reid Sych

Aimee Reid Sych, a master Biblical expositor who serves on the pulpit faculty of The Tabernacle, is in great demand as a guest speaker throughout the world. Aimee has been a pastor and senior worship leader in her home church for more than eighteen years. A rich anointing of the Holy Spirit is evident upon her worship, her preaching, and her writing.

Like her father, she is a dreamer by nature who has a unique ability to inspire and teach others to dream.

Iain MacDonald

Iain MacDonald dreams of a world where every person is living out their God-given destiny. He believes there is a God-dream for everyone's life and contained in the Scriptures are the tools to accomplish it.

He earned his Business degree in 1984 and set out to make his mark in the business world. Iain worked for General Motors and then started two successful marketing and consulting firms. He thought he had found his calling, but God had other plans and called him into full-time ministry. Marked with passion, Iain and his family founded Victory Church in Fort Erie, Ontario. Victory is designed to create an environment that facilitates personal transformation and dream-centered maturity. He co-pastors Victory with his wife Tina and their three children. People come from all over the world to Victory to encounter God and to discover His plan for their lives. He also travels with Tommy Reid teaching the power of dreams.